Wills of
Chester County
Pennsylvania

1713-1748

Based on the Work of
Jacob Martin

HERITAGE BOOKS
2007

HERITAGE BOOKS
AN IMPRINT OF HERITAGE BOOKS, INC.

Books, CDs, and more—Worldwide

For our listing of thousands of titles see our website
at
www.HeritageBooks.com

Published 2007 by
HERITAGE BOOKS, INC.
Publishing Division
65 East Main Street
Westminster, Maryland 21157-5026

Copyright © 1993 F. Edward Wright

All rights reserved. No part of this book may be reproduced or transmitted in any form or by any means, electronic or mechanical, including photocopying, recording or by any information storage and retrieval system without written permission from the author, except for the inclusion of brief quotations in a review.

International Standard Book Number: 978-1-58549-261-9

INTRODUCTION

The wills of Chester County were first abstracted by Jacob Martin of Marshallton, Pennsylvania and indexed by the indefatigable Gilbert Cope. The abstracts done by Jacob Martin appear to be accurate and complete. Recently it was noted by the Chester County Historical Society that the abstract of the will of James Whitaker was in error in that Martin had incorrectly given Whitaker's son's name as Edward Clayton which during mid 1700s would have suggested that Edward was a son-in-law and husband to daughter Ann Clayton. An examination of the original will showed Edward Whitaker to be son of James Whitaker while daughter Ann Clayton is mentioned as having a husband, but unnamed.

ERROR BY ABSTRACTOR: I have examined two slightly different versions of the abstracts, same handwriting, both purporting to have been prepared by Jacob Martin and indexed by indefatigable Gilbert Cope. In the case of the abstract of James Whitaker (see above) - in one version the name Clayton was initially omitted and later added above a caret while the other version (held by the Chester County Historical Society) initially included the name Clayton. [Thus each was incorrect.]

ERROR BY RECORDING CLERK: In the case of the will of Elizabeth Newlin (Liber A, folio 48) the original will shows a daughter Rachel Jackson. The official record as transcribed by the county clerk erroneously introduces an additional daughter Rebecca. One version of the Martin's abstracts shows the false name Rebecca crossed through and the correct name Rachel written above. This would suggest that the abstracts were taken from the county recorded wills and at a later point someone made a comparison back to the original will. In any event this proves the point that one should eventually examine the original document whenever possible. It also suggests that the annotations made to Martin's abstract (perhaps by Martin himself) are valid. Because numerous annotations have been added to the abstracts of administrations based on information other that the probate records themselves we have placed brackets around these entries with the caution that this information should be verified from other sources.

The first date given is normally the date that the will was written; the second date is usually the date of probate or court action following the death of the testator.

Dates are frequently given numerically in the following order: month, day and year. Prior to 1752, March 25th (Feast of the Annunciation) was the first day of the new year by traditional acceptance of the ecclesiastical calendar. Later as the Gregorian calendar was being accepted the double dates were used from January 1st until March 25th.

Basic information on the records of adminstrations was included in Martin's work and likewise is included here. This information is especially helpful when there was no will (died intestate).

F. Edward Wright
Westminster, Maryland 1993

BEESON, EDWARD. Nottingham, being sick.
6/20/1712. March 9, 1713/4. A. 1.
To son Edward, 1421 acres of land, "laying by Nessamony." To son Richard tract of land near South Ampton, Bucks County containing 290 acres, also 25 acres of liberty land by Schulkill. To son William, my West "look" in Nottingham, also £48 for building him a house and wearing apparel. To daughter Ann Cloud £20. After former wife's children have had their portions personal estate to be divided between widow and daughter Elizabeth. Widow [not named] - to have plantation whereon I live during widowhood, afterward to daughter Elizabeth. Also provides for child that wife is "now great with."
Executors: wife and son Richard.
Witnesses: Andrew Job, James King.
Mentions land purchased of Daniel Wharley and warrant for survey September 14, 1709.

ADAMS, SAMUEL. Darby, Woolcomber.
September 23, 1713. 3/3/1714. A. 3.
Provides for wife Elizabeth and what remains after her death to daughter in England, not named. No mention of real estate.
Executors: Saml. Levis Sr., Saml. Levis Jr.
Witnesses: John Hood, William Smith, Wm. Levis.

POWELL, THOMAS. Upper Providence, yeoman.
December 8, 1714. January 5. 1714. A. 4.
To wife Sarah, all real estate and personal estate which I now have. Also what shall fall to me at the death of my mother. She paying the following legacies. To two daughters Anna and Susanna Powell £100 each when of age or married. Reversion of real estate to brother Joseph Powell. Bequeaths Kate Pullen to wife to serve her time. To Richard Clayton £5 and £5 towards building a house for the Minister of Chester. To brother Joseph £5 also executor with wife Sarah.
Witness: Peter Worrell, Richard Elwell, Jos. Elly.

SWAFFER, JAMES. Chester County. Caln, carpenter.
3/6/1714. February 1, 1714/5. A. 6.
To son in law Robert Pyle of Birmingham 5 shillings and to my daughter Elizabeth his wife 15 shillings and to their two daughters Sarah and Hannah 10 shillings each. To wife Elizabeth all estate real and personal to be disposed of as she pleases with the advice and consent of my brother Wm. Swaffer of Nether Providence yeoman, Esther Bezer and friend John Bezer.
Executor: wife Elizabeth.
Witnesses: John Kinsman, Mathew Wood, Mary Martin.

HARLAN, GEORGE. Kennett on Brandywine Creek, yeoman.
2/21/1714. 8/2/1714. A. 7.
To son Aaron, my clock and great brass kettle. To brother Michael Harlan, young Susquehanna mare. To servant Mary Mathews an expiration of time. Cow and calf and mare. Directs body to be buried by wife's in new burying ground on Alphonsus Kirk's land.
Executors: sons Ezekiel and Aaron. Brother Michael and son Saml. Hollingsworth trustees and assistants to executors. Remainder of

estate to be equally divided among all children, sons and daughters
alike, not named.
Witnesses: Danl. McFarson, Nathan Maddock, Thos. Peirson.

CHANDLER, GEORGE. Chichester.
November 12, 1713. 8/5/1715. A. 9.
To wife Ruth and children all estate as follows. All children to have
equal shares except eldest son, his share and his mother's to be
double than of the other children.
Executors: wife Ruth and brothers Swithin and Thomas Chandler Cod.
Same date gives to mother Jane Bayliss £5.
Witnesses: Walter Martin, Wm. Chandler, John Simcock.

MILLER, JOHN. New Garden. Joyner.
August 17, 1714/5. December 8, 1714/15, A. 10.
To wife not named 1/3 of real and personal estate. To son Joseph, the
plantation I now live upon containing 300 acres. Paying to son in law
Joseph Hutton £20 and to daughters Martha and Sarah Miller £20 each
when 16. To son James 300 acres of land lying on south side of above
mentioned plantation extending to James Starrs line. To son William,
400 acres of land with mill, he paying £60 as follows. To daughters
Elizabeth, Susanna and Elinor, £20 each when 16.
Executors: wife Mary and son Joseph.
Witnesses: Joel Baily, Gayen Miller, John Wily.

GOTTY, MARY.
6/18/1713. 3/3/1714. A. 11.
To daughter Sarah and her husband Benjamin Chandlee the lot whereon we
now live. To grandsons Abel Cottey and Cottey Chandlee my south lott
of land adjacent Andrew Job. To son John Cottey "if he shall come into
these parts again" £10. Remainder to son and daughter Benjamin
Chandlee and Sarah his wife also executors. Witnesses: Andrew Job,
John Churchman. [Benjamin Chandlee son of William Chandlee of Kilmore
County. Kildare Ireland and Sarah Cottey, daughter of Abel Cottey of
Philadelphia, married March 25, 1710, Philadelphia, Mtg.]

CHADS, FRANCIS. Birmingham, yeoman.
1/15/1712. A. 13. Copy of the original will in Philadelphia dated May
6, 1717. To eldest daughter Sarah Chads £30. To eldest son John when
21 my plantation I now dwell on, also 1/2 of my corn mill. To second
daughter Grace Chads £30 at 16. To third daughter Betty Chads £30 at
16. To fourth and youngest daughter Ann Chads £30 to be paid each of
them when 16. Also at death of wife 1/2 of corn mill. To wife Grace
1/2 of corn mill and other provision during life, also executor.
Witnesses: Edward Bennett, Sarah Bennett, John Parker.

POWELL, THOMAS, SR. Upper Providence. Gentleman.
December 4, 1714. December 24, 1714. A. 15.
To the use of the church in Chester 4 lotts in James St. over
against the church. To wife Anna 1/2 of estate real and personal

during life. To my 3 sons, John, Joseph and Thomas 1 shilling
each. To son John Powell's children there being 4 sons of them
viz Joseph, John, Thomas and Benjamin £10 each and to his 2
daughters Mary and Margaret £5 each. To son Thomas after wife
deceases the other 1/2 of estate real and personal.
Executors: wife Anna and son John.
Witnesses: John Humphreys, Thomas Weston, Joseph Elly.

MAXEL, JOHN. Uwchlan.
March 14, 1714/5. 1/14/1715. A. 16.
To sister Jane, horse and side saddle. Estate to son John in case he
dies in his minority. Plantation to brothers and sister Jane and for
support of mother. Reference to deceased wife's daughter Mary Spark.
Executors: James Thomas and Jerermy Jerman who are to see that son is
educated in the doctrines of Church of England. Testimony signed.
Witnesses: John Evan, Richard Thomas, Rees Jones.

TODHUNTER, JOHN. Westtown. Husbandman.
January 13, 1714. 4/10/1715. A. 17.
Plantation and personal estate to be sold and proceeds equally
distributed between wife Margaret and daughter Sarah Todhunter. To
wife's 3 children Mary Ann and Stephen Beale 30 shillings each when of
age.
Executors: wife, James Gibbons and Geo. Ashbridge.
Witnesses: Daniel Hoops, John Warrilaw, John Goulding.

HARRIS, RODGER.
10/11/1714. 4/20/1715. A. 18.
To wife Sarah 1/2 of estate real and personal the other 1/2 to
children viz Rebecca, Elizabeth and Rachel Harris and one to be born.
Wife Sarah executor and friends John Salkeld and Nicholas Fairlamb
trustees for children. (Widow on Danl. Worsley). Witnesses: John
Tyler, James Barber. (Daughter Eliz married John Passmore, daughter
Rachel married David Black).

STEWART, ALEXANDER. Kennett.
10/30/1714. 4/20/1715.
To well beloved wife, 5 horses, 5 cows, sheep and all moveables
belonging to the plantation. To daughter Jane, son Robert, daughter
Ann and Mary, each a mare. To father Joel Baily Sorrel pacing mare. To
Henry Nayle, a young horse. To Riche Jones a pair of leather britches.
To John Stewart, best suit of apparel, buttons excepted. To Saml. Hall
my new vest. To son Robert my plantation when 21, he paying the other
children above named £10 each when 21.
Executors: father-in-law Joel Baily and Henry Nayle.
Witnesses: Vincent Caldwell, Gayon Miller and William Weble.

MASON, RICHARD.
1/9/1714-5. 6/30/1715. A. 20.
All real estate in Aston Township which I had of my father
Richard Mason to be sold. To sister Mary Powell £5. To Nathaniel
Richard £5. To Elizabeth Kirk £5. To cousin Nathaniel Richards

clothing and chest.
Executors: James Todd and John Abernathey.
Witnesses: Edward Stephens, Richard Story, John Todd.

HANES, JOHN. Darby.
September 7, 1815. 8/7/1715. A. 21.
Describes himself as "late of Great Britain."
To my mother Dorothy Wallis £5 to be paid out of the money due me in England. To my sister Dorothy about the sum of £5. To cozin John Abbot £7-10 to be paid out of that £25 due me in England. To cozin Rebeckah Abbot, ditto. To brother John Wallis £3. To friend John Dodson £3. To friend Lewis Davis £3.
Executorst Friends John Wallis and John Davis. Witnesses: William Davis, Ann Davis, Katherine David.

SMITH, JOHN. Darby, yeoman.
12/10/1714/5. 9/8/1715. A. 22.
To daughter Mary wife of William Garret £5. To daughter Sarah, wife of Samuel Sellers £5. To daughter Martha, wife of Richard Parker £5. To my grandchild viz daughter Mary's child and daughter Marthals child 5 shillings each when of age. To daughter in law Jane's children Samuel and Ann Bethel 2/6 each when 21. To son William all remaining real and personal also executor. Friends Thomas Hood and Michael Blunston, overseers. Witnesses: John Blunston, Thomas Worth, Thos. Bradshaw.

BENNETT, EDWARD. Thornbury.
1/25/1714. 8/8/1715. A. 24.
To son John 200 acres of land being the north half of tract of 400 acres in Sadsbury adjacent Geo. Leonard, Saml. Nutt and Thomas George, also a great Bible which did belong to my father John Bennett. To son Jacob 250 acres in Sadsbury between lands of Thos. George and Wm. Brinton. To son Edward 200 acres being the south part of above tract of 400 acres. All estate real and personal in Thornbury to be sold and divided equally among 7 youngest children, viz Jacob, Esther, Edward, Sarah, Joseph, William and Elizabeth all being minors. Brother in law Wm. Horne and wife to have the bringing up of 2 youngest daughters Sarah and Elizabeth.
Executors: friends Nicholas Pyle and Philip Taylor.
Witnesses: Nicholas Newlin, Richard Woodward, William Pyle, Joseph Brinton, Nicholas Rogers.

DUNBABIN, THOMAS. Aston.
11/10/1715. 11/14/1715/6. A. 26.
To brother John Dunbabin of Overwalton, Cheshire, England, his children viz John, Thomas and Margaret £8 each. To sister Mary Poulston's children of Norton in same county viz Thomas and Mary £8 each. To cozin Samuel Heald of Kennett £8. To cozin John Crosby of Ridley £2. To cozin Katherine Fairlamb £10 and to her husband £2. To Elizabeth, wife of Moses Key and to each of their 5 children, 20 shillings.
Executors and residuary legatus Robert Carter and Moses Key.
Witnesses: John Dutton and Wm. Rattew.

JACKSON, ROGER. Chester.
January 23, 1711. 11/15/1715. A. 27.
To friends Joseph Baker Sr. of Edgmont and Thomas Powell of Providence all my lotts of land in and near Chichester and dwelling house and lotts in Chester and all other real estate in trust to be sold and proceeds divided among such or so many of my relations in England as shall within 7 years come over here. Executors: Thomas Powell and Joseph Baker. Letters to Baker the other being deceased.
Witnesses: John Baldwin, Nicholas Fairlamb, John Remington and David Lloyd.

HENDRICKSON, ALBERTUS. Chester County. 11/5/1714. 11/20/1715/6. A. 29.
To son Tobias, my whole plantation and personal estate paying legacies. To son Albertus £5. To sons James and Johannes 5 shillings each. To grandson Albertus Steve 5 shillings. To my 3 daughters, viz., Elizabeth Bright, Isabel Venaman and Katharine Harred 5 shillings each. To granddaughter Helchey, daughter of son Tobias £20 at 21 or marriage.
Executors: son Tobias and friend John Salkeld.
Witnesses: David Willson, Johan Devenport and John Wright.

WOODWARD, JOSEPH. Goshen.
November 28, 1715. 12/18/1715/6. A. 30.
All real and personal estate to be sold. To mother Jane Woodward £40. Remainder to wife, not named, and child or children if she be with child.
Executors: brothers Thomas and Edward Woodward.
Witnesses: William Penil, Joseph Lewis, Mary Butterfield, widow Elizabeth married William Vestal, 1716, see Deed Book A3, 420.

BROWN, JAMES. Nottingham.
11/15/1715. 1/1/1715/6. A. 30.
To sons William Brown, Jeremiah Brown and daughter Margary Pigot, to grandchild James, son of William, Patience and Jeremiah, children of Jeremiah, and Margary Pigot daughter of Margary and John Pigot £5 each when 21. To son Daniel the lott of land between Dorsons and Robert Williams containing 500 acres. To daughter Mary Brown £20 at 20. To wife Honor and son James all my estate paying the above legacies also executors. Nothing to be done or disposed of without the consent of Mercer Brown and son Jeremiah Brown.
Witnesses: James Wright, Wm. Howell and John Bruss.

WILLIAMS, ROBERT. Nottingham.
12/25/1711/2. 3/14/1716. A. 32.
To friend William Brown Sr. of Nottingham house and lott of land in Nottingham. To Joseph Brown, shoe making tools. To Messer Brown, all carpenter tools. To friends of Nottingham Meeting £3. To friend Andrew Job 20 shillings. To friend Jane Brown, rod and kettle. To Hannah Brown, great Kettle. To Saml. Brown £5. To John Brown, wolf trap. To William son of Wm. Brown my gun. To Richard and Thomas Brown 10 shillings each. To Mary Brown one piece of gold that is in my chest. Remainder to Wm. Brown Sr. also

executor.
Witnesses: James King, Samuel Finler.

WORRALL, JOHN. Marple.
3/3/1716. 3/25/1716. A. 33.
To son John £30 when 21. To son Peter £30 when 21. To daughters Mary and Hannah Worrall £30 at 21 or married. To son Joshua 140 acres of the lower end of my land next to Crum Creek when 21 paying to executor £15. To wife Mary all remaining of personal estate and use of all my land until son Henry is 21. And then son Henry shall have 1/2 of said land and remainder on wifes decease. Executors: wife Mary and friend Bartholomew Coppock to assist her.
Witnesses: Daniel Brown, Mord. Massey, Joseph Selby. Mentions brother in law Henry Lewis of Radnor.

MUSGRAVE, ABRAHAM. Haverford.
January 7, 1714/5.
Adm. to Gainer Musgrave and William Lewis.

LOWDIN, JOHN.
May 3, 1714.
Adm. to Margaret Lowdin.

BOOTH, CHARLES. Providence.
January 12, 1714/5.
Adm. to Elizabeth Booth.

BALDWIN, JOSEPH. Chester. March 29, 1715.
Adm. to Elizabeth Baldwin.

LAMPLUGH, NATHANIEL. Chichester.
December 7, 1715.
Adm. to Nathaniel Lamplugh.

BAKER, ROBERT. Middletown.
May 9, 1716.
Adm. to Joseph Baker, father.
Susanna the widow, renouncing.

BROWN, JOSEPH.
August 14, 1716.
Adm. to Margaret Brown.

BROWN, JOHN.
August 14, 1716.
Adm. to William Brown.

RICHARDS, WILLIAM.
August 28, 1716.
Adm. to Nathaniel Richards.

PENICK, JOHN.
December 26, 1716.
Adm. to Nathl Newlin.

FIERRE, MARY.
November 28, 1716.
Adm. to Daniel Philip and John Fierre.

BAKER, JOSEPH. Edgmont.
12/19/1714/5. 7/24/1716. A. 34.
Provides for wife Mary. To daughter Sarah wife of Thos. Smedley £50. To son Robert £5. To son Joseph 20 shillings. To son John the remainder of my land in Thornbury which is the reversions of the tract my son Joseph's land was taken out of. Also to son John all my land in Edgmont by estate, 500 acres and all other estate. Executors: son John.
Witnesses: John Worrilow, Wm. Hickin, Joseph Selby.

SCOTT, JOHN.
1/28/1716, died 1/30/1716. 6/28/1716. A. 36.
Non cupative will. All estate to wife Mary except a gun to John

Rice. Letters to wife Mary.
Witnesses: Nicholas Fairlamb, Samuel Tomlinson, Jacob Howell, Caleb Coupland, John Salkeld.

PHILLIPS, GRIFFITH. Whiteland in the valley.
August 24, 1716. 8/8/1716. A. 37.
To wife Jennet, all estate real and personal and if my nephew John Phillips arrives in Pennsylvania his passage shall be paid out of my estate.
Executors: wife Jenett Phillips.
Witnesses: Evan Lewis, Grace Thomas, Griffith Lewis, Richd. Thomas.

HARRIS, WILLIAM. Caln.
5/2/1715. 8/15/1716. A. 37.
Describes himself as "late of Long Compton county of Warwick in Great Britain." To friend George Peirce of Thornbury my best greah coat and buckskin breeches. To Gainer son of said Geo. Peirce wearing apparel Geo. Fox's Journal. To Isaac Taylor of Thornbury practitioner of physicks in whose house I now am articles of wearing apparel. Remainder to brother Edward Harris of Redway under near Edge Hill in Warwickshire, Great Britain.
Executors: George Peirce and Isaac Taylor.
Witnesses: Daniel Evan, Wm. Hannams, John Taylor.

SMITH, WILLIAM. Darby.
8/29/1716. 8/30/1716. A. 38.
To sister Mary Garrett, wife of Wm, 5 shillings. To sister Sarah Sellers 5 shillings. To sister Martha Parker, wife of Richard, 5 shillings. To Saml. and Ann Bethell, my son and daughter in law, 5 shillings each. To my 2 servants John Smith and Elizabeth 2/6 shillings each. To wife Jane all personal estate, also executor of real estate during widowhood, but if she marry, 2/3 of real estate to go to bringing up my child or children. Letters to Jane Smith sole executor. Brothers in law Richard Parker and Wm. Garrett, overseers.
Witnesses: Jonathan Bentley, Sarah Marshall, Benjamin Cliffe.

MERCER, THOMAS. Thornbury.
3/17/1715. 9/13/1716. A. 40.
Provides for wife Mary. To eldest son Thomas after wifes decease or marriage, my new dwelling plantation containing my estate 238 acres. To son Thomas, son Daniel 1/2 of 500 acres of land in Marlborough which lieth next to Nathl Newlins land. To son Joseph the other 1/2 said 500 acres whereon son Thomas now lives. To my 3 daughters, viz Mary, Elizabeth and Ann, £20 each. To sons in law Wm. Pennil, Joseph Woodward and Joshua Peirce one pistole each. Remainder of moveables to wife and son Thomas.
Executors: wife Mary.
Witnesses: Francis Pullen, Thomas Pierson, Rose Pierson.

PARKER, JOHN, Darby.
9/3/1716. November 30, 1716. A. 41.
To brother William Parker of Long Clason in Leicestershire in England £40. To Mary Campen of same place 40 shillings. To Sarah

Blunston of Darby £15 at 21 or marriage. To Barbara Bevan and Ann
Hood 40 shillings each. My great Bible to Ann Gilbertharp.
Remainder to cousin Richard Parker Jr. also executor.
Witnesses: Ann Hood, Barbara Bevan, John Hay.

SMITH, JANE. Darby. Widow of William. 9/4/1716. 10/20/1716. A. 42.
To son Samuel Bethel and daughter Ann Bethel articles of furniture
named. To son John Smith his grandfathers bed and furniture. To sister
in law Mary Garrett 5 shillings. To sister in law Sarah Sellers 5
shillings. To sister in law Martha Parker 5 shillings. To Elizabeth
Broom 20 shillings. To servant John Smith one ewe. Remainder to
father, Richard Parker also executor. Witnesses: John Marshall, Sarah
Marshall, Elizabeth Broom. Mentions brother Richard Parker and brother
in law William Garrett.

SIMCOCK JR, JACOB. Ridley.
1/10/1716/7. 12/21/1716/7. A. 43.
To wife Sarah, part of plantation during life and afterward to son
Joseph, to said son remainder of land on East side of little Crum
Creek, also £10 when 21. To daughter Sarah £100 at 18.
Executors: wife Sarah and brother in law Richard Walln.
Witnesses: Jacob Simcock, Benj. Simcock, John Hood.

GARRETT, THOMAS. Willistown, yeoman. Noncupative.
12/13/1716/7. 12/28/1716/7. A. 45.
To son William at 21, 492 acres of land in Willistown. To wife
Rebecca, all personal estate to bring up my two daughters Susanna and
Hannah till 18 and then pay each of them £20.
Executors: wife, brother Saml. Garrett and Geo. Ashbridge. Will not
signed. Witnessed by Wm. Garrett, George Garrett.

HOSKINS, JOHN.   DUBLE, JEROME.
January 1, 1716.   10/13/1716.
Adm. to Ruth Hoskins.   Adm. to Henry Millard and Isaac Bellarby.

BLUNSTON JR, JOHN. --   NORTHUM, WILLIAM.
November 30, 1716.   March 8, 1717.
Adm. to Ann Blunston.   Adm. to Margret Northum.

WOODYER, GEORGE. Chester Township.
January 25, 1714. 5/20/1717. A. 46.
Directs body to be buried in Friends burial place in Upper Providence
by first wife. To my 7 grandchildren the children of my daughter Mary
Phips. All estate real and personal to be equally divided among them,
except 6 shillings to son in law John Turner.
Executors: John Sharpless and Jacob Howell. Son in law Joseph Phipps
to have wearing apparel.
Witnesses: John Tyler and Evan Morgan.

HALL, THOMAS. Concord.
September 11, 1704. August 21, 1717. A. 47.
Land and plantation to wife during life and afterward to son Thomas if living otherwise to son John, also names daughters Sarah and Mary.
Executors: wife, who is not named.
Witnesses: Thomas Gartwright, William Rattew.
Widow Sarah Hall married George Robinson, May 10, 1708, St Paul's Ch, Chester.

NEWLIN, ELIZABETH, widow. Concord.
August 18, 1714. 2/10/1717. A. 48.
To daughter Rachel Jackson £65. To son in law Ephraim Jackson 20 shillings. To daughter Rachel Jackson, furniture and wearing apparel. To the children of said Ephraim and Rachel Jackson £50 to be divided at 20 years age. To son in law William Pagett late of Ireland, 20 shillings. To granddaughter Mary Burton late of Ireland, £10. To the 3 daughters of my daughter Elizabeth and Wm. Pagett, late of Ireland, £5 each. To grandson Nicholas Newlin late of London, £10. To granddaughter Elizabeth Lewis, £40. To daughter in law Mary Newlin, 20 shillings. To Nicholas, Nathaniel, John, Jemima, Kezia and Mary Newlin, children of son Nathaniel, £5 each. To son Nathaniel all remainder of estate, also executor.
Witnesses: George Pearce, John Fred., John Mendenhall.

PYLE, NICHOLAS. Concord. Gent.
October 6, 1715. Codicil: 12/18/1716/7. 2/10/1717. A. 49.
To eldest son Nicholas the plantation I now live on in Concord containing 450 acres when he is 21, he paying to his mother in law Ann Pyle £10 yearly during her widowhood and an annuity to his grandmother as is -already settled, Sarah Bushell. Mentions legacy of £23 due son Nicholas from his grandfather Joseph Bushell. To son Samuel 257 acres of land at the southern part of my tract in Kennett that was surveyed originally to James Wallis for 515 acres, also £27 when 21. To son Joseph the remaining half of above mentioned tract of land also £27 when 21. To daughter Mary Sharp £30 and to her daughter Abigail Sharp £10 to be in the hands of her father Joseph Sharp until she is 16. To daughter Edith Pyle £77. Also mentions legacy of £23 to daughter Edith from her grandfather Joseph Bushell. To daughter Sarah Pyle £77 when 16. Provides for wife Ann. Remainder to son Nicholas. Executors: brother Robt. Pyle, Nathl Newlin and Wm. Pyle, son of Robt. Letters to Newlin the others renouncing.
Witnesses: Wm. Hill, Isaac Taylor, Ellis Lewis, John Vastow.

BAKER, JOSEPH. Thornbury.
12/26/1716/7. 2/10/1717. A. 53.
To daughter Sarah Baker, £30 when 21. To daughter Hannah Baker, £30 at 21 or married. Also provides for a possible child yet to be born. All remainder of estate to wife Mary for bringing up the children.
Executors: wife Mary and friend Isaac Taylor.
Witnesses: Ann Worrilow, John Cluse, Jos. Selby.

FLOWER, WILLIAM. Chichester. Yeoman.
July 16, 1717. August 5, 1717. A. 54.
To wife Sarah, £20 and household goods which she brought with her and 20 shillings more. To son in law John Flower all my lands, messuages, etc.
Executors: son Enoch and son in law John Flower.
Witnesses: Richard Edwards, John Riley.

TYLER, JOHN. Chester. Tailor.
July 23, 1717. August 26, 1717. A. 56.
To wife Esther, sons William and John, daughters Deborah and Katherine all personal estate to be equally divided. Authorized Tobias Hendricks and Saml. Thomlinson to sell and convey his real estate in Chester and elsewhere.
Executor: wife Esther.
Witnesses: Geo. Simpson, Geo. Brown, Richard Marsden.

ARNOLD, JOHN. Thornbury. Cooper
1/17/1714/5. 6(7?)/27/1717 (both months given). A. 57.
200 acres of land in Bradford to be sold and all estate divided into 10 equal parts. To father Richard Arnold one part. To mother Sarah Arnold one part. To sister Grace Eavenson, brother Thomas Arnold, brother Josiah and William, sister Elizabeth Arnold, brother Richard, sister Sarah Arnold and brother Anthony Arnold each on part.
Executors: brother Thos. Arnold.
Witnesses: Sarah Bennett, Wm. Pyly, Isaac Taylor, Jos. Townsend.

ROBINSON, GEORGE. Concord, yeoman.
August 19, 1717. 6/31/1717. A. 58.
To son in law John Hall after death of wife the plantation I own in Aston containing about 60 acres. To wife Sarah all personal estate during life and after her decease to be equally divided between her 3 youngest children, viz John, Sicilly and Margaret. To Thomas Amans one mare.
Executor: wife.
Witnesses: Francis Pullen, Ann Clerk.
George Robinson married the widow of Thomas Hall of Concord.

COMPTON, JONATHAN. Birmingham. Cooper.
July 4, 1717. 7/25/1717. A. 60.
To daughter Eleanor Palmer 1 shilling. To wife, not named, 1/3 of real and personal estate. To son John all remaining at 21.
Executors: John Beckingham and John Palmer. Letters to Beckingham, the other renouncing.
Witnesses: Robert Stevens, Saml. Scott, Jr., John Chalfant Jr.

HOOD, THOMAS. Darby, yeoman.
September 7, 1717. 8/7/1717. A. 60.
To eldest daughter Sarah wife of David Thomas £50. To daughter Hannah wife of George Wood, £50. To daughter Ann, wife of Enoch Bonsall, £50. To daughter Mary £50. To daughter Martha wife of Jacob Bonsall, £50. Land and plantation in Darby to be sold for the use of said 5 daughters children. Executors to make title to the 200 acres of land in Abingdon sold to Geo. Godshett.

Executors: sons in law, David Thomas, George Wood, Jacob and Enoch
Bonsall. Brother John Hood and his son Jonathan to be overseers.
Witnesses: John Maris, Thomas Taylor, John Hood.

PYLE, ROBERT.
May 16, 1717.
Adm. to Eliz Pyle and Wm. Pyle.

PYLE, JACOB.
August 16, 1717.
Adm. to Alice Pyle.

ALCOCK, JEFFREY.
March 28, 1717.
Adm. to James Gibbons.

EDWARDS, JOSEPH.
April 15, 1717.
Adm. to Mary Edwards.

TAYLOR, ISAAC.
April 15, 1717.
Adm. to Sarah Taylor and Isaac Taylor.

EVAT, FRANCIS.
October 1, 1717.
Adm. to John Mendenhall.

HANNUM, JAMES. Concord, yeoman.
August 24, 1717. November 26, 1717. A. 62.
To brother Robert Hannum all my land in Birminham containing 200
acres. To friend Ann Martin £15. Remainder to 2 brothers George and
John and 3 youngest sister, Margery, Sarah and Ann in equal shares.
Executors: father John Hannum.
Witnesses: Thomas Smith, Francis Pullen.

BUSHELL, SARAH. Widow. Concord.
2/9/1716. January 18, 1717/8. A. 62.
To Margaret wife of James Chivers of Concord and friends Mary, wife of
Robt. Chamberlin and Rachel daughter of Joseph Gilpin, wearing
apparel. To kins woman, Mary daughter of Wm. Webb in Great Britain,
£5. To James son of brother Samuel Webb formerly of Derets in of the
Parish of Chipman, County of Wilts. All remainder of estate with
revisions in case of his death without issues. To the youngest
daughter of Joseph Gilpin named Alice, youngest daughter of Vincent
Caldwell named Ruth and youngest daughter of Richard Webb, named
Elizabeth.
Executors: friends George Pierce and Joseph Gilpin.
Witnesses: Thos. West, William Hill.

ERWIN, WILLIAM. Chester.
December 25, 1717. 12/3/1717/8. A. 65.
To Thomas Coeburn Jr. £3. To Joseph son of Thos. Coeburn Sr. 40
shillings. Remainder to friend Thos. Coeburn Sr. also executor.
Witnesses: Joseph Weldon. Jo. Parker.

MORGAN, BLANCH. Widow. Newtown.
11/18/1717/8. May 28, 1718. A. 66.
To grandchildren as follows. To Elizabeth £10. To Ann £10. To Mordecai
£2-10. To Benjamin £5 when 21. Toward the repairing of the graveyard
at Newton 20 shillings.
Executors: son in law, Jon. Griffith.
Witnesses: Rees Howell, Wm. Lewis.

TEST, JOHN. Darby. Innkeeper
June 15, 1718. June 27, 1718: A. 66.
All estate to wife Margaret during widowhood and afterward to 3
children. Thomas, John and Margaret Test.
Executors: wife Margaret.
Witnesses: Owen Owen, John Reece.

LEWIN, EDWARD. Darby. Weaver.
December 2, 1718. January 1, 1718/9. A. 68. All estate to wife Mary
Lewin also executor.
Witnesses: David Thomas, Jona Bentley, Richd. Parker, Jr.

HAYES JR, HENRY. Marlborough.
October 9, 1717.
Adm. to Richard Hays of Marlborough, Bond £60, sureties, Jach
Butcher of Upper Providence and John Brackenbury of Marlborough.
Witnesses: Susanna Lownes, Agnes Salkeld. Inv August 18, 1717 by
Mordcay Cloud, Jeremias Cloud. Accounts filed December 19, 1719,
disbursements £9-3-4.

WORTH, JOHN.
November 12, 1717.
Adm. to Kathrine Worth.

EDWARDS, WILLIAM.
January 1, 1717.
Adm. to Joseph Pratt. Jane the widow, renouncing.

MORTONSON, MORTON. Calking Hook.
November 21, 1718. January 1, 1718/9. A. 69.
To son David all real and personal estate, paying to son Andrew, one
English shilling and to sons John and Mathias, daughters Katherine and
Margaret, one shilling.
Executors: son David.
Witnesses: Mathias Netsellis, Swan Boon, Wm. Patterson.

COPPOCK, BARTHOLOMEW. Marple.
5/10/1718. May 9, 1718/9. A. 70.
To son Bartholomew, articles named. To wife Margaret, all remaining
moveables. To son Bartholomew's 5 daughters viz Margret, Rebecca,
Sarah, Esther and Martha Coppick £5 each. To daughter in law Jane,
widow, wife of Jonathan the use of my land in Springfield for the
bringing up of said sons 3 children until the 12 month, 1727. Then to
be sold and divided among said daughter in law and 3 children, viz
Sarah, Rachel, Hannah. To grandson Moses, son of Bartholomew Coppock,
tract of land in Marlborough, containing about 338 acres.
Executors: wife Margaret and son Bartholomew.
Witnesses: Hannah Massey, Mordecai Massey, Jos. Selby.

LAWRENCE, DANIEL. Haverford.
2/1/1719. May 5, 1719. A. 72.
To mother, not named, use of plantation during life, afterward to
brother, Thos. Lawrence in trust for his son David paying to my
brother Henry £50, after he is 21. To his sister Rachel and his

brother William Lawrence, £5 and to my sister Elinor's son Daniel
William and her daughter Sarah William, £15. To the use of Haverford
Meeting £5, servant David Jones mentioned.
Executors: brothers Henry and Thomas Lawrence.
Witnesses: Richd. Hayes, David Lewis, Henry Lewis.

ROMAN, ROBERT.
January 22, 1717/8.
Adm. to Jacob Roman. Hannah the widow renouncing.

STREATOR, ROBERT.
April 19, 1718.
Adm. to James Streator.

CROSBY, RICHARD.
May 22, 1718.
Adm. to John Crosby.

ROBINETT, ALLEN.
August 20, 1719.
Adm. to Joseph Carter.

LEWIN, MARY. Widow. Darby.
April 23, 1719. May 5, 1719. A. 73.
To Hannah Ceary daughter of brother, John Ceary in Great Britain and
to Margaret daughter of brother, Wm. Ceary in same place. Articles
named, to kinsman Wm. Ceary of Philadelphia, gold ring and my husbands
weaving apparel, forgives servant Elizabeth Andrews the judgment of
Court which is against her. Remainder to brother, Samson Ceary and my
3 kinsman, Wm. Sharpe and Saml. Ceary, brother Samson Ceary, executor.
Witnesses: Fr. Gandovett, Enoch Bonsall, Richd. Parker.

MARTIN, WALTER. Chichester.
August 4, 1715. June 27, 1719. A. 73.
Refers to the legacies given to his children by their grandfather
Joseph Bushells will and names mother in law Sarah Bushell. To son in
law Wm. Clayton 20 shillings, also to daughter Mary 20 shillings.
Provides for wife Mary. To daughter Ann Martin certain lots in
Chichester and 4 acres of woodland, also £5. Also to daughters
Elizabeth and Sarah Marter certain described lotts and a tract of
woodland each. Messuage and plantation I now live on to be sold [about
160 acres] and proceeds, except £10, to be invested for the
maintenance of son Stephen during life and after his death, divided
among other heirs. Mentions granddaughters Mary and Hannah Marten.
Executors: brothers in law Nicholas Pyly and Daniel Williamson.
Witnesses: Francis Routh, Thomas Linville, Wm. Chandalar.

BULLER, WILLIAM. Kennett.
6/19/1719. October 12, 1719. A. 78.
To eldest daughter Hannah Branton, daughter Eliz Buller and 3 sons
Thomas, John and Richard, household goods and wearing apparel as
described.
Executors: brother John Buller and son Thomas, son Richard to be

apprenticed.
Witnesses: Robert Stevens, Robert Wry.

WHITAKER, JAMES. Darby.
October 30, 1719. 12/8/1719/20. A. 79.
To friend Elizabeth Levis Jr. £5. To friend Sarah Levis £5. To friend Rebecca Davis, walnut chest. To friend Ann Need El. To friend Joseph Lewis £3. To friend Christopher Spray £3. To friends John Davis, Wm. Levis and Saml. Levis Jr., working tools and Boards.
Executors: Saml. Levis, Jr.
Witnesses: James Treviller, Michl. Harlan, Thomas Bird.

MARTEN, JOHN. Middletown, yeoman. 8/20/1705, February 25, 1719/ 20. A. 80.
To only son and heir Thomas, all estate real and personal in Middletown subject to provision for wife Elizabeth.
Executors: son Thomas, Robert Pennil and John Crosby, wifes Feoffe to see her rents and duly paid.
Witnesses: Nicholas Fairlamb, Edward Beeson.

STEVENS, ROBERT. Birmingham.
February 18, 1712. 1/1/1719/20. A. 81.
Describes himself as of St Johns Wapping, Co. of Midx. and "outward bound on a voyage to sea." Devises all estate to wife Mary Feencers, also executor.
Witnessed by John Joy and John Allen Jr. Acknowledged in Birmingham Township, February 26, 1719/20 in presence of Nathan Newlin, James Houston, Mary West, Joseph Gilpin.

WEBB, RICHARD. Birmingham, yeoman.
March 2, 1719. 1/14/1719/20. A. 82.
To wife Elizabeth all estate real and personal, to sell the same and pay debts and legacies as follows. To son William daughter Mary wife of George Brown, daughter Sarah wife of William Delwarth, dau. Esther wife of Jacob Bennett son Joseph, son Benjamin, son Daniel, son John and son James, £1 each.
Executors: wife Elizabeth.
Witnesses: Henry Nayle, John Bennett, Joseph Brinton.

DAVIS, JOHN. Thornbury.
March 3, 1719/20. 1/18/1719/20. A. 83.
To son Abraham, tract of land in Bradford containing 200 acres. To son John,, tract of land in Bradford containing 200 acres boundary on north by Robert Jeffrey, son Daniel, tract of land in Bradford containing 166 acres. To wife Mary, plantation in Thornbury containing 158 acres, until son Isaac is 21, when he shall inherit it. To wife Mary and 4 daughters Mary, Hannah, Susanna and Charitie, all remainder of estate.
Executors: wife Mary and Moses Key overseer.
Witnesses: James Webb, Charles Turner, John Taylor.

FRED, JOHN. Birmingham. Cooper.
March, 1/9/1719/20. 1/19/1719/20. A. 85.
To daughter Rachel, 200 acres of my land next to Daniel Davis and 1/3 of moveables. To wife and son Nicholas the plantation I now dwell on containing 246 acres of land and 300 acres of land adjacent, being the remainder of the tract I bought of Joseph Phibo and 2/3 of moveables. Mention of servant maid Margret Mathews. To son Benjamin, my oxen, servant man John Kitchen £5.
Executors: sons Benjamin and Nicholas.
Witnesses: James Johnson, Mary Minner, Margt. Mathews.

HILL, JAMES.
September 23, 1719.
Adm. to Thomas Hill.

HOWELL, WILLIAM.
March 10, 1719/20.
Adm. to Ralph Pyle.

BENNETT, ANN.
November 3, 1719.
Adm. to John Bennett.

WHITAKER, CHARLES.
April 8, 1720.
Adm. to Anthony Lea.

CAIN, JOHN.
November 11, 1719.
Adm. to Ann Cain.

TAYLOR, JOSEPH.
March 24, 1720.
Adm. to Rachel Taylor.

EVANS, JOHN.
February 23, 1719/20.
Adm. to Benjamin Vining.

STEVENSON, GAIEN.
April 4, 1720.
Adm. to Grace Stevenson.

TREVILLER, JAMES. Marlborough.
1/1/1720. 1/25/1720. A. 87.
To brother Henry, the plantation I now live on, subject to the maintenance of his mother during life. To brother Richard £3, 2 horses, wearing apparel etc. To sister Katherine £2. To sister Ann El. Remainder to Henry.
Executors: Samuel Levis, Jr., Wm. Levis.
Witnesses: Danl. McLister, Robt. Jones, Roger Peniston.

BROWN, GEORGE. Middletown.
March 1, 1719/20. 2/20/1720. A. 88.
All estate to wife Mary, also executor, friends Richard Webb and William Webb, overseers.

Witnesses: Edward Pilkington, James Underwood, Thos. Barnes.

CALDWELL, VINCENT. Marlborough.
8/15/1715. 2/15/1720. A. 88.
Tract of land on north side of west branch of Brandywine Creek in township of Bensalem containing 450 acres to be sold and money equally divided among 5 daughters, viz, Anne, Betty, Mary, Hannah and Ruth. Plantation whereon I now dwell to be at wifes disposal for breeding up and educating children.
Executors: wife Betty and father in law George Peirce of Thornbury.
Witnesses: Jas. Gibbons, Wm. Webb, Joshua Harlan, Wm. Levis.

WITHERS, THOMAS. Chichester.
March 29, 1720. 2/15/1720. A. 90.
To son Robert, all my right to my improvement on tract of land in
Nottingham near Octararo Creek and moveables on the same. To son
Ralph, my plantation in Chichester containing 232 acres, subject to
life int of wife Jane. To daughters Mary Hughs, Jane and Elizabeth
Withers £16 each. Mentions that Jeremiah Collet Sr. late of Chichester
devised into his 5 children above named, £15 each which had not all
been paid, evidently their grandfather. Remainder to wife, also
executor.
Witnesses: Wm. Brown Sr., Henry Reynolds, Wm. Reynolds.

ALLIN, JOHN. Newton.
2/8/1720. 2/22/1720. A. 92.
To sister Sarah Ashton, £20. To Robert Keath, John Cloose and Joseph
Beaker, articles of wearing apparel. Remaining real and personal to
wife Alice.
Executors: wife and John Williamson.
Witnesses: Danl. Williamson, Thos. Smedly, Sarah Harrey.

COPPOCK, BARTHOLOMEW. Springfield. 2/5/1720. 2/22/1720. A. 93.
To my 3 sons and their wives, viz Richard Woodward and wife, my
daughter Mary, Wm. West and my daughter Deborah, and Robt. Williamson
and my daughter Hannah 5 shillings each. All remainder of estate, real
and personal to wife Ellen, for her maintenance during life, with
power to dispose of what remains at her death among her children. Just
signed B.
Executors: brother in law Danl. Williamson and Evan Lewis.
Witnesses: Jonathan Heacock, John Scholar, Jane Scholar.

WEST, WILLIAM. Springfield.
2/9/1720. 2/22/1720. A. 94.
To 2 brothers Thomas and John West, all wearing apparel. To brother in
law Robt. Williamson and wife Hannah, 20 shillings each. To kinswoman
Deborah daughter of Peter Britain, deceased, £5 at 21 or married.
Executors to sell all remainder of estate real and personal and
proceeds to wife Deborah during widowhood with rev to Wm. West
youngest son of brother Thomas.
Executors: wife Deborah and brother Thomas. Letters to widow, brother
renouncing.
Witnesses: John Maris, John Lea, Jacob Simcock, Bartholomew Coppock,
John Gleave.

JAMES, GEORGE. Springfield.
1/28/1720. April 23, 1720. A. 96.
Provides for wife Anne, remainder of estate real and personal to be
sold and money divided as follows. 1/3 to wife Anne and of the
remainder a double share to son Mordecai, equal shares to 6 daughters,
viz Sarah, Mary, Jane, Hannah, Anne and Eliz. James at 21 or married.
Son Mordecai to be apprenticed.
Executors: brother in law Richard Woodward of Bradford and Kinsman
David Register.
Witnesses: John B. Broomall, Thomas Taylor, Susanna Taylor.

EDGE, JACOB. Nether Providence.
2/3/1720. 2/25/1720. A. 97.
To each of my daughters, viz Hannah, Jane, Abigail and Sarah, £50.
Executor to pay to 3 eldest daughters £12-6 which their grandmother
Jane Edge bequethed them, viz to Abigail £5-12. To Hannah £3-7 and to
Jane £3-7. To wife Sarah all remainder of estate real and personal for
bringing up and educating children. Refers to his share 1/3 of
Providence Mill.
Executors: wife Sarah and father in law Ellis David and brothers
John Edge and Richard Jones. Friends Henry Miller, Jacob Howell,
Wm. Lewis and Thos. Vernon, Guardians
Witnesses: John Powell, Jacob Vernon, Henry Hastings.

SWAFFER, WILLIAM. Nether Providence. 2/15/1719. 3/16/1720. A. 99.
To wife Mary, 40 acres of land being N.W. corner of the land I now
dwell upon, during life and after her decease, to son Jacob. Also to
said son the remainder of said land in N. Providence, paying £50
towards discharge of debts. Executors to sell land in Westtown
containing 300 acres-. To daughter Rebecca, son Joseph, daughters
Mary, Phebe, Ann, Sarah and sons William and Thomas, £5 each, when 21.
Remainder for maintenance of younger children.
Executors: wife Mary and friend Jacob Edge. Letters to widow.
Witnesses: Thomas Dell, John Sharpless.

TRAGO, JACOB. Middletown, yeoman.
June 9, 1720. 4/20/1720. A. 100.
To wife Mary 1/2 of estate during widowhood and remainder to 3
children Hannah, John and Rachel. Son John to have £5 over his equal
share.
Executors: wife Mary, brother Wm. Trago and kinsman John Davis of
Darby.
Witnesses: Thos. Marten, Danl. Cookson, Joseph Jervis.

CARPENTER, ISAAC. Bethel. Laborer. 6/20/1720. 8/6/1720. A. 101.
To Joseph Pyles 3 children, viz Robert, Joseph and Ralph £4, when 21.
To Deborah Dix £4. To John Garten all my clothes. Remainder to Joseph
Pyle also executor.
Witnesses: John F. Garten, Ralph Everson.

TAYLOR, PETER. Caln.
5/5/1720. 9/6/1720. A. 102.
To sons John and Saml. the plantation whereon I dwell subject to
maintenance of their mother, not named. To daughter, not named, £16
with that she has already received. To son Peter 20 shillings beside
what he has received. To son William 20 shillings.
Executors: wife, not named and son Peter.
Witnesses: Hugh Davis, Richard Thomas, test signed P.

BULLER, THOMAS. Kennett.
November 18, 1720. 10/6/1720. A. 104.
All real and personal estate to be sold and equally divided between
brother Richard and sister Elizabeth Buller when of age, except £5 to
eldest sister Hannah Brinton and £20 to cosin Hannah

Whittington with rev to her son Saml. Whittington.
Executors: Uncle John Buller and Wm. Brinton Sr.
Witnesses: Robert Way, Pierce Power.

HELSBY, JOSEPH.
June 27, 1720.
Adm. to Joan Helsby.

MARTIN, JOHN.
December 7, 1720.
Adm. to Robert Jones.

STEDMAN, JOHN.
November 3, 1720.
Adm. to Joseph Stedman.

CARPENTER, JAMES.
October 29, 1720.
Adm. to Edward Bezer.

LE TORT, ANN.
November 19, 1720.
Adm. to James Le Tort.

CLOUD, WILLIAM. Caln. Cordwainer 2.
11/19/1716/7. December 16, 1720. A. 105.
To wife Grace, my plantation etc. during life and after her decease, to son Jason also all personal estate. To son Joseph £5 and wearing apparel. To son Richard, son William and daughters Susanna and Ann 5 shillings each.
Executors: wife and son Jason.
Witnesses: Thos. Pierson, Aaron Mendenhall.

ARNOLD, RICHARD. Thornbury.
10/7/1720. 10/30/1720. A. 105.
To wife Sarah my plantation in Thornbury containing 140 acres during life and after her decease that part of the same which lies east of the road adjoining Benjamin Mendenhall and Jacob --non, supposed to contain 115 acres. To son Anthony, he paying to son William £10. To daughter Sarah remainder of land, about 25 acres. To sons Thomas, Joseph and Richard 5 shillings each. To daughters Grace wife of Ralph Eavenson and Elizabeth wife of Richard Pritchard 5 shilling each. Remainder to wife Sarah also executrix.
Witnesses: Ann Vernon, Wm. Cluse, John Taylor. [Did widow marry Zerubabel Thatcher?, more probably the daughter Sarah.]

MORRIS, DAVID. Marple.
November 25, 1720. January 17, 1720/1. A. 107.
To eldest son David the North half of my land in Marple
by estate, 400 acres, he paying to my daughter Elizabeth Morris £30.
To son Mordecai the other 200 acres of said tract, he paying to daughter Elizabeth £10. To son Isaac, my plantation in Whitemarsh Township containing 324 acres, paying to daughter Elizabeth £25.
To son Jonathan my 1/3 of grist mill in Haverford and land etc.

belonging and all my share of the trading stock in co. with Richard Hayes.
Executors: son David and brothers Henry and Saml. Lewis, overseers.
Witnesses: Wm. Plamer, Andrew Robison, Saml. Lewis, Henry Lewis.
(David Jr. married Mary Philips (------ all) and had 3 children.
Deed Book A. 395, Del Co.)

SHARPLESS, CALEB. Ridley. Weaver.
2/25/1720. 12/19/1720/ A. 109.
To father John Sharpless all estate real and personal also executor.
Witnesses: Joseph Vernon, John Powell.

BOWATER, FRANCES. Concord, widow.
January 29, 1720/1. 12/28/1720/1. A. 110.
To daughter Mary Ails £10. To daughter Eliza Pusey £5. To daughter Ann Chanler £16. To daughters Eales Mendenhall remainder of household goods. To daughter Phebe Scarlet £25. To grandson Saml. Pyle £4 at 21, to be paid his mother Ealse Mendenhall.
Executors: sons in law, Wm. Pusey, Moses Mendenhall.
Witnesses: Wm. Brinton, Nathan Newlin, Jean Brinton.

GIBBONS, JOHN. Bethel.
11/2/1720. 1/25/1721/ A. 110.
To brother Robert Gibbons £5 if living 12 months after date of will. To grandson John Gibbons my half of the house I now live in and plantation belonging which land is three score and fifteen acres, when 21. To granddaughter Rebecca Gibbons, a plantation and the land which is 200 acres, when 21. To daughter in law Sarah Gibbons 5 shillings. To son James, remainder of estate, also executor.
Witnesses: Francis Fervis, Rachel Fervis, Marsi Booth.
To sister in England £10 if living 12 months after date of will.

JOHN, DAVID. Youplian. Laborer.
March 24, 1721. 2/6/1721. A. 112.
To friend David Jenkins £1-15. To friend James Pugh Jr. Ell. To friend John Harris £3-10. To friend Jeremiah Jarman and Jas. Pughs 2 daughters, pewter. Remainder to executors friends Wm. Phillips and Wm. Williams.
Witnesses: James Pugh, David Jenkins.

KINSMAN, JOHN. Chichester, yeoman. 1/4/1718/9. 2/14/1721. A. 114.
To grandson Kinsman Dutton, the plantation I now live upon in Chichester containing 200 acres, when 21, paying to his two younger brothers Jacob and Joseph £10 each, when 21. To granddaughter Hannah Dutton, £10 at 21 or married. To granddaughter Mary Dutton £10 at 21 or married. To Robert Pule for repair of Chichester meeting house £5. To friends Robert Pyle and John Salkeld £5 each. Remainder real and personal to daughter Elizabeth Dutton also executrix. Codicil gives plantation to dau Elizabeth Dutton during life and then to her son Kinsman.
Witnesses: Wm. Griffith, Robert Pyle, Jo. Parker.

Codicil March 15, 1720-1.

WHITAKER, JAMES. Chichester, yeoman.
1/25/1721. 2/15/1721. A. 117.
To wife Mary 1/2 the land I now live on containing about 200 acres during life. Mentions having given to son Abel, a tract of land in Rockland Manor, Newcastle Co. containing 100 acres. To son Edward Whitaker, daughter Ann Clayton and her husband, 5 shillings each, having already provided for them. Remainder of land and stock to be sold and money divided among 3 daughters, Hannah, Sarah and Mary.
Executors: wife Mary and friend John Bezer of Chichester.
Witnesses: Humphrey Scarlet, Nathan Wood, Thos. Barnard, Thos. Linval.

BARTON, ISAAC. Sadsbury. Smith.
May 18, 1721. 3/31/1721. A. 119.
To wife Sarah 1/2 of estate real and personal. To my 7 children, viz Abraham, Isaac, Mary, Elizabeth, Jacob, Joshua and Benjamin 5 shillings each. Remainder to executors for use of children.
Executors: wife Sarah and Jacob Weldon.
Witnesses: Arthur White, Wm. Marsh, Robt. Sanford and Joseph Griffiths.

HENDRICKS, JOHN. Ridley, yeoman.
April 10, 1720. 4/5/1721. A. 121.
To 3 sons Andrew, John and Israel, all real estate to be equally divided, Andrew to have his part where I now dwell but all to be at disposal of wife during widowhood, for bringing up the younger children. Personal estate to wife and daughters who are not named except Mary, "which is married."
Executors: wife Magdalena and son Andrew.
Witnesses: John Archer, Jacob Archer, Geo. Campinet.

TALBOT, JOHN. Middletown, yeoman.
June 12, 1721. 5/22/1721. A. 122.
To wife Mary all real and personal during widowhood. To my children by wife Elizabeth, viz Mary, Joseph, Benjamin, John, Elizabeth, Sarah, Rachel and a child my wife is now with all my estate, sons to have £10 each more than daughters.
Executors: wife Eliz and friend Jonathan Haycock.
Witnesses: John Gibson, John Chapman, Peter H. Hunter. Letters to Mary Talbot.

YARNALL, FRANCIS. Willistown.
4/3/1721. 6/6/1721. A. 124.
To eldest son John, 150 acres of land which was part of Thos. Brasies tract, which he now lives on. To son Moses, the remainder of said tract being 127 acres. To son Joseph, the tract of land in Springfield, containing 120 3/4 acres paying to daughter Sarah £30. To daughter Sarah £20. To son Mordecai at 21, 100 acres of land. To son Daniel £60 at 21. Mentions having deeded land to sons Peter and Francis. To wife the place I now live on until son Amos is 21, when he shall inherit it.
Executrix: wife, not named.

Witnesses: Geo. Smedley, Philip Yarnall, Sarah Smedley.

HEAD, BENJAMIN. Chester. from Ireland, died July 1, 1721. 6/5/1721.
9/14/1721. A. 126.
To daughter Mary Head £50. To wife Sarah all my estate (from whom I derided it] to be disposed of as she sees fit. Also executors friends Thos. Dell and Thos. Vernon, Assistants.
Witnesses: Joseph Townsend, William Clerke.

SMITH, RICHARD. Darby.
January 12, 1722. 12/9/1721/2. A. 127.
To sister Ann Smith £10. Remainder equally divided between 3 sisters Mary Smith, Elizabeth Smith and Sarah Taylor.
Executors: Thomas Smith and Isaac Taylor.
Witnesses: Jonathan Watson, Saml. Sellers, Wm. Kirk.

BROOM, JAMES. Chester.
7/13/1721. 12/19/1721/2. A. 127.
To son Alexander all my real estate in Marshfield County of Gloucester, England with revision in case of death before he is 21, to my daughter Edith Broom all estate real and personal in Chester County to be sold and proceeds invested for use of said son and daughter when 21. All estate in west New Jersey to be sold and proceeds for son Alexander.
Executors: William Hammons of Concord.
Witnesses: William Pyle, John Hughes, John Taylor.
Executor to send son Alexander to England when four years old unless he understand his relations are dead or not willing to receive him.

SWAINE, FRANCIS. Marlborough.
2/14/1721. 1/26/1722. A. 131.
Provides for wife, not named. To daughter Sarah £20. To son William the smith tools and my watch. To son Francis £25. To daughter Jean £5. To son Edward the plantation when 21 paying above legacies.
Executors: wife and son William.
Witnesses: William Webster, Chas. Hollman, John Wickersham.

POWELL, ANN. Wife of David. Marple. 3/4/1722. 3/11/1722.
To son in law Richard Moris of Springfield and daughter Elizabeth his wife £120, he paying to my husband David Powell, £5 yearly, so long as he continues unmarried and at his decease pay to their 3 daughters, viz, Mary, Elizabeh and Ann £30 each. To son in law Evan Lewis and my daughter Mary his wife £10, they paying to husband £5 yearly. To kinswoman Rachel Merick of Philadelphia £10. To friends John Salkeld, John Lea and Joseph Selby £5 each. To my husbands 2 daughter, viz Lydia wife of David Harry and Mary wife of Lewis Lewis 20 shillings each and to the 2 eldest children of Lewis Lewis, that is Anne and Phineas 10 shillings each. To John Powell of Marple 40 shillings. To granddaughter Hannah, daughter of Evan Lewis, bed etc. Mentions Ann daughter of Evan Lewis. To my husband's son Saml. Powell 20 shillings. Remainder to Elizabeth Mario.

Executors: sons in law, Richard Maris and Evan Lewis.
Witnesses: John Broomfield, Mary Broomfield, Lidia Thompson.

BALDWIN, WILLIAM. Chester. Mason.
July 20, 1722. 6/2/1722. A. 135.
To brother Anthony Baldwin 10 shillings. To wife Mary all estate real and personal. Letters to widow.
Witnesses: John Griest, Thomas Baldwin, Edward Carter.

HENDRICKSON, ANDREW. Ridley.
June 27, 1722. 6/6/1722. A. 136.
Directs body to be buried in grave yard of Swedes Church at Wickaco. To eldest son Henry 5 shillings. To daughter Katharine a horse. To wife Katherine 1/3 personal estate and use of plantation until eldest son John comes of age. To daughters Elinor, Mary Christian and Rebecca, articles named. To son Jacob 18 shillings. To 3 sons, John, Peter and Gabriel, all remainder of estate real and personal.
Executors: wife Katherine and neighbor George Vanculin.
Witnesses: John Crosby, George Vanculin.

BUTCHER, EDMUND. Birmingham. Worsted comber.
December 21, 1720. 7/22/1722. A. 139.
Provides for wife Isabella. To daughter Susanna Butcher £30 at 18. To my brother in law John Beckingham, one cow. To my 4 sons, viz Zachariah, Edmund, Thomas and William, all remainder of estate real and personal.
Executor: brother John Beckingham.
Witnesses: John Wyeth Jr., John Wyeth, W. Haydon.

EFFORD, THOMAS.
October 2, 1721.
Adm. to Silas Prior.

WITHERS, JOHN.
January 22, 1721.
Adm. to Benjamin Moulder.

FREDERICK, ISAAC.
November 30, 1721.
Adm. to John Frederick.

CARTHEDGE, JOHN.
November 19, 1722.
Adm. to Elizabeth Carthedge.

MORTON, ANDREW.
November 8, 1722.
Adm. to Margret Morton.

JONES, THOMAS.
June 9, 1722.
Adm. to Richard Story.

DAVIES, THOMAS. Uwchlan.
July 24, 1722.
Adm. to Elizabeth Davies.

BROWN, ALEXANDER.
September 22, 1722.
Adm. to Ellenor Brown.

JOB, ANDREW. Nottingham. Farmer.
March 30, 1722. 9/13/1722. A. 140.
To son Jacob the 1/2 of the lot where he is now settled. To son Abraham, the other 1/2 of said lot. To son Enoch the tract of land upon little Elk river. To son Thomas 200 acres of the south end of the lott whereon I live. To son in law John White £5. To my 3 grandchildren, William, John and Mary White, 20 shillings each when 10 years old. To grandson Nathan Job 40 shillings when 10.

To wife Elizabeth my plantation whereon I live during widowhood and
afterward to 2 younger sons Caleb and Joshua, they paying to their 2
younger sisters Hannah and Patience £10 each when of age. Wife
Elizabeth executrix.
Witnesses: John Beals Sr., Jacob Beals.

ROBISON, JOHN. Conestogue. Farmer.
March 7, 1721/2. 9/29/1722. A. 141.
To my sister Elizabeth 5 shillings. To friend James Patterson all
remainder of estate real and personal, also executor.
Witnesses: Geo. Oatway, Edward Douherty, John Morris.

THOMAS, DANIEL. Merion.
10/1/1722. January 1, 1722/3. A. 145.
To nephew John Thomas of Haverford £40 and to Elizabeth his daughter
£20 when she is 12. To Abednego Vichan of Darby £9. To Thomas Vichan
£6. To Griffith Vichan £2. To Margaret youngest daughter of David
Lewellin £5. To Hannah youngest daughter of Henry Lewis £5. To Morgan
David of Merion £4. To James Mortimer £2. To Mary David £2. To Thomas
Mills El. To Haverford Meeting £3-10. To sister Elizabeth Thomas of
Langiby Co, Cardigan, Great Britain £10. To sister Gwen Thomas and
brother Joshua Thomas of same place £10 each. To sister Elizabeths
daughter and her 2 children £10 to be divided.
Executors: Henry Lewis and David Lewellin and authorizes them to found
a school at Haverford with contingent remainder of estate. Witnesses:
John David, Thomas David.

CHENEY, JOHN. Middletown.
October 30, 1722. January 1, 1722/3. A. 145.
To sons John and Thomas all estate real and personal here and in
Great Britain to be equally divided, except £20 to son Thomas and
E5 to Cheyney Walderon in Great Britain.
Executors: sons John and Thomas.
Witnesses: Edward Lawrence, Edward Pilkington, Ephraim Jackson.

SCHOLLAR, JOHN. Springfied, yeoman.
March 15, 1722/3. May 16, 1723. A. 147.
To wife Jane the house and lands where I now dwell and all other
estate also executrix.
Witnesses: Jonathan Haycock, Saml. Levis Jr., John Pearson.

SMEDLEY, GEORGE. Willistown.
2/28/1723. 3/29/1723. A. 148.
To daughter Alice Woodward £10. To grandchildren that is the children
of John Edge, 1/2 of all estate at 21 and 18. Land in Willistown,
containing 200 acres to be sold and all personal
estate and proceeds divided between sons Thomas and George and
son in law John Williamson who are also executors.
Witnesses: Sarah and Harry, William Lewis.

DOUGHERTY, OWEN.
October 1, 1722.
Adm. to Robert Richardson.

PEIRSON, THOMAS. (of Caln).
October 4, 1722, died 29 September.
Adm. to John Mendenhall. Inventory by John Earl and Jos. Cloud,
November 19, 1722. £74 :15 :10.
Surveying instruments and what belongs thereto. £1.

HOLLINGSWORTH, JOHN.
October 6, 1722.
Adm. to Stephen Jackson of Philadelphia, Katherine the widow,
renouncing.

FAIRLAMB, NICHOLAS.
October 22, 1722.
Adm. to Katherine Fairlamb.

COEBURN, JOSEPH. Aston. Gent.
3/28/1723. 4/5/1723. A. 149.
To wife Sarah, the tract of land where I now dwell in Aston during
life afterward to 2 sons, Caleb and Joshua. To daughter Sarah Coeburn,
£50 at 21. To the child with which my wife is now pregnant, the tract
of land which was my wifes in Sadsbury containing about 300 acres. To
3 daughters, Dinah, Lydia and Susanna, the money due by bond from
James Gibbons. To son Thomas 1 shillings. To son Joseph 1 shilling and
to his children 1 shilling each. To daughter Elizabeth Pedrick and her
children 1 shilling each.
[The daughter Sarah married John Harris and John Coppock.]
Remainder to wife Sarah who is also executrix.
Witnesses: John Churchman, Arthur Barratt, Jos. Coeburn Jr. The widow
married John Weldon.

MASSAR, MARY. Westtown.
4/30/1723. 6/3/1723. A. 151.
To eldest daughter Mary Penal £5. To daughter Elizabeth £5. To 2 sons
Thomas and Joseph Masser, remainder of estate also executors. Will not
signed.
Proven by: James Gibbons, Ann Gibbons.

BLUNSTONE, JOHN. Darby, yeoman.
5/7/1723. 6/28/1723. A. 151.
Provides for wife Margaret, to daughter Sarah Fern £10 and to her
husband and child £10. To daughter Katharine Rhodes ditto. To the 2
children of son John, viz Sarah and Hannah £15 each. To son Samuel all
lands & messuages, after wifes decease, he paying to my 2 trustees £20
each.
Executrix: wife Margaret.
Trustees John Salkeld of Chester and John Smith of Marlborough.
Witnesses: Obadiah Bonsall, Benj. Pearson, Saml. Bunting.

FREDD, KATHERINE. Widow, late of Birminham.
8/23/1723. 9/12/1723. A. 154.
To son Nicholas Fred El. To daughter in law Ann Fred £1. To John
and Mary, children of son Nicholas, £5 each when 10 years old. To
cousin Deborah Starr £1-4. To cousin Mary Hutton El-4.
To daughter in law Deborah Fredd and daughter Rachel Miller,

articles named. To Sarah the child of my daughter Rachel Miller £20, when 10 years of age. To son Benjamin Fred, £20. To brother in law Thomas Jackson, £1-4.
Executors: son Benjamin and brother in law Thos. Jackson.
Witnesses: Mary Jackson, Saml. Jackson, Isaac Jackson.

TODHUNTER, MARGARET. Widow. Westtown.
December 14, 1723. 10/17/1723. A. 156.
To son John Todhunter £140 at 21, to be brought up and educated at charge of my son Stephen Beakes. To daughters Mary wife of John Boune and Ann wife of Caleb Perkins £3 each. To son Stephen Beakes all remainder of estate.
Executors: son Stephen Beakes and friend Geo. Ashbridge of Goshen. Will not signed.
Witnesses: John Taylor, Thomas Smedley, Bery Hickman.

NATSELLERS, MATHIAS. Darby, yeoman.
February 11, 1723. 12/25/1723/4. A. 158.
To daughter Christian 1 shilling and to son in law Gunrod Nethermerk her husband, 6 acres of upland. To son Otto, all remainder of my plantation in Darby. Remainder to son Otto and 5 younger daughters, viz Catharine, Mary, Elizabeth, Dorothy and Margaret.
Executor: son Otto; overseers: Richard Parker Jr. and Zachariah Cook.
Witnesses: Richard Parker Jr., Benjamin Pearson, Rose Bethel. [Son in law of Otto Ernest Cock, Penna. Mag. ii 228. A deed recorded in Philadelphia, says he was son in law of Peter Putcon who acknowledged a deed to him at Chester Court 1702-3. ... See Archives XIX 555.]

JOHNSON, JAMES. Nottingham.
12/18/1723/4. March 11, 1723/4. A. 160.
Real and personal estate to be sold, 1/3 thereof to wife Barbara and 2/3 to my 3 children John, James and Elizabeth Johnson. Refers to "my estate that I have in North Britain."
Executrix: wife Barbara.
Witnesses: Elisha Gatchell, Thos. Job, Abraham Job.

PUGH, JAMES. Uchlan.
October 7, 1723. August 25, 1724. A. 161.
To son Hugh, the plantation on which I now live. To son John, 200 acres of land upon French Creek. To son Thomas, 200 acres of roughland adjacent son Johns, next to Simon Meredith. To son James, £6. To daughters Joan and Sible Pugh, £10 each. 40 shillings towards enlarging Uwchlan Meeting house. Remainder to children, viz Hugh, John, Thomas, Joan and Sible.
Executors: sons Hugh and John, friends David Pugh and David Price, assistants.
Witnesses: Richard Thomas, Samuel John.
[Joan married Wm. Williams, Sibilla married John Edwards.]

REYNOLDS, HENRY. Chichester.
April 12, 1720. 8/16/1724. A. 164.
To son Francis the plantation where I live in Chichester

containing 290 acres, he paying his brother William when 21, £20. To
son John, tract of land in Chichester, containing 210 acres, paying
his brother Wm. £20. To son Henry tract of land in Nottingham
containing 490 acres. To son Wm, tract in Nottingham [being a south
lott], containing 490 acres. To each of my daughters, viz Margaret,
Prudence, Deborah and Hannah 1 shilling each. To wife Prudence all
personal estate, also executrix. Witnesses: William Clayton, John
Hanby.

MORTON, JOHN. Ridley, yeoman.
February 6, 1724/5. 12/20/1724/ A. 166.
To wife Mary the use of plantation, containing 135 acres in Ridley,
during widowhood unless we have a child which lives to maturity
otherwise at her decease to brother George Culins children by my
sister Margaret, viz John, George, Morton, Daniel and Jonas, remainder
to wife.
Executors: brothers George Culin and Adam Archer, both of Ridley.
Witnesses: John Hallowburton, Andrew Archer, Thos. Worth Jr.

MAGIILL, DANIEL.
February 18, 1723/4.
Adm. to Thomas Hill.

EMBRUGH, JOHN.
November 26, 1724.
Adm. to John Mendenhall.

HUNTLY, FRANCIS.
May 29, 1723.
Adm. to James Bruce.

HEAD, SARAH.
November 28, 1724.
Adm. to Mary Head.

BRAND, HANS.
July 1-, 1723.
Adam Brand, Adm.

HOWELL, DAVID.
December 24, 1724.
Adm. to Penelope Howell and
Griffith Howell.

CLOUD, DANIEL.
October 2, 1723.
Adm. to Jeremiah Cloud.

HOWRY, WOLRICK.
June 2, 1724.
Adm. to Barbary Howry.

MARTIN, MARY.
December 28, 1723.
Adm. to Thos. Taylor, Jos.
Powell and Francis Routh.

WYTH, JOHN.
January 4, 1725.
Adm. to John Wyth, Jr.

LEWIS, DAVID.
March 25, 1723/4.
Adm. to Jane Lewis.

KENDRICK, HENRY.
March 30, 1725.
Adm. to Martin Kendrick and
John Harr, the widow Barbary,
renouncing in favor of brother
in law Martin Kendrick.

NEILD, JOHN.
May 18, 1724.
Adm. to Elizabeth Neild.

STAPLER, STEPHEN.
August 15, 1724.
Adm. to James Stapler.

COEBURN, THOMAS. Chester, yeoman.
January 13, 1724. April, 1, 1725. A. 167.
To daughter in law Hannah Cockfield £5 at 16. To wife Elizabeth the messuage & etc. where I dwell containing 170 acres, also my share in the mill and all other estate also executrix.
Witnesses: Thos. Coeburn, Joseph Parker.
Elizabeth Hudson married Joshua Cockfield and Thomas Boeburn.

VERNON, RANDLE. N. Providence.
6/2/1715. May 4, 1725. A. 160.
Provides for wife Sarah. To daughter Hannah and her husband Caleb Harrison 5 shillings each. To son Jacob 5 shillings. To daughter Sarah and her husband Jacob Howell 5 shilling each. To son Joseph all estate real and personal paying above legacies also executor.
Witnesses: Thomas Minshall, Jacob Vernon, Joseph Ely.

CHURCHMAN, JOHN. Nottingham.
10/7/1724. May 10, 1725. A. 170.
To eldest son George, part of my lott supposed to contain 150 acres. To son John the plantation whereon I dwell inc 70 acres since added by survey. To son Thomas part of my lott supposed to be 250 acres. To 2 youngest sons, viz Edward and William, tract of land which is run out upon Jordan, being about 300 acres. To 2 daughters Dinah and Susanna tract of land which is surveyed upon Chestnut Hill being about 300 acres, also £20 each. To 2 youngest daughters Miriam and Sarah £5 each at 18. Provision for wife.
Executors: wife Hannah and son George.
Witnesses: Aaron Coppock, Esther Brown, James Wright.

CHALFORT, JOHN. Birmingham, yeoman.
August 12, 1725. August 25, 1725. A. 172.
To wife not named, all estate real and personal during life and what remains at her death to my 2 sons, Robert and John. John's part to be in trust for his 3 eldest sons, viz John, Solomon and Robert.
Executors: son Robert and John Beckingham.
Witnesses: Mary Stevens, Edward Partridge.

ROWAN, CORNELIUS. New London.
August 18, 1725. 7/1/1725. A. 173.
Describes himself as late from Ireland. To wife Ann now in Ireland and to son Abraham, all estate real and personal and failing them to my grandson David Rowan.
Executors: James Cochran of octoraro and James Moor, New London.
Guardians: Rev Wm. Boyd of Octoraro and cousin Robert Finney.
Witnesses: James Mole, Patrick Moore, Joseph Houston.

WILSON, HUGH. Fallowfield.
April 12, 1725. September 2, 1725. A. 175.
To daughter Katherine Wilson £10. To son Gideon £15. Also 50 acres of the land I bought from Geo. Leonard. To son Samuel the remainder of land bought of Leonard, being 150 acres, when he is of age, he paying to his 2 youngest sisters Marth and Sarah Wilson £14 each, when of age. Provides for wife Ann and a possible child. To son William a heifer. To son Joseph wearing

apparel and gun.
Executors: Adam Boyd and John Devor.
Witnesses: Arthur Parke, William Wilson.

ENGLISH, JOSEPH, of Mansfield, Burlington Co. N.J., yeoman.
September 4, 1725. 8/14/1725. A. 177.
To son Joseph the tract of land whereon he now lives, [on the river], also equal part of tract containing 80 acres and £30. To son John £4 having been advanced. To son William the plantation whereon he lives, after wifes decease. To daughter Rachel wife of Thomas Green all the cattle in my name at Egg Harbor. To son in law Peter White tract of land at head of Abscom river. To duaghter Hannah wife of John Wells 5 shillings. To grandson Thomas English £10 to his brother Joseph £10. To granddaughter Hannah English daughter of son Joseph £5. To granddaughter Jean Wells £5. To wife Hannah, the plantation containing 200 acres, which lieth in the forks of Brandywine in Chester Co. and all remainder of estate, also executrix.
Witnesses: Geo. Aston, Daniel M. Lester, Hannah Nickles.

BETHEL, JOHN. Darby.
April 13, 1725. 8/15/1725. A. 179.
To son William £10 at 21. To son Joseph £5 at 21. To daughter Frances Bethell £5. To daughter Eliza Bethell £5 at 18. To wife Rose, all remainder of estate real and personal also executrix.
Witnesses: Abadiah Bonsall, Job Harvy, Richard Parker.

LIGHTFOOT, THOMAS. Darby.
1/7/1724/5. November 9, 1725. A. 180.
Provides for wife Margaret who was widow of John Blunston late of Darby. To daughter Katherine Miller, 2 sons William and Michael, daughter Abigail Wiley. Elizabeth Jones and Mary Starr and my late wifes 2 children, viz John Wiley and Mary Jackson 5 shillings each, all being married and having had their portions. To son Jacob 60 pounds to be paid out of my real estate in New Garden Township when 21. Remainder of estate real and personal to son Samuel also executor. Son Michael and son Thomas Jackson of Marlborough, overseers.
Witnesses: Richd. Parker, David Thomas, Benj. Pearson.

BOON, HANCE. Darby, yeoman.
No dat. November 30, 1725. A. 182.
Provides for wife Barbara. To son Andrew the plantation whereon I now dwell. To son Swen the house and land which was Mathias Martins. To 3 daughters Katherine, Ann and Bridget £50 each, £20 when they marry.
Executors: wife and son Andrew.
Witnesses: Benj. Cliff, Thomas Dwyer, Esther Dwyer.

OWEN, RICHARD. Whiteland, yeoman.
November 21, 1725. December 25, 1725. A. 183.
Executor to sell real estate subject to rights of mother as bequeathed her by my deceased father. To brother John, my Welsh Bible in lieu of 10 shillings which my father ordered me to pay him, remainder of estate divided into 3 equal shares, one to wife

Elinor, she applying £5 to Baptist Congregation in Tredyffrin.
Remaining 2 parts for bringing up and educating of 2 daughters, Rachel
and Rebecca. Also provides for child with which wife is now pregnant.
Executors: father in law, John Evans and friends Thomas John of
Glandy, Alexander Owen and Griffith John of Tredyffrin.
Witnesses: James Cooper, Geo. Evans, Richd. Jones.

TAYLOR, THOMAS. Springfield.
8/12/1725. December 28, 1725. A. 186.
Executor to sell plantation where I now live when youngest son Isaac
is 14. To my 4 sons, Thomas, Mordecai, Jonathan and Isaac, £20 each.
To my mother Mary Selby £5. To daughters Mary, Susanna, Esther and
Hannah, articles named. Remainder to above named 8 children.
Executors: brothers Barth Coppeock of Marple and Henry Lewis of
Haverford.
Witnesses: Robt. Taylor, Jo. Taylor, Mordecai Massey.

WAY, ROBERT. Kennett.
April 25, 1725. February 7, 1725/6. A. 188.
Joseph and Jacob 5 shillings each. To daughter Elizabeth furniture at
18 or married. To son Francis £5 when 21. Remainder divided among the
rest of my children, viz Caleb, Joshua, James, Benjamin and Elizabeth
when 21.
Executors: Philip Taylor, William Pyle.
Witnesses: Wm. Madcaff, Saml. Pyle, Pierce Power.

MUSGRAVE, MOSES. Sadsbury, yeoman.
1/5/1725/6. April 7, 1726. A. 189.
Provides for wife Elizabeth including all personal estate she paying
to son youngest, John, £30 when of age. To eldest son Moses, the place
I now live on containing 250 acres, subject to provision for his
mother during widowhood. To son Aaron 250 acres adjacent to Roger
Diers in ye great Valley. Executor to buy the same for him for £37-10.
To daughter Jean Musgrove, horses, colts etc.
Executors: wife and friend Abraham Marshall.
Witnesses: John Walter, Caleb Peirce, John Musgrove.

DAVIS, LEWIS.
December 1, 1725.
Adm. to Maudlin Davis.

DAWSON, ---.
December 6, 1725.
Adm. to Elizabeth Dawson.

HAIR, ABRAHAM.
December 14, 1725.
Adm. to Abraham Hair.

TOOBY, JOHN.
December 21, 1725.
Adm. to Mary Tooby.

BREWBACK, JOHN.
December 30, 1725.
Adm. to Jacob Croydens.

LAWRENCE, EDWARD. Middletown.
March 9, 1725/6.
Adm. to Mary Lawrence.

WILLIAM, DAVID.
April 2, 1726.
Adm. to Alexander Bane.

FLEMING, WILLIAM.
May 5, 1726.
Adm. to Mary Fleming.

TAYLOR, ISRAEL. Mattinicuck Island. Chirurgeon.
November 17, 1725. April 16, 1726. A. 191.
Directs burial by wife in burial place appointed by me in my orchard
where several of my children lieth. Bequeaths the whole of the island
above mentioned to the 3 sons that now liveth with me, viz
Christopher, Benjamin and Israel, to be dividied as will directs. To
son Samuel tract of land in township of Strasburg township containing
1300 acres. To son Thomas £100. To daughter Dinah Cartmell £50. To
daughter Sarah Heal El. To daughter Ellen, Martha and Hannah £100 each
at 21 or married. To daughter Mary Sandeland, the debts [£97] I paid
for her husband Jonas Sandelands.
Executors: sons Christopher, Benjamin and Israel.
Witnesses: James Dicken, Jonn Rose, John Wright.

NAYLE, HENRY. Thornbury.
June 11, 1726. August 20, 1726. A. 193.
Provides for wife Deborah. To grandson John son of Richard Woodward
the plantation, where I now dwell containing by estimate 200 acres,
when 21. Also team of horse. To daughter Mary Woodward £10. Remainder
of personal estate to the other children of said daughter. Gives £5 to
the church now building in Concord. To Elizabeth daughter of Henry
Peirce £5.
Executors: friend Henry Peirce and son in law Richard Woodward of
Thornbury.
Witnesses: John Cox, Richard Hendra, John Neil.

IDDINGS, RICHARD. Nantmell. Husbandman.
January 25, 1724/5. October 1, 1726.
To sons Richard and William, daughter Ann and Elizabeth 1 shilling
each. To son John 1 shilling and wearing apparel. All remainder to
wife Sarah, also executrix.
Witnesses: Edward Thomas, Reece David, Morgan Tyson.

PARRY, JAMES. Tredyffrin, yeoman.
December 28, 1725. October 1, 1726. A. 198.
Gives £1 toward the building of Presbyterian Meeting house in
Tredyffrin. Provides for wife Ann. To son David £25 as also
"one years diet if he continues teaching school in the place
where he now is in the township of Tredyffrin." To daughter
Lettice wife of Lewis William El. To daughter Elizabeth wife of
James Davies, El. To daughter Margaret Parry £25. To daughter
Mary Parry £20 when 21. To daughter Hester Parry £20 at 21. To
eldest son John all lands & messuages, also executor.
Witnesses: Thomas David, John William, Thomas Lloyd.

RICHARDSON, ISAAC. Whiteland, yeoman.
October 14, 1726. November 12, 1726. A. 200.
Provides for wife Catherine. To son John and daughters Mary,
Elizabeth, Elinor and Martha, all my land and personal estate to be
equally distributed.
Executors: wife Catherine, Isaac Melin and Wm. Paschall of Whiteland.
Witnesses: John Bennett, Edward Pugh, Eliz. Johns.

EVENSON, THOMAS. Thornbury, yeoman.
June 10, 1726 or August 20, 1726. November 30, 1726. A. 201.
Provides for wife Margaret. Remainder of estate in 3 equal parts one to wife and the others not further mentioned. To sons Richard and Joseph 5 shilling each. To daughter Hannah Arnold and Sarah Buffington £10 each. Remainder to son Ralph also executor.
Witnesses: Henry Pierce, Edward Milsam.

OSBORN, RICHARD. Nottingham.
9/24/1726. November 30, 1726. A. 203.
Describes himself as formerly of New Jersey. Bequeaths all lands & etc. in Hopewell, West New Jersey to Andrew Smith of said place and all effects in Nottingham and Maryland to Messer Brown of Nottingham except my riding horse, which I give to Benjamin Mattison of or near Susquehanna hundred.
Executor: Messer Brown.
Witnesses: John Harris, John Beckett, Thomas Hampton.

COPPOCK, AARON. Nottingham
10/3/1726. December 17, 1726. A. 205.
To son John the plantation whereon I live when he comes of age, subject to wifes life interest, the tract containing 100 acres or there about. To daughter Lydia and Merian Coppock £10 each. To daughter Sarah Frazer 5 shillings. To daughter Martha Robinson 5 shillings. To daughter Mary Sinclair 5 shillings. To son in law Ralph Thomson the money that is due me 40 shillings. To son in law John White 5 shillings. To son in law Saml. White 5 shillings. To daughter in law Elizabeth White 5 shillings.
Executors: wife Miriam, James King to be assistant.
Witnesses: James Wright, Samuel Lighter.

BEALS, JOHN. Nottingham.
8/11/1726. December 17, 1726. A. 206.
To eldest son John, bed and furniture and £5, he paying to his 5 children, viz Sarah, John, Thomas, Ann and Phebe, 10 shillings when of age. To daughter Mary Harrold 8, she paying to each of heir children, viz Elizabeth, Rachel, Jonathan and Richard 10 shillings when of age. To son Jacob £12, he paying to each of his 4 children, viz John, Jacob, Mary and William 10 shillings when of age. To daughter Patience Jones the £8-15 that is due of bond of her husband and £5 more paying to their 4 children, viz Judith, Mary, Sarah and Charity 10 shillings each, when of age. To kinswoman Mary Davis of Philadelphia 20 shillings.
Executors: sons John and Jacob.
Witnesses: James McMullin, Wm. House.

BUTCHER, THOMAS. Birmingham.
December 4, 1726. December 24, 1726.
To mother, not named, £5. To sister Susanna Butcher £5. Remainder real and personal to be equally divided between 2 brothers Zachariah and Edmund Butcher.
Executor: brother Edmund.
Witnesses: Annanias Higgins, Jas. Purtell, John Day.

YARNALL, DANIEL. Willistown.
10/17/1726. December 29, 1726. A. 208.
To brother Mordecai Yarnall £20. Remainder to mother, brothers and sisters to be equally divided.
Executor: brother Francis Yarnall.
Witnesses: John Williamson, Amos Yarnall.

STONEMAN, NICHOLAS.
March 12, 1725/6.
Adm. to Christian Brenaman.

GROVE, JOHN.
March 1, 1725/6.
Adm. to Ann Grove.

SHANK, CHRISTIAN.
March 1, 1726, 1732.
Adm. to Henry Shank.

RAWLINS, THOMAS.
August 20, 1726.
Adm. to Joseph Haines.

MOORE, DAVID.
November 3, 1726.
Adm. to Mary Moore.

EYRE, ANN.
November 21, 1726.
Adm. to William and Robert Eyre.

PHILLIPS, THOMAS.
November 28, 1726.
Adm. to Jonas Sandelands. Mary the widow renouncing.

RYALL, PETER.
December 6, 1726.
Adm. to John Willis.

CODRY, THOMAS. Birmingham, yeoman.
December 24, 1726. January 2, 1726/7. A. 208.
To son Thomas 50 acres of my land next to Anthony Baldwin. To wife Elizabeth all remainder of land and all other estate paying legacies. To daughter children Susanna Henry and Elizabeth Codry 5 shillings each when of age.
Executors: wife Elizabeth and son Thomas.
Witnesses: Thomas Codry Jr, Joseph Webb.

LINDLEY, JAMES. Londongrove. Smith.
10/8/1726. January 2, 1726/7. A. 210.
To wife not named 200 acres of land being 1/2 of the tract I now live on and all personal estate she to pay for the 600 acres I have got an order to have surveyed of the land of Sir John Faggs. To sons Thomas, James, Robert and William 200 acres of land each when 21, that is the above 600 acres to be divided into 3 equal parts and the remaining half of the tract I now live on. To son Jonathan the plantation I now live on at death of wife. To daughter Rachel £20 at 21. To daughter Margarey £20 at 21. To daughter Elizabeth £20 at 21. To daughter Hannah £20 at 21. Also provides for a child yet to be born. To son James the smith tools.
Executors: wife Elinor and son Thomas.
Witnesses: Susanna Wilcocks, Elish Maxwell, John Jordan.

SCOTT, JOHN. Kennet, yeoman.
December 2, 1726. January 9, 1726/7. A. 212.
To wife not named until child or children are 18 paying to Owen Thomas 10 shillings and to my mother in law 10 shillings.

Mentions that his wife was with child and there was a daughter not named. If children die under age after wife decease £20 to be given the Baptist Society in Birminham and the remainder to children of brothers and sisters and wifes brothers and sisters children.
Executors: John Heath and Wm. Buckingham.
Witnesses: Joseph Garrett, Margaret Buckingham, Wm. Webb. [the widow married John Garrett].

WICKERSHAM JR, THOMAS. Marlborough, yeoman.
December 23, 1726. January 10, 1726/7. A. 214.
To wife Abigail, plantation where I now dwell and all personal estate, she paying to eldest daughter Sarah £20 on day of her marriage and to youngest daughter Hannah £30 on her marriage. To only son Robert all remainder of lands, paying to his sisters Sarah and Hannah £5 each. To my brother John and sister Ann 20 shillings each.
Executrix: wife Abigail.
Witnesses: Richard Wickersham, Cales Johnson, Wm. Webb.

TAYLOR, THOMAS. Thornbury.
December 12, 1726. January 25, 1726/7.
All estate to brother Simeon Taylor of Nottingham, laborer, also executor.
Witnesses: Jo. Bernard Duplese, Geo. Bostock, Philip Taylor.

LEA, JOHN. Springfield. Weaver.
10/25/1726. February 28, 1726/7. A. 217.
Executors to sell plantation I live on in Springfield and other estate and provide for wife during life and what remains at her decease, divided among 3 children, viz Isaac, John and Hannah.
Executors: son Isaac, Saml. Levis, Wm. Levis.
Witnesses: Sarah Bonsall, Arthur Borradail, Francis Pearson.

PREW, CALEB. Kennet, yeoman.
December 15, 1726. March 1, 1726. A. 218.
To wife Hannah all personal estate and 1/2 of real estate during life and at her decease, the place I now live on to my daughter Susanna, she paying 1/3 of the value thereof to each of her 2 sisters, Sarah and Mary. To daughter Betty the land purchased of Reece Thomas adjacent the former containing 112 acres.
Executors: Jeremiah Cloud of Marlborough and John Cloud of New Castle.
Witnesses: James Maginly, Wm. Webb, Edward Terret.

TREVILLER, HENRY. Marlborough, yeoman.
December 9, 1726. March 1, 1726/7. A. 219.
Provides for wife Mary, remainder to 3 children now born, viz Ann, James, Thomas and the child wife is now pregnant with.
Executors: friend Wm. Levis and brother Joseph James and authorizes them to sell all lands.
Witnesses: Robert Carter, Wm. Webb, Richd. Hays.
[Widow married John Earl. See book A p. 65, Taylor papers, survey, etc.]

PUSEY, CALEB. Marlborough, yeoman.
1/11/1725/6. 1/14/1726/7. A. 220.
To 2 step sons, Francis and Henry Worly £50 each. To granddaughter
Susanna Painter £10 at 21 or married with rev to above named stepsons,
Francis and Henry Worley's, 2 sons viz Caleb and Daniel Worly. To
granddaughter Lydia Smith £20 at 21 or married. To cousin Caleb Pusey,
my largest dictionary. To son in law John Smith and wife Ann my tract
of land lying south of that they now live on, being 200 acres.
Executors: son in law John Smith and kinsmen Wm. L Caleb Pusey Sr.,
trustees.
Witnesses: Wm. Swain, Wm. Lowdon, Joseph Skeen.

SCARRIOT, JOSEPH.
January 2, 1726.
Adm. to Nathaniel Newlin.

WORRILOW, JOHN.
January 2, 1726.
Adm. to John Taylor.

WILKINSON, EDWARD.
February 3, 1726.
Adm. to John Wade.

COX, WALTER. Cock of
Marlborough.
January 20, 1726/7.
Adm. to Robert Jones. [Walter
Cock left widow Rebecca who
married -- Feagan and only issue
James Cock. See deed book M.
75.]

BLAND, ISAAC.
January 30, 1726/7.
Adm. to George House, widow
Susanna renouncing in favor of
"my son Geo. House."

JACK, PATRICK.
December 22, 1726.
Adm. to Elinor Jack.

RUE, WILLIAM.
February 16, 1726/7.
Adm. to George Dandison.

CLARK, JONATHAN.
April 24, 1727.
Adm. to Nathan Dicks.

COPPOCK, ELINOR. Springfield.
11/28/1720/1. 1/20/1726/7. A. 222.
To son in law Richard Woodworth and his wife Mary my daughter 10
shillings each. To son in law Robt. Williamson 10 shillings. To
daughter Hannah wife of Robt. Williamson.
Executors: brother in law Daniel Williamson of Newtown.
Witnesses: Jona Heacock, Ann Heacock, Jos. Selby.

CARTER, GEORGE. Bradford, yeoman.
12/24/1726/ March 27, 1727. A. 223.
To wife Elizabeth the home plantation and stock during life. To
daughters Rachel, Elizabeth and Mary £40 each when 18, also the
plantation on wifes decease. To eldest daughter Ann Carter £80 and
articles named. To eldest son George my upper plantation when 21. To
son John, my share of the mill and horse. Woodward renounced.
Executors: wife Elizabeth, Richd. Woodward (renounced), Samuel Nutt.
Witnesses: Abiah Taylor, Joseph Townsend, Thomas Ward.

LEWIS, EVAN. Whiteland,, yeoman.
February 16, 1726/7. March 28, 1727. A. 224.
To wife Maud, my plantation whereon I now live, containing 150 acres during widowhood and afterward to son Griffith Lewis, he paying to daughter Catharine £40. To daughter Mary £60. To daughter Elizabeth 10 shillings.
Executrix: wife Maud.
Witnesses: David Howell, Jane George, John Howell.

RICE, JOHN. Chester.
February 9, 1726/7. March 28, 1727. A. 226.
Gives £1-5 to the minister that shall preach my funeral sermon and £5 for repairs on the Protestant Church in Chester. To wife Catherine 1/2 of all estate real and personal and the remaining during life and at her decease to my brothers Edward and Henry Rice of Bandon in Ireland.
Executors: Alex Hunter and Wm. Weldon.
Witnesses: Jos. Reyners, John Minshall, Nathan Pickles.

FABIAN, WILLIAM. Uwchlan.
March 25, 1727. April 3, 1727. A. 227.
To daughter Elizabeth £8 with interest from this date to the daughter of her age. All remainder to wife Sarah also executrix. Witnesses: John Elleman, Owen John.

STEDWELL, THOMAS. Ridley. Laborer.
March 15, 1726/7. April 3, 1727. A. 228.
Non cupative will. To son Ebenezer £50 when 21. Remainder to wife Dinah.
Executors: brother in law John Hendrickson and wife Dinah.
Witnesses: Magdalen Hendrick, John Hendrickson, Mary Morton.

MOORE, JOHN. Caln.
11/12/1726/7. April 10, 1727. A. 229.
To mother £8 per annum during life. To sister Mary Fleming £5. To brother in law Mathias Kerlin and my sister Susanna his wife, my negro man Jo, to my brother Joseph Cloud £5. To sister Mary Kerlin £5. To sister Ann Engle £5. To brother Benjamin Moore £7. To cousin Stacy Moore £2 when 12. To Thomas Cook a new blanket. To Wm. Orson a new hat. To brother Thomas Moore all remainder of estate real and personal, also executor.
Witnessed by Richard Hughs, Thomas Jones.

BRADSHAW, THOMAS. Darby, yeoman.
7/9/1725. April 18, 1727. A. 231.
To daughter Hannah £30. To daughter Mary £10. To daughter Sarah Bradshaw £10. Remaining real and personal equally divided among all children, viz Hannah, Mary, Sarah, Elizabeth.
Executors: cousin Saml. Levis Jr and daughter Hannah.
Witnesses: Saml. Bunting, Benj. Pearson, Josiah Fern.

GARRETT, WILLIAM. Darby.
1/3/1726/7. April 18, 1727. A. 232.
Provides for wife, not named. To children, viz Elizabeth, Isaac, Martha, Joshua, Mary and William £40 each, sons at 21 and

daughters at 18. To son John when 21, the plantation I now live on and farming implements. Remainder equally divided among my 7 children, viz Elizabeth, Isaac, Martha, Joshua, Mary, Hannah and William. Appoints brothers Richard Parker and Samuel Seller, guardians for children.
Executors: wife, brother Joseph Pennell and Saml. Levis Jr.
Witnesses: Michael Blunston, John Marshall, Josiah Hibbard.

BOOTH, ROBERT. Bethel, yeoman.
2/1/1727. April 27, 1727. A. 234.
To son Joseph part of my land formerly belonging to Wm. Fleming containing 130 acres. To daughter Mercy £5 and all my right and interest to the moneys in England. To son Robert when 21 the land whereon I live containing 130 acres. To son John £30 at 21 to be apprenticed at 14. To daughters Mary and Ann £10 when 21. Remainder to wife Elizabeth.
Executors: wife Elizabeth and friend John Bezar.
Witnesses: Robert Pyle, John Hopton, William Wilton.

COHLAN, JOHN. Sadsbury.
April 3, 1727. April 28, 1727. A. 235.
To brother Cornelius Cohlan, my gun and bible. To sister Mary Murphy 30 shillings and the remainder to Wm. Smith, for his trouble and charge that he has been at for me. Letters to Wm. Smith.
Witnesses: Stephen Heard, James Kelly.

REYNOLDS, WILLIAM. Ches Co., yeoman.
April 16, 1727. May 8, 1727. A. 235.
To wife Mary, my plantation, stock etc. To son Robert £100. To son David £100. To 2 daughter Agnes and Martha Reynolds £70 each.
Executors: wife Mary, Robert Reynolds Sr and Robert Reynolds Jr.
Witnesses: James Donald, James Wright, Wm. Porter.

BATTERTON, HENRY. Nantmeall.
April 9, 1727. May 13, 1727. A. 237.
All real and personal estate to wife Patience to breed up my children in a Christian like manner. She paying to eldest son Robert £5 and to the 3 others - Mary, Martha and James £4 each, when 21. Letters to wife.
Witnesses: Richard Jones, Thomas Weight, William Arnold.

LITTLER, SAMUEL. Nottingham.
3/8/1727. May 30, 1727. A. 238.
To wife Rachel 200 acres of land at the north end of the lott whereon I now live until son John is of age. To son Joshua the remainder of the aforesaid lott, when of age. To son Samuel the 200 acres of land I bought of Richard Jones when of age. To son Mincher 200 acres of land upon the branches of Pigeon Creek when of age. To daughter Sarah Littler £20 when of age.
Executors: wife Rachel and son John.
Witnesses: Alexander Ross, John Ruddell.

LANGWORTHY, JENESIS. Newtown.
2/7/1727. May 30, 1727. A. 240.

To son Henry 5 shillings. To son William 15 shillings. To daughter
Elizabeth Evans 5 shillings. To daughters Sarah, Margaret and Mary,
furniture.
Executors: daughters Sarah and Mary who are to pay Thos. Reece's child
20 shillings. Letters to Sarah and Mary Harris.
Witnesses: William Hary, John Reece, Thomas Reece.

MALIN, JACOB. Upper Providence, yeoman.
11/3/1726/7. May 30, 1727. A. 241.
To wife Susanna use and profits of the plantation I am now settled on
containing 150 acres during widowhood for support and maintenance of
children who are not named.
Executors: wife Susanna and brother Isaac Malin.
Witnesses: Randal Malin, Henry Miller.

HUGHS, MORGAN. Easttown.
November 21, 1726. May 31, 1727. A. 242.
Provides for wife Elizabeth. To eldest son Benjamin my plantation
where I dwell containing 100 acres and farming implements. To son
Edward £40 at 21. To daughter Elizabeth £10 and household goods. To
daughter Dorothy 20 shillings.
Executors: wife Elizabeth and son Benjamin.
Witnesses: Wm. Davis, Morgan Hughs, Richard Iddings.

THOMAS, JOHN. Darby.
3/6/1727. May 31, 1727. A. 244.
To son Lewis Thomas all my land and plantation in Darby. To eldest son
John 5 shillings. To grandson Joseph Thomas 5 shillings. To
granddaughter Sarah Thomas 5 shillings. To grandson John Thomas £5 at
10 years of age. To granddaughter Susanna Thomas 5 shillings. To
daughter Elinor Shelton £30. To daughter Susanna Thomas £25. Remainder
to son Lewis also executor. Witnesses: Adam Roades, Henry Lewis.

RITTER, JOHN. Coventry.
May 17, 1727. June 7, 1727. A. 246.
To sons John, George and Paul Ritter £5 each when 21. To son in law
Gerrard Hangel £2. To daughter Katherine Hangell £3. To daughter
Margaret Ritter £5 at 18. To daughter in law Sarah Ritter Widow of
Frederick Ritter 1 shilling. Remaining both real and personal to wife
Margaret, also executrix.
Witnesses: Benjm. Hickman, Thomas Smedley, John Cheney.

ELLIS, THOMAS. Easttown.
6/24/1726. June 16, 1727. A. 246.
To sister Elizabeth Price £45. To brother Joseph Ellis £4. To my 3
brothers Evan, William and Benjamin 40 shillings each. To sister
Bridget Davis £3. To sister Rebecca Ellis £3. To Rees Prices 4
children 5 shillings each. To Mary wife of Abrahm Lewis £5 and 20
shillings to be divided among her 5 children. To friend Abram Lewis
£10. To Ann wife of Lewis David of Haverford £3.
Executors: Mother Lydia Ellis and Abraham Lewis.
Witnesses: Thomas Jones, John David Lewellin.

MESSAR, ROBERT. New London. Weaver.

May 13, 1727. August 1, 1727. A. 248.
Appoints friend James Smith of Nottingham and Robert Smith of New London executors and guardians of children with power to dispose of estate for benefit of wife and children who are not named. Letters to above named executors.
Witnesses: Andrew Steel, John Morrison, Abm. Emmit Jr.

OGDEN, JONATHAN. Chester. Innholder.
6/17/1727. August 31, 1727. A. 249.
To daughter Katherine articles of furniture named at 21. Executors to sell house and lott where I now dwell and all other real estate and invest proceeds for use of 2 sons David and Joseph and daughter Katherine Ogden, to be equally divided when 21.
Executors: father in law, George Robison and cousin Jacob Howell.
Witnesses: Martha Ogden, Peter Grashoe, Jo. Parker.

WOOD, AUBREY.
May 2, 1727.
Adm. to Ellen Wood.

WOODWARD, RICHARD.
June 23, 1727,
Adm. to Mary Woodward.

WALL, JOSEPH.
May 6, 1727.
Adm. to Mary Wall.

MARSHALL, WILLIAM.
August 28, 1727.
Adm. to Mary Marshall.

CROSS, JAMES.
May 29, 1727.
Adm. to John Spencer.

VALLELEY, ARTHUR.
September 1, 1727.
Adm. to Hugh Reiney.

BROWN, WILLIAM.
June 2, 1727.
Adm. to Messar Brown.

GREGORY, JOHN.
September 27, 1727.
Adm. to Mary Gregory.
(William Nichols and wife Mary, widow and adm. of John Gregory of Caln file accounts June 29, 1734; charge for bringing up dau. Rebecca for 18 months, daus. Thamer and Ann 3 months. other children were Wm. Gregory, Sarah Strong and Esther Gregory. Tamer m. about 1743 Ralph Forrester an Irish schoolmaster and lived in Goshen. Wm. Gregory and Margaret Lowe m. Apr. 16, 1736, Swedes Church, Wilmington.]

JACKSON, THOMAS. Marlborough. Weaver.
2/25/1727. September 16, 1727. A. 251.
Provides for wife Mary including use of plantation I now live on containing 140 acres until son Ben is 21 and servants Saml. Hughes, Elizabeth Iriscall and Joseph Kelly. To son Samuel 180 acres of land adjacent on south side of above mentioned tract. To son Isaac 180 acres on south side of Samuels. To son Benjamin this plantation on which I live when he is 21, paying to daughter Ruth Martin £20 [wife of Joseph Martin in Ireland]. Remainder to wife and 3 sons.

Executors: wife Mary and son Samuel. Overseers brother in law Michael Lightfoot and cousin Benjamin Fred, both of Newgarden. Witnesses: Wm. Beverly, Abigail Wickersham, Francis Windle.

WORRALL, HENRY. Marple.
7/1/1727. October 7, 1727. A. 254.
To father in law John Broomfield of Whiteland and mother Mary Broomfield his wife £5 each. To brother Joshua Worrall my plantation in Marple containing 150 acres also £20, he paying to my brother Peter and sisters Mary and Hannah Worrall £20 each. Executors to sell plantation purchased of Enoch Pearson in Marple.
Executors: brother Joshua Worrall and Mordecai Massey.
Witnesses: Mary Jones, Peter Worrell, Jos. Selby.

JONES, THOMAS. Upper Providence, yeoman.
September 13, 1727. October 17, 1727. A. 255.
Provides for wife Ann. To daughter Mary Jones £20, horse, cows, sheep. To son Peter all real and remainder of personal estate paying debts and legacies.
Executor: wife Ann and friend Isaac Minhall.
Witnesses: Peter Jones, Pete Taylor, Peter Dicks.

MILLER, JOSEPH. New Garden.
7/26/1727. October 24, 1727. A. 257.
To wife Ann all personal estate and plantation until sons are 21. To sons John and Isaac this plantation containing 300 acres to be equally divided by a north and south line, when they are 21, with reversion in case of their death to brother Wm. Miller he paying £100 to wife and £100 to brother James and sisters Mary Hutton, Marth Jordan, Sarah Hutton, Elizabeth, Susanna and Elinor Miller.
Executive: wife Ann and brother Wm. Miller.
Witnesses: Michael Lightfoot, John McKillip, James Starr.

MOOR, FRANCIS. New London. Farmer.
September 21, 1727. December 11, 1727. A. 258.
To son James £10 and cow. To daughter Elizabeth £6. To daughter Jean £6. To daughter Margaret £6 at 18. To daughter Jenneh £6 at 18. To son Francis my plantation on which I live which is 200 acres. To wife Jean all other personal estate and use of plantation during life, after her decease, what remains to three youngest children, viz Margaret, Jenneh and Francis. Wife Jane executrix.
Witnesses: Robb Smith, John McKrakin, Abm. Emmich Jr.

ROE, JOSEPH. Pequa.
December 1727. December 1727.
Estate to wife and children who are not named except son Joseph. Wife executrix. Witnessed by James Johnson, Joseph Davis, James Cole, Magnus Tate.

DAVIS, HAZEHIAH.
November 6, 1727.
Adm. to John Jones.

POWELL, JOHN.
November 28, 1727.
Adm. to Sibella Goodbolt.

WEAVER, WILLIAM.
December 14, 1727.
Adm. to Mary Weaver.

COCHRAN, JOSEPH.
December 7, 1727.
Adm. to Ephraim Moore.

MIER or MYER, WOOLRICH.
December 7, 1727.
Adm. to Martin Milen.

HICKMAN, ROBERT.
January 8, 1727/8.
Adm. to Ralph Withers.

CLEMENTS, NICHOLAS.
January 9, 1727/8.
Adm. to William Clayton.

ROBINSON, THOMAS.
January 11, 1727/8.
Adm. to Catherine Robinson.

SMITH, WILLIAM. Darby.
April 9, 1726. January 8, 1727/8. A. 260.
Provides for wife Elizabeth. Refers to an agreement made before married with her and also to her son Philip Pritchard deceased. To son Edward the plantation being the purchases I made of Thomas Brasey. Jacob Simcock and John Hallowell, during life afterward to his children also my tract of land bought of John Estaugh agent of the London Co also my share of the lands which he and I bought jointly of John Hood in Darby. To son William 5 shillings having done sufficiently for him. To daughter Rose Bethall £40. To grandson Saml. Pritchard £20 at 21. To daughter Elizabeth £40. To daughter Mary £40. To grandchildren Wm. and Elizabeth Bartram, Ellen Fretwell, Frances William, Joseph and Elizabeth Bethell, William and Benjamin Pearson, Martha, William and Sarah Smith, Saml. Pearson, Joice, Simon, John and Wm. Smith £10 each, when of age. Executors to sell land in the great valley in Chester Co. To sons in law David Thomas, John Smith and Enoch Pearson 5 shillings each.
Executors: son Edward and Saml. Levis Jr.
Witnesses: William Shipley, Mary Shipley, Isaac Tunecliff.

PERTT, SIMON. Conestogoe. Sadler.
January 4, 1727/8. January 13, 1727/8. A. 263.
All estate to Tobias Hendricks Esq. also executor. Will "to be of no force or effect in any other place but this Province."
Witnesses: Samuel Taylor, John Hendrick, Joshua Lowe.
Appraisers, John Postlethwait and Joshua Lowe.

ROE, ELIZABETH. Pequea.
November 18, 1727. February 7, 1727/8. A. 264.
Plantation and all moveable estate to be sold "in ye spring" and £20 taken for the raising of the 2 children Joseph and Priscilla being ye youngest and then an equal division be made of ye rest, between all my children excepting a mare that my husband left my son Joseph and my daughter Sarah shall have my side saddle, clothes.
Executors: brothers Richard and William Hiddings.
Witnesses: Jas. Johnston, Joseph Davis, James Cole.

SMITH, ELIZABETH. Darby.
3/3/1721. February 20, 1727/8. A. 265.
To son Edward Pritchett, daughter Elizabeth Calvert, son Richard Pritchett [mentions his wife Elizabeth] and grandson Samuel Pritchett, each 1/4 of estate. Refers to "my present husband", but does not name him.
Executors: sons Edward and Richard Pritchett.
Witnesses: Saml. Levis Jr, Edward Smith, Mary Smith. Codicil mentions son in law Danl. Calvert and granddaughter Elizabeth Calvert.

CLAYTON, WILLIAM. Chichester, yeoman.
10/24/1725. February 22, 1727/8. A. 267.
Provides for wife Elizabeth. To son Richard 5 shillings. To son in law Thomas Howell 10 shillings and to daughter Rachel his wife 20 shillings. To sons Edward and Ambrose lott of land in Chichester remainder to 5 sons, viz William, Edward, Thomas, Abel and Ambrose, except 40 foot lot in Philadelphia to son Richard.
Executors: sons Edward, Thomas, Ambrose and Abel.
Witnesses: John Weldon, Robt. Plummer, Joseph Bond.

SWAFFER, JACOB. Nether Providence.
12/10/1727/8. March 2, 1727/8. A. 269.
All estate real and personal to be sold and proceeds equally divided among my 3 brother and 5 sisters, viz Joseph, William, Thomas, Mary, Phebe, Ann, Sarah and Hannah Swaffer.
Executors: brother Joseph and cousin John Sharpless Jr.
Witnesses: John Sharpless, Thos. Vernon, Caleb Cowpland.

WILLIAMSON, DANIEL. Edgmont, yeoman.
March 7, 1725/6. March 8, 1727/8. A. 270.
To wife Mary my plantation with all the stock during life, also £60. To son Robert all the money due to me from him. To son Daniel ditto. To son John the cane cousin Mary Lewis gave me. To son Thomas the plantation after his mothers decease, he paying £5 to each of my 2 daughters, viz Margaret Thompson and Abigail Yarnall. To daughter Mary and son in law Myrick Davis £5. To son Joseph 1 shillings.
Executors: wife Mary and sons John and Thomas.
Witnesses: John Houldston, Ephraim Jackson.

YEARSLEY, ELIZABETH. Widow. Concord.
1/11/1728. March 25, 1728. A. 271.
To son in law Peter Hatton £15 and articles named. To son John articles named. Remainder of goods and wearing apparel to 4 daughters, viz Ann wife of Jacob Vernon, Elizabeth wife of Moses Key, Hannah wife of Peter Hatton and Martha wife of John Palmer. Remainder of money to Jacob Vernon, Moses Key, Son John and John Palmer. To friend Thomas Marshall 10 shillings, also executor. Witnesses: Peter Hatton, Harmah Dutton.

MORGAN, HUGH. Nottingham.
7/28/1727. April 6, 1728. A. 273.
To wife Mary all personal estate to bring up the children. To son John all my right to a tract of land that I look up in Co. with

Thomas Jackson of Marlborough, lying next to the north of John
Rentfroes. All the rest of children to have equal parts of personal
estate as they come to age. Sons Robert, Joseph, Moses and David and
daughter Sarah being named.
Executors: wife Mary and son Hugh Morgan.
Witnesses: John Cook, Robert Oldham, John Ruddell.

REYNOLDS, PRUDENCE. Chichester.
November 17, 1726. April 15, 1728. A. 274.
To my daughters "as many as shall be in being" all household goods. To
son Francis, eldest son Henry Reynolds one silver cup value 40
shillings. Remainder of estate to all children in being, none named.
Executor: son Henry Reynolds.
Witnesses: Robert Howard, Mathew Keasby, John Lea.

WOOD, JOHN. Darby.
4/27/1728. August 9, 1728. A. 278.
To sons George and John and daughter Ann wife of Owen Owens 5
shillings each. To son Abraham and daughter Hannah Wood £25 each. To
son William 1/2 the money he owes me. To grandson Aubrey Wood by son
Aubrey, deceased, £20 at 21. Remainder real and personal. To son
Joseph at 21 subject to provision for wife Rebecca inc 1/16 part of
Brigateen Mary Ann, now upon a voyage to sea.
Executors: wife Rebecca and son Joseph.
Witnesses: Benj. Bonsall, Saml. Bethell, Thomas Worth Jr.

MYLEN, JOHN.
January 29, 1727/8.
Adm. to John Mylen.

SWOAP, YOAST.
January 29, 1727/8.
Adm. to John Swoap.

PERKINS, HUMPHREY.
February 5, 1727/8.
Adm. to Jane Perkins.

ROADS, BENJAMIN.
February 10, 1727/8.
Adm. to Elizabeth Roads.

THOMAS, JAMES.
February 27, 1727/8.
Adm. to George Ashbridge.

MILLER, HENRY.
March 9, 1727/8.
Adm. to Barbary Miller.

FREY, HANCE.
April 2, 1728.
Adm. to Jacob Kendrick.

EBY, DORUS.
April 1, 1728.
Adm. to John Eby.

SANDELANDS, JONAS.
April 17, 1728.
Adm. to Mary Sandelands.

COPE, REBECCA.
May 16, 1728.
Adm. to Hugh Blackwell.

GOLDING, JOHN.
May 23, 1728.
Adm. to Thomas Howard.

WOOD, MATHEW.
May 24, 1728.
Adm. to Nathan Wood.

CLOUD, JOSEPH.
May 31. 1728.
Adm. to Ruth Cloud.

KENDRICK, JACOB.
June 29, 1728.
Adm. to Michael Downer.

ROBERTS, ROBERT.
September 13, 1728.
Adm. to Hannah Roberts.

BAKER, ROBERT.
September 13, 1728.
Adm. to Caleb Baker.

TAYLOR, ISAAC. Thornbury. Practitioner of Physick.
May 14, 1728. June 4, 1728. A. 275.
To wife Martha the plantation I now live on in Thornbury containing 146 acres, during life and after her decease to son Philip. To son John my plantation in Concord containing 100 acres, purchased of James Chevers. To son Jacob the northern half of my tract of 500 acres in Bradford, also my large surveying instruments. Authorizes executor to make title to 100 acres in Aston sold to Jas. Widdows and 100 acres in Kennet sold to Joseph Taylor. Remainder of real estate to be sold and divided among wife and 5 children, viz John, Philip, Jacob, Ann and Mary in equal shares.
Executors: wife Martha and son John. Brother Jacob and brother in law Philip and Jacob Roman to be assistants.
Witnesses: William Pyle, Olive Pyle, Richd. Eavenson, Saml. Savage.

HARRYS, EVAN. Kennet, yeoman.
9/25/1727. August 15, 1728. A. 280.
To wife Elizabeth all personal estate also use of plantation during widowhood for education and breeding up of children after wifes decease or marriage the plantation to son Daniel paying to his sisters, viz Mary, Elizabeth, Ann, Hannah and the child yet unborn, £5 each when they come of age.
Executors: brothers Willam Harry and Thos. Speakman (Spikman).
Witnesses: Wm. Webb, Elizabeth Eaches, Alen Underwood.

CHEYNEY, THOMAS. Thornbury.
August 31, 1728. August 30, 1728.
To daughters Mary and Ann Cheyney £80 each at 25 years. To brother John Cheyney all wearing apparel, also 50 acres of land to be taken off my tract of 200 acres which lies down Chester Creek. To wife Elizabeth 60 acres of my tract of 500 acres in Thornbury. Remainder of land to be sold and after provision for a possible posthumous child, the proceeds given to wife Elizabeth for bringing up and education children.
Executors: wife Elizabeth and brother John Cheyney.
Witnesses: Benjamin Hickman, Ann Hickman.

JOHNSON, CALEB. New Garden.
4/26/1728. October 1, 1728. A. 283.
To brother James Johnson, £15. To brothers Joshua, Robert and Benjamin £15 each. To sister Abigail wife of Isaac Baily of Marlborough £15. To sister Ann wife of Saml. Jackson late of Eegmont £15.
Executors: father Robert Johnson [of New Garden, Glazier] and with mother Margaret Johnson, residuary legatees.
Witnesses: Samuel Jackson, James Cooper.

IRWIN, JOHN. Caln, yeoman.
September 19, 1728. October 16, 1728. A. 284.
To brother Robert Erwin the plantation whereon I dwell containing 200 acres and all personal estate paying to my sister Jane £40, £20 to be paid her the day of her marriage and £20 the day she bears the first child. To Elizabeth daughter of Joseph Darlington £5 at 15 or married. Names brother Theophilus.
Executors: brother Edward Erwin and Hugh Cowen.
Witnesses: Saml. McKinley, Sarah Erwin, Jos. Griffiths.

PENNELL JR, JOSEPH. Edgmont, yeoman.
August 28, 1728. October 19, 1728. A. 286.
To mother Eliz. Pennel my silver watch. To sisters Ann and Mary Pennell and friend Ann Hoopes, article named. To sister Hannah's 4 children, viz Ephraim, Rachel, Ealis and Joseph Jackson 20 shillings each. To father Joseph Pennell 300 acres of land in Edgmont and all other remaining estate, also executor.
Witnesses: Wm. Lang, Wm. Oliver, John Wogan.

REED, JOHN. Nottingham.
(died) January 18, 1728. January 22, 1727/8. A. 287.
Non cupative will. To only son James Reed the plantation when he comes of age. Wife Elizabeth executrix.
Witnesses: John McDaniel, Janet McDaniel. No record of letters.
Witnesses aff. before Elisha Gatchell Esq.

WHITTAKER, CHARLES. Ridley.
February 12, 1807/8. April 8, 1720. A. 453.
to my 2 daughter by former wife, viz Sarah and Mary Whittaker, articles of household furniture to be divided among them by their uncle Joseph Baker and their aunts Mary Cobourn and Hannah Yarnall. To wife Hannah 1/3 of estate, remainder to children Samuel, Elizabeth, Susanna and Ann Whittaker. Directs that son Samuel be placed with Jonathan Hood of Darby. Elizabeth with John Simcock of Ridley. Susanna with John Blunston of Darby and Ann with Jacob Simcock of Ridley, to serve until daughter are 18 and son 21.
Executors: John Maris, Francis Yarnall.
Witnesses: Jacob Simcock. John Simcock Jr, Wm. Smith.
Executors refused to act. Letters cta to Anthony Lea.

DAVIS, THOMAS. Unchlan.
1/22/1721/22. July 18, 1722. A. 454.
All estate to wife and children. Elizabeth Davis, John Evans and Mary Evan during her widowhood. To grandson Thomas Evans, my plantation I now live on containing 200 acres, when 21 and if he die under age the to be divided between rest of the children. To son in law John Evans and wife Mary, the other 200 acres during life and afterwards to whom the survivor shall think best. Letter
C. T. A. to Elizabeth Davis.
Witnesses: Samuel John, Thomas John, Hugh Davis.

BOWEN, EVAN. Whiteland.
September 14, 1724. December 29, 1724. A. 455.
To son John £40 at 21 with reversion to brother John Bowen and

sister Anne Bowen. To wife Gainor all remainder of estate real and personal. Also executrix.
Witnesses: John Richard, Thomas Davis.

MAGIL, DANIEL.
February 10, 1723/4. March 3, 1724. A. 456.
Non cupative will at house of Arthur Parke. Cousin John Young to have his plantation and brothers son in Scotland should have £25 due to him in England and that his library should go to the use of the Synod and confided in Arthur Park to see him buried like a gentleman. Letter adm. had been granted.
Witnesses: Barnet Cuningham, William Wilson.

NICHOLAS, AMOS. Ridley.
April 31, 1724. January 6, 1725. A. 457.
To sons Edward and John tract of land whereon I dwell or for want of a title to the same, my tract of land in west New Jersey now in possession of John Friend. To my 3 children, viz Edward, John and Ann £100 now in the hands of Robert Love in Maryland and all other estate son John not yet of age.
Executors: son Edward and daughter Ann Nicholas.
Witness: John Crosby.

EACHUS, ROBERT. Goshen, yeoman.
December 3, 1727. November 26, 1728. A. 287.
To wife Elizabeth 1/2 of plantation whereon I live containing 200 during life. To son John the other 1/2 of said plantation and the whole of same at death of wife. To son William 200 acres north of the above and to have liberty to work upon the same when 19. To youngest sons, Robert, Enoch and Daniel £10 each to be put apprentices at 14. To my 3 daughters, viz Elizabeth, Ann and Alice £5 each at 18.
Executors: wife Elizabeth and son John.
Witnesses: Isaac Vernon, John Collins, Richard Jones.

WORRALL, JOSHUA. Marple, yeoman.
November 13, 1728. December 11, 1728. A. 289.
Provides for wife Margaret, authorizes executor to make title to land sold to Lewellin Parry and provides for a possible posthumous child. Remainder to sisters, sisters Mary and Hannah and brother Peter Worrall. Sister Mary Bromfield, brothers John and Thomas Bromfield.
Executors: David and Jonathan Morris.
Witnesses: James Dicken, Thos. Worrilow, Joseph Hawley.

ALLISON, JOHN. Donegal.
November 6, 1728. February 20, 1728/9. A. 291.
Provides for wife Janet. To eldest son James, my black suit of clothes. To second William £20 and the improvements of the plantation I bought of James Brownler. To son Patrick young horse. To sons John and Robert, the improvements of this plantation I live upon, with stock. To daughter Jean 10 shillings "to be paid att meeting." To daughter Margaret £30.
Executors: wife Jenneh and Rev Jas. Anderson to decide all disputes.

Witnesses: Richard Allison, James Cook, Alex Hutchison.

PENNELL, ROBERT. Middletown, yeoman.
May 22, 1727. February 25, 1728/9. A. 293.
To grandson Joseph son of Joseph Pennell 200 acres of land being part of 500 acres purchased of Wm. Smith in Edgemont he paying £30 to his 4 sisters the same being their grandfather's legacies and also £6 per year to his grandfather Robt. Pennell during life. To granddaughter Hannah Jackson, to granddaughters Alice, Ann, Jane and Mary Pennell £5 each and the £10 formerly given to grandson Robt. Pennell deceased. To grandson Thos. Pennell £10. To James Pennell £10. To Hannah Pennell £5. To Ann Pennell £5. To Robt. Pennell £10. To Wm. Pennell £10. To daughter Ann and Benjamin Mendenhall, my bed. To John Sharpless 10 shillings and 5 shillings to each of his children. To Jane and Saml. Garrett £1 and 5 shillings to each of their children. To Robt. Taylor 2/6 shillings. To Phebe Lewis 5 shillings. To Hannah Mercer 5 shillings. Remainder to sons Joseph and William also executors.
Witnesses: John Cooper, Mark Fester, Eph. Jackson.

HANRY, ULRICH.
Died July 13, 1723. February 28, 1728/9. A. 295.
Non cupative will. All estate to wife Barbary, but concerning the said Hanry brothers and sisters they altogether shall have 30 shillings of his estate.
Witnessed by Peter Yorte and Hance Herr and five other Dutchman whose names cannot be read.

STEVENSON, GRACE. Widow. Birmingham.
October 8, 1726. March 4, 1728/9. A. 295.
To son John Chads all my lands tenements, also all personal estate and executor.
Witnesses: Saml. Scott Jr, John Day, Andrew Haydon.

BRADSHAW, SAMUEL. Darby.
12/18/1728/9. March 18, 1728/9. A. 296.
To the eldest son of my sister Mary Smith of Wignmorpoor in Nottinghamshire, England, my house and lott in Darby also £5. To kinswoman Mary wife of Benj. Tomlinson of Philadelphia £10. To the children of sister Mary Smith £60. To Benj. Pearson all wearing apparel. To Saml. Bunting 50 shillings. Remainder to kinswoman, Sarah and Elizabeth Bradshaw of Darby.
Executors: Friends Saml. Levis Jr, John Davis.
Witnesses: Isaac Lea, Benj. Pearson, Saml. Bunting.

BULLERBY, ISAAC. Newtown.
10/15/1728. March 25, 1729. A. 297.
To brother John Bullerby my tract of land in New Castle Co containing 200 acres, also reversion of my land in parish of Dunston Somersetshire, England. To said brother, sisters Mary and Susanna Bellerby all personal estate.
Executors: friends Henry Miller Sr of Providence and Jacob Howell.
Witnesses: Wm. Whittyman, Geo. Mathew, James Mark.

CLOUD, WILLIAM.
September 16, 1728.
Adm. to Jason Cloud.

BALDWIN JR, JOHN.
November 12, 1728.
Adm. to John Baldwin.

ELLIS, WILLIAM.
November 16, 1728.
Adm. to Benjamin Ellis.

WITTMORE, JOHN.
December 17, 1728.
Adm. to Christian Hidey.

PASCHALL JR, THOMAS.
February 10, 1728/9.
Adm. to Margaret Paschall.

REYNOLDS, JOHN.
February 10, 1728/9.
Adm. to Martha Reynolds.

MCKINLEY, MATTHEW.
February 26, 1728/9.
Adm. to Saml. McKinley.

SELBY, JOSEPH.
March 28, 1729.
Adm. to Saml. Levis, Jr.

MORRIS, DAVID.
March 25, 1729.
Adm. to Mary and Jonathan Morris.

HAGGATHY, NICHOLAS.
March 12, 1728/9.
Adm. to John Mather.

PARKER, RICHARD. Darby, yeoman.
2/6/1726. March 25, 1729. A. 298.
To grandson Saml. Bethell £1. To-granddaughter Ann Bethell £40 at 21.
To grandson John Smith £1 at 21. To son Richard children, viz Mary,
William, John, Joseph and Martha 5 shillings each at 21. To son
Richard my plantation whereon I live in Darby and all other estate
paying above legacies, also executor.
Witnesses: Benj. Clift, John Paschall, David Enoch.

THOMAS, ANN. Goshen.
11/19/1729. April 21, 1729. A. 299.
To friends of Goshen meeting £4. To Kennet meetings £4. To father
articles named. To sister Rachel Davis, saddle and bridle. Remainder
to father, brother and 3 sisters (not named). To friend Ruth Jones
pair of sheets. To Alice and Phebe daughters of Moses and Alice
Mendenhall 10 shillings each at 18.
Executors: friends Ellis Lewis and Moses Mendenhall.
Witnesses: Jacob Chandler, Francis Mathews.

FINIKIN, RICHARD. Chester Boro.
January 1, 1728-9. May 16, 1729. A. 300.
To Prudence Dangor £5. Remainder to friend John Mather who is to see
me decently buried in the churchyard with Tombstone placed over my
grave. Letters to Mather.
Witnesses: J. Reyners, John Young, Josiah Gates.

HARLAN, MICHAEL. Londongrove.
12/13/1728/ July 1, 1729. A. 301.
To son George 1/2 the land I purchased on a branch of Elk river. To
son in law Richard Flower that part of said tract he now dwells
upon. To son James the tract of land upon Octorara Creek being
400 acres paying to daughter Dinah Harlan £30. To son Michael 150
acres of land in Londongrove with 40 acres of the tract I now

live upon. To son Solomon my dwelling house and plantation except
above 40 acres. To son Thomas £10. To son Stephen £10. To
granddaughter Dinah son George's daughter £5. Remainder of land to be
sold. Refers to wife thirds but does not name her.
Executors: sons George, Thomas and Stephen.
Witnesses: Edward Flower, Jer. Starr.

BROOMALL, JOHN. Nether Providence, yeoman.
4/20/1729. August 21, 1729. A. 303.
To son John my plantation in N. Providence subject to wifes 1/2 int
during life, he paying to daughters Lydia, Ellen, Mary and Jean £4
each. Remainder to wife.
Executors: wife Mary and friend John Crosby her assistant.
Witnesses: Susanna Crosby, Wm. Biron, Andrew Crozer.

SIDWELL, HUGH. W. Nottingham, yeoman.
July 6, 1729. August 26, 1729. A. 304.
Provides for wife Elizabeth. To son Richard the plantation whereon I
live with brick house and barn. To sons John and Hugh my right in the
proprietors lott.
Executor: son Richard.
Witnesses: William Harris, John Harris, Thomas Rogers.

SPENCER, JOHN. Londongrove.
August 28, 1729. October 1, 1729. A. 305.
Wife who is not named to have house and plantation during widowhood
and directs that the land be purchased if possible and is so to go to
son Thomas at 21, he paying to his sisters Dinah and Elizabeth and
"the child my wife is now with" £10 each when of age.
Executors: father in law Thomas Black, Wm. Miller, Jeremiah Starr.

BOON, SWAN. Darby.
November 2, 1729. November 26, 1729. A. 306.
To daughter Catherine Rambo, a piece of land lying upon Relkenhood
Island containing 3 acres. To son Andrew remainder of lands and all
moveables, also executor.
Witnesses: Neels Boon, Andrew Boon, Benj. Pearson.

DAVID, THOMAS. Whiteland.
October 22, 1729. November 29, 1729. A. 307.
To wife Catherine and son James my land and plantation whereon I live
during their lives and after their decease to son David. Refers to
articles of agreement with son David dated October 28, 1728 in regard
to Fulling Mill and 15 acres of land. To daughter Sarah now in Wales
£10 provided she comes over. To daughter Ann 5 shillings and to her
daughter Elizabeth spinning wheel. To son John great iron pot and to
each of his 6 children 1 shilling. To son Thomas all wearing apparel
and to his daughter 1 shilling. To daughter Ann's 3 children, viz.
Thomas, Evan and Elizabeth 1 shilling each.
Executors: wife Catharine and son James.
Witnesses: Isaac Malin, Wm. Paschall.

STOCKIN, THOMAS. Whiteland.
October 1729. November 29, 1729. A. 309.
To wife Ann 1/3 of all estate. To servant Wm. Scall, Wm. Brown and Martha Hood, 1 year of their time. To my father Francis Stockin remainder of estate real and personal if living. To mother in law Catherine Freviller £3. To John Lecock £6. To brother in law Wm. Treviller, wearing apparel in case my father is deceased I give £50 toward building a church intended to be built near Thomas Davids.
Executrix: wife Ann.
Witnesses: Wm. Paschall, Griffith Lewis, David Meredith. Mentions Michael Wills. [Widow Ann married February 28, 1730-1 Richd. Rickison.]

MARSHALL, JOHN. Darby, yeoman.
9/8/1729. December 1, 1729. A. 310.
To wife Sarah 110 acres of land in Blockley Township, Philadelphia Co. and all personal estate except legacies. To eldest son John 5 shillings and to his children, viz Thomas, Abraham, Sarah, Margaret and Joanna 1 shilling each. To children of son Thomas, viz Ann, Benjamin and Thomas 1 shilling each.
Executrix: wife Sarah.
Witnesses: Samuel Seller, Edward Ease, Saml. Bunting, son Thomas and cousin Abraham Marshall, overseers.

JACKSON, MARY. Widow of Thos. Marlborough.
8/28/1729. December 20, 1729. A. 310.
Mentions that she is now at sea aboard the "Sizargh" of Whitehaven, Jeremiah Cowman master bound for Philadelphia." To sons in law, Saml., Isaac and Benjamin Jackson 20 shillings each. To daughter in law Ruth Martin in Co Cavin, Ireland, £20. To brother John Wiley in Pennsylvania £40. Remainder to executors. Executors: Michael Samuel and Jacob Lightfoot, Abigail Wiley, Eliza Jones and Margaret Starr.
Witnesses: James Miller, Lambert Emerson, Robert White.

ROMAN, PHILIP. Chichester, yeoman.
9/25/1728. January 21, 1729/30. A. 312.
Provides for wife Dorothy. To son Philip my plantation in Chichester containing 205 acres paying as follows. To daughter Martha late wife of Isaac Taylor £30. To son Jonah £10. To son Jacob the messuages, land in Chester purchased of John Child also all he owes me. To son Jonah, my tract of land in Caln containing 170 acres, but not to sell the same with out consent of sons Philip and Jacob and grandson John Taylor the object being to secure said land for the benefit of Jonah's children, viz Jonah, Joshua, Rachel and Mary. To daughter Martha £120. To grandson William son of Robert Roman £20 at 21 and to grandson Thomas son of Robert Roman £20 at 21. To grandson John Taylor £5. To Sarah wife of Saml. Grave and daughter of Wm. Bezer deceased £5. To Wm. Harlan son of Ezekiel and Mary his wife who was daughter of said Wm. Bezer £5. Remainder to son Philip and grandson John Taylor who are also executors. Robert Pyle and John Bezer, assistants.
Witnesses: Joseph Bond, William Hughs.

MARSHALL, ANN. Widow. New Garden.
9/30/1729. February 10, 1729/30. A. 314.
Describes herself at "late from Ireland." To sons, John and William all estate to be equally divided when 21.
Executors: friends Wm. Halliday and Benjamin Fred of New Garden.
Witnesses: John Griffith, Sismer Wright, Wm. Read.
[She was daughter of John Griffith and had brother Christopher as appears by Ecrs Accts.]

EMMITT, ABRAHAM. Ches Co., yeoman.
February 13, 1729/30. March 25, 1730. A. 315.
To wife Jane 1/3 of estate real and personal. To son Josiah the land he now lives on being part of a tract of 625 acres [described] containing 132 acres. To son Abraham my right to a tract in Prince George Co, Maryland on Eastern branch of Potomac containing 504 acres, also £10. To son William £30. To son David remainder of personal estate plantation I now live on and 1/2 of Grist Mill paying the legacies herein bequeathed. To grandson Josias Emmitt 100 acres of land called Carlok between the branches of Elk river in Cecil Co., MD, also £21-10. To granddaughter Sarah Emmitt 1661 acres of land lately purchased of Robt. Smith in New London.
Executor: son David. Brother in law David Miller and Andrew Miller and cousin James Smith, assistants.
Witnesses: Wm. Gelaspy, Joseph Houston, David Wallace.

MONTGOMERY, JOHN. New London.
September 26, 1729. June 18, 1730. A. 318.
Provides for wife Ann inc real estate until son William is 21 and all person al estate except legacies. To son Robert the grey filly. To my 3 daughters Alice, Joan and Ann £5 each at 21 or married. To daughter Margaret 5 shillings. To son Michael £20 at 21. To son John £20 at 21. To son William all real estate at 21.
Executrix: wife Ann and son Robert, overseer.
Witnesses: Abraham Ayers, William Roe.

NEWLIN, MARY.
5/9/1730. July 23, 1730. A. 319.
To grandson in law Nathan son of Nathaniel Newlin £5. To Sarah daughter of John Newlin £5. To Mary daughter of Ellis Lewis £5. To Mary Everson £5. To granddaughter in law Mary Baily £5. To kinswoman Hannah Shewin £3 and the remainder of her time to my father. To sisters Rebecca Bennet and Sarah Swain all wearing apparel. Remainder to father and brothers Jonathan and John Fincher and sisters Rebecca Bennet and Sarah Swain and to my sister Elizabeth Cox's 3 children.
Executors: father John Fincher and brother Francis Fincher.
Witnesses: William Swain, Martha Mullin.

MILLER, MARY. Widow. New Garden.
5/12/1730. August 10, 1730. A. 320.
To son William Miller all my real estate lying upon White Clay Creek paying £80 towards legacies. To son James a colt. To daughter Martha Jordan £20. To daughter Susanna Miller £15. To granddaughter Mary Jordan £12 at 18 or married. To kinsman John

Tos a colt. Remainder to 6 daughters, viz Mary Hutton, Martha Jordan, Sarah Hutton, Elizabeth Chambers, Susanna Miller and Elinor Chambers, they paying £30 in my executor's hands to pay the passage of 3 of my brother Andrew Ignews children coming to this country provided they come within 2 years of my decease.
Executor: son William.
Witnesses: James Miller, Nathl. Richards, Michael Lightfoot.

WICKERSHAM, THOMAS. Marlborough. Husbandman.
June 16, 1730. August 20, 1730. A. 321.
To wife Alice the plantation I now possess during widowhood afterward to son James paying to son Richard £10. To son Isaac £10. To son Thomas 1 shilling. To son John 5 shillings. To son William 5 shillings. To daughter Ann and Alice 5 shillings each. To daughters Elizabeth and Jane 20 shillings each. To son in law Wm. Wilton the 2 city lotts.
Executors: wife Alice and son Richard.
Witnesses: Joel Baily, Betty Caldwell, Henry Hays.

PYLE, ROBERT. Bethel, yeoman.
1/2/1729/30. August 29, 1730. A. 322.
To wife Susanna £100 and 1/2 household goods. To son William £50 and to his children £50 to be divided at 21. To son John all my right title to that 200 acres of land in Marlborough which I lately leased to one Holt on condition that he pay to his son Moses £30 when 21 also to his daughter Sarah Pyle £20 at 21 or married. To son Joseph £30. To grandson Robert son of Joseph my tract of land in Marlborough containing 224 acres. To son Daniel £70 paying to his daughters Susanna and Mary £15 each at 21 or married. To daughter Mary Moore £50, she paying to each of her children £5 at 21 or married. To grandson Aaron Vernon £15. To granddaughter Rachel Green £15. To George, James and Dorothy Turner my now wifes children £4 each. To grandchildren Saml. Pyle and the 3 daughters of son Robert 10 shillings each.
Executors: wife Susanna and sons Wm. and Joseph.
Witnesses: John Hopton, Rachel Hopton, Jos. Bradford.

GUNSTON, HENRY. Birmingham, yeoman.
August 20, 1730. September 29, 1730. A. 324.
To wife Ann all real and personal estate also executrix.
Witnesses: Elizabeth Sharp, David Eckhoff.

GUNSTON, ANN. Birmingham.
October 2, 1730. October 20, 1730. A. 326.
To my friend John Green all my land messuages and other estate, also executor.
Witnesses: Eliza. Sharp, David Eckhoff.

WOOD, JOSEPH. Darby, yeoman.
April 27, 1730. October 5, 1730. A. 325.
To sister Hannah Wood £100 at 21 also riding horse. To my mother Rebecca Wood of Darby all my land in Darby also a marsh in Kingsess and all personal estate.
Executors: mother Rebecca Wood and friend Thomas Worth Jr.
Witnesses: Isaac Lea, Jos. Hibbert, John Pearson.

REYNOLDS, ROBERT. New London, yeoman.
January 18, 1730/1. January 24, 1730/1. A. 327.
All estate into 3 parts, one to wife and the other 2 for use of my child and if child should die its portion to be divided between wife and my sister Margaret Reynolds. To niece Mary Brown I bequeath her indentures. Also to Wm. Brown and niece Agnes Brown one year of their time. To sister Margaret Brown and her family 20 bushels of Indian Corn. (name spelled Ryandel in the original papers].
Executors: Johh McClenahan and Wm. McCain.
Witnesses: Wm. Waugh, Archibald Scott.

MATHEWS, EDWARD.
April 23, 1729.
Adm. to Joshua Harlan.

McCONNEL, ALEXANDER.
May 19, 1729.
Adm. to Elizabeth McConnell.

HOWELL, HUGH.
May 20, 1729.
Adm. to Ann Howell.

WALL, JAMES.
May 26, 1729.
Adm. to Martha Wall.

KINIKIN, JAMES. May 26, 1729.
Adm. to Joseph Kinikan.

NEWLIN, NATHANIEL.
May 29, 1729.
Adm. to Nicholas Newlin. Mary the widow renouncing.

LOCKRY, JAMES.
September 13, 1729.
Adm. to Edmond McKollagh.

CRAWFORD, JOHN.
December 26, 1729.
Adm. to Mary Crawford.

HANNUM, JOHN. Concord, yeoman.
July 13, 1730. February 8, 1730/1. A. 328.
Provides for wife Margery. To daughter Mary wife of Thos. Smith £10. To daughter Elizabeth wife of Thomas Broom £10. to daughter Margary wife of Anthony Baldwin 50 shillings. To daughter Ann wife of John Way 50 shillings. To daughter Sarah wife of Jacob way 50 shillings. To son Robert £5. To son John my plantation in Concord containing 231 acres with stock. Reminder to wife. Executors: son Robert and sons in law Thos. Smith and Thos. Broom.
Witnesses: Henry Pearce, John Palmer.

MCCAIN, SUSANNA. New London.
December 28, 1730. February 21, 1730/1. A. 329.
To sons William and Thomas McCain the 400 acres of land I now possess with stock. To daughter Barbara Murrah £30 to be paid by sons. To sons John Craghton 2 ewes. To son in law John Henderson 1 shillings and to daughter Margt. Henderson 1 shilling. To Mr. Saml. Gelston 20 shillings. Servant maid Rachel the last year of her time.
Executors: sons John Greaghton and Wm. and Thos. McKean.
Witnesses: John Ross, Wm. Waugh.

FEARN, JOSIAH. Darby.
March 10, 1730. March 30, 1731. A. 330.

To daughter Sarah Bunting 5 shillings. To daughter Rebecca Fearn £100 also lott of ground when 21. To granddaughter Elizabeth Hibbert £10 when 21. To grandaughter Mary Bunting £5 when 21. To son Josiah all remainder of estate real and personal.
Executors: friend Saml. Sellus and son Josiah.
Witnesses: Benj. Lobb, Richd. Parker, Benj. Cliffe.

SMITH, EDWARD. Darby.
March 10, 1730/1. April 3, 1731. A. 331.
To wife 50 acres of land purchased of John Hood adj the place I now live on and 300 acres of land and 1/2 the sawmill lying over the river in partnership with Saml. Shivers. To son William the land I now live on when of age, he paying to his sister Martha £40. To son John 1/2 of the 500 acres purchased of John Easto in Londongrove paying to sister Martha when she is of age £40. To son Edward the other 1/2 of said tract paying to sister Martha £40 when he is of age.
Executrix: wife Mary.
Witnesses: Bernhard Vanleer, Martha Deacon, Benj. Yard.

WORTH, THOMAS. Darby, yeoman.
3/9/1729. Codicil 2/2/1731. April 15, 1731. A. 332.
To son Thomas my plantation in Darby being 222 acres. To 3 granddaughters Sarah, Hannah and Mary daughters of eldest son John deceased, my 500 acres of land in Bradford Township in forks of Brandywine also £10. To son Thomas, 4 daughters Susanna, Lydia, Rebecca and Hannah £10 to be divided and to Saml. and Ebenezer Worth one guinea in gold. Remainder to son Thomas and son John's 3 daughters. Cod gives to son Thomas 6 acres of the above 500, at the mine hill adj to Richard Woodwards.
Executors: Saml. Garrett, John Davis.
Witnesses: Benj. Cliff, David Thomas, Benj. Pearson.

WHITING, SAMUEL.
December 29, 1729.
Adm. to John Littler.

PENNICK, JOHN.
February 7, 1729/30.
Adm. to John Taylor.

JACKSON, JOHN.
August 1, 1730.
Adm. to Wm. Betty and Colin Campbell.

ARMSTRONG, DAVID.
August 1, 1730.
Adm. to David Betty.

RICHARDS, NATHANIEL.
August 25, 1730.
Adm. to Margaret Richards.

CHALFANT JR, JOHN.
November 14, 1730.
Adm. to Solomon Chalfant.

EWING, JOHN.
December 23, 1730.
Adm. to Robert Jackson.

HUNTER, PETER.
December 31, 1730.
Adm. to Jonathan Hunter eldest son. Esther the widow renouncing, December 30th.

LARKE, THOMAS.
January 25, 1730/1.
Adm. to Samuel Ash. Widow Donti renouncing.

CLEMENTS, JEREMIAH.
January 28, 1730/1.
Adm. to Richard Barry.

LEA, GEORGE.
March 13, 1730/1.
Adm. to Isaac Lea.

SCAWTHORN, NATHAN.
April 1, 1731.
Adm. to Mary Scawthorn.

EVANS, EVAN.
May 12, 1731.
Adm. to Margaret Evans.

JOHN, THOMAS.
May 12, 1731.
Adm. to Gwen John and John Elliman.

PUSEY, WILLIAM.
May 14, 1731.
Adm. to Elizabeth Pusey.

LOCKHART, JOHN.
May 20, 1731.
Adm. to John Lockhart.

LLOYD, DAVID. Chester. Gent.
March 29, 1724. April 15, 1731. A. 333.
To the children of my niece Jane wife of Thomas Smith now on late living in New England £50. To servant Jane Fen £10. To wife Grace all remainder of estate real and personal, also executrix.
Witnesses: Francis Knowls, Owen Owen, Joshua Lawrence.

BALDWIN, THOMAS. Chester. Blacksmith.
March 17, 1730/1. July 2, 1731. A. 334.
To son Thomas 1 shilling. To heir of son Joseph deceased 1 shilling. To heir of son William deceased. To son Anthony 1 shilling. to daughter Mary Baldwin 1 shilling. To daughter Martha Grice 1 shilling. To daughter Elizabeth Weaver 1 shilling. To wife Mary remainder of estate and executrix.
Witnesses: Wm. Rattew, Gouldsmith Edward Folwell, John Pike.

LEWIS, WILLIAM. Newtown, yeoman.
6/5/1731. Codicil: 6/8/1731. October 1, 1731. A. 335.
Provides for wife Lowry Lewis. To son Nathan 20 shillings besides what I have already confirmed to him. To son William my plantation whereon I live in Newtown containing 200 acres, also £50 towards bringing up and educating my younger children, viz Joseph, Gideon, Ann, Ambrose and Japhet. To sons Jeptha and Enos, my tract of land in Gwynned purchased of Humphrey Bate containing 307 acres. Also to Enos £50 and to Jeptha £20. Remainder to younger children Joseph, Gideon, Ann, Ambrose and Japheth. Cod states that Joseph and Ann are now deceased and gives their shares to all surviving children, viz Nathan, Wm, Jephtha, Enos, Gideon, Ambrose and Japheth.
Executors: wife Lowry and son Wm.
Witnesses: Thomas Evan, John Goodwin, Richd. Jones.

MORGAN, JOHN. Providence, yeoman.
8/5/1731. October 11, 1731. A. 337.
To wife Margaret all lands and plantation forever. To 3 brothers David, Evan and Thomas Morgan a bond of Wm. James. To my niece, brother David's second daughter, my bible. To Owen Thomas the baptist minister £10. To ye baptist meeting at Philadelphia £3. To John Beckingham £5.
Executors: wife Margaret, brother Thomas and father in law John Powell.

Witnesses: Peter Taylor, John Needham, Rebecca Minshall.

MOULDER, BENJAMIN. Chichester. Marriner.
April 27, 1731. November 19, 1731.
Provides for wife Prudence including house and lott lately purchased of Abel Clayton in Chichester during life. To son Joseph a lott of 300 ft. front on Delaware river. To son Robert the house where I now dwell with remainder of land. To sons Benj. and Wm. my tract of land in Manor of Rockland, New Castle Co. To daughter Mary Moulder £200. To sons Benj. and Wm. the house devised to wife after her decease. To the 3 children of brother Thomas deceased, viz Peter, Elizabeth and Deborah Moulder £5 each at 21.
Executors: wife Prudence and son Robert.
Witnesses: Wm. Weldon, James Boydon, Jo. Parker.

MORRIS, THOMAS. London, Britain.
November 26, 1731. December 16, 1731. A. 340.
To eldest brother Evan Morris 1 shilling. To sister Elinor wife of David Thomas £1. To nephew Solomon David £1. To Owen Thomas and Richard Whitting for the use of the meeting house that is in the Indiantown in London, Britain £2. Remainder to wife Elinor also executrix.
Witnesses: John Jones, John Devonald.

HARLAN, EZEKIEL. Kennet, yeoman.
November 14, 1730. December 14, 1731. A. 341.
Mentions "being about to take a voyage into old England." To sons William and Ezekiel, daughters Mary wife of Daniel Webb and Elizabeth wife of William White 5 shillings each. To sons Joseph and Benjamin 500 acres of land part of the tract of which I dwell. To daughter Ruth Harlan £50 bringing up and education minor children, also executrix.
Witnesses: Joseph Robinson, Wm. Webb Jr., Wm. Henderson.

CRIGHTON, JOHN. New London.
December 24, 1731. January 6, 1731/2.
To sister Barbara Murray my plantation at £80 to be paid to my sister Margaret and brothers Wm. and Thomas. To cousin Wm. Waugh my best cow, also to Mr. Gellson a cow. Remainder to brothers. Mentions servant Dugal.
Executor: brother Thomas McKane.
Witnesses: Wm. McKane, John Henderson.

DUTTON, THOMAS. Aston.
10/9/1731. January 10, 1731/2. A. 343.
To son Richard house and tract of land on which I live in Aston containing 200 acres paying to son John £15 at 21 and to my daughters Lydia, Mary and Sarah Dutton £15 each at 18. To son David my tract of land in Middletown purchased of Aaron Coppock, containing about 50 acres. To son Jonathan my tract of land in Aston purchased of Aaron Coppock lat John Neelds containing 50 acres. To son John £30 when 21. To children Richard, David, Jonathan, John, Lydia, Mary and Sarah all remainder of estate in equal shares.

Executors: friends Thomas Banet of Aston, Wm. Pennell of Middletown.
Witnesses: Thomas Cummings, John Carter.

PENICK, EDWARD. Bethel, yeoman.
April 29, 1731. January 18, 1731/2. A. 345.
To brother John Penicks 8 children, viz Joshua, Edward, Ruth, Roman, Lydia Whitaker, Mary Perkins, Rachel Stapleton, Sarah and Hannah Penick 1/6 shillings each. To brother Christopher Pennock of Bethel all remainder of estate real and personal and executor. Executors: John Bezer, Esther Bezer.

JONES, PETER. U. Providence, yeoman.
10/29/1731. January 25, 1731/2. A. 346.
Estate to wife Ann and unborn child. To mother 8 bushels of wheat per annum. If child dies under age to sister Mary Jones £10.
Executors: wife Ann, Peter Taylor and Amos Lewis. Letter to wife and Lewis. Taylor renouncing.
Witnesses: John Neddham, Daniel Broom, Robt. Livingston.

MINSHALL, ISAAC. Providence, yeoman.
December 9, 1731. February 1. 1731/2. A. 347.
Provides for wife Rebecca inc. plantation in Providence until son Isaac is 21 for bringing up my younger children when Isaac is to have 100 acres at S. W. corner and son Samuel to have 108 acres at N.E. corner when 21 and son Edward. 100 acres at S.E. corner when 21 and son Jacob the dwelling house at N.W. corner 700 acres in all. To sons Aaron and Griffith my tract of land in Goshen cont 200 and odd acres they paying their sister Rebecca Minshall £40.
Executors: son Aaron and Griffith and friend Peter Dicks.
Witnesses: Bartho. Coppock, Jacob Minshall, Thos. Minshall.

CRAFFORD, JOHN. New London.
March 6, 1730/1. February 28, 1731/2. A. 348. To wife Rebecca all estate also executrix.
Witnesses: Hugh Stewart, Robt. Linton, Henry Geesbred.

NEWLIN, NATHANIEL. Concord, yeoman.
January 10, 1731/2. February 29, 1731/2. A. 349.
Provides for wife Jean. To son Nathaniel my plantation where I dwell with 275 acres of land at the west end when 21 also stock. To son Joseph 400 acres of land being part of a tract in -Township, next to land of Henry Hayes also £20 and the gun that was his grandfathers, when 21. To son Nicholas 400 acres being part of 785 acres on Doe Run also £20 at 21. To son Nathan 125 acres part of my home tract also £25 at 21. To daughters, viz Rachel, Elizabeth, Jane, Mary and Martha £50 each at 18.
Executors: wife Jane and Edward Woodward of Middletown.
Witnesses: Jos. Pyle, John Robertson, Robert Green.
Trustees: John Newlin, Ellis Lewis.

BALDWIN, JOHN. Chester Borr.
Codicil: 9/9/1731 and November 11, 1731/2. April 2, 1731. March 7, 1731/2. A. 352.
To grandson John Baldwin the house lot wharf where I now dwell in

Chester with rev to grandson Joshua. To grandson Joshua the house and lott on easterly end of Chester Bridge also to said grandsons various properties in Chester and vicinity and my 600 acres of land in Caln Township. To brother Thomas £5 per year during life to be paid on 29th day of 7 months yearly.
Executors: Mercer Brown, Peter Dicks and Joseph Parker.
Cod. gives to Thos. Baldwin son of brother Thomas £20 and to Anthony son of bro. Thomas, and Thomas and John sons of brother Francis £10 each. Also £5 towards building a school house upon the lott I lately conveyed for that purpose. £5 to Martha Thomas and £5 towards repairing the meeting house and names Thomas Cummings as executor. Letters to Peter Dicks and Thos. Cummings. Messer Brown being deceased and Jos. Parker renouncing. Witnesses: Richd. Barry, Robt. Willson, Benj. Kendall, John Tomkins.

PENICK, CHRISTOPHER. Bethel, yeoman.
January 22, 1731/2. March 7, 1731/2. A. 355.
To cousin Edward Penick son of brother John that part of my land of N.E. side of road to Concord. To cousin Ruth Roman and cousin Rachel Stapleton £10 each. To cousins Lydia Whitaker, Mary Perkins, Sarah Penick and Hannah Penick 5 shillings each. To cousin Joshua Penick that part of my land on S.W. side of Concord road also remainder of personal estate and executor.
Witnesses: John Bezer, Moses Key.

CHAMBERLIN JR, ROBERT. Concord, yeoman.
December 28, 1731. March 10, 1731/2. A. 356.
To wife Ciecly use of plantation during widowhood for bringing up children afterward to 5 children, viz Jacob, Susanna, Robert, John and James. Son Robert being lame to have £5 more than the others.
Executors: wife Cicely and Jonathan Munroe of Concord.
Witnesses: Wm. Arnent, Elizabeth Arment.

DUTTON, EDWARD. Bethel, yeoman.
10/24/1731. March 14, 1731/2. A. 357.
To wife Gwin 100 acres of land where I now live during life and after her decease to son John. To son William if living £20 to be paid him within 3 years of his coming here. To daughter Mary wife of Daniel Davis £5 at wifes decease. Wife Gwin executrix. Witnesses: Wm. Lindley, Mary Mackall, Moses Key.

OBORN, WILLIAM. Concord.
12/7/1731/2. March 25, 1732. A. 358.
To wife Elizabeth all personal estate and use of the house and plantation for 12 years then to be rented until the child my wife is now big with comes to age. With rev in case of childs death to sister Hannah and Susanna.
Executors: Father Henry Oborn and Thos. Hollingsworth.
Witnesses: Ralph Eavenson, Thomas Gilpin.

COOKSON, ELIZABETH.
September 2, 1731.
Adm. to Joseph Jervis.

RAWSON, ANDREW.
September 25, 1731.
Adm. to Sarah Rawson. [Left child Gantree under 1 year. Widow married James Causey or Casey. Andrew Rossen and Sarah Bloair married July 28, 1780, Swedes Church, Del.]

BOOTH, JONATHAN. January 1, 1731/2.
Adm. to Philip Taylor.

MILLSON or MILLSOM, EDWARD.
January 24, 1731/2.
Adm. to Kathrine Millson. [Children John, Thomas and Mary.]

JOB, ENOCH.
February 15, 1731/2.
Adm. to Abigail Job.

ANDREWS, THOMAS.
February 16, 1731/2.
Adm. to John Ketton.

GRAHAM, JAMES.
February 25, 1731/2.
Adm. to Colin Campbell.

BARNES, WILLIAM.
March 2, 1731/2.
Adm. to James Few. Elizabeth the widow renouncing.

GIBBONS, JOHN, of Bethel. March 9, 1731/2.
Adm. to Sarah Gibbons [who married Joseph Pyle November 10, 1732. Inventory filed 18 April, 1732 by Joseph Pyle and Robert Gwen, apparently about £42 15-6. One child Mary Gibbons.]

KILGORE, JOHN.
March 9, 1731/2.
Adm. to John McClehan.

BAKER, RICHARD.
March 15, 1731/2.
Adm. to Elizabeth Baker.

HEALD, JOSEPH.
March 25, 1731/2.
Adm. to John Heald.

HARLAN, STEPHEN.
April 8, 1732.
Adm. to Hannah Harlan.

SHEWARD, JAMES.
April 8, 1732.
Adm. to Elizabeth Sheward.

HARLAN, SOLOMON.
April 12, 1732.
Adm. to James Harlan. C.J.A.

ROADS, JOSEPH.
April 7, 1732.
Adm. to Abigail and John Roads and Mordecai Massey.

GRAY, NIGEL. New London. Gent.
February 4, 1731/2. February 29, 1731.2. A. 360.
To son George my plantation, horses. Remainder of estate to wife Mary and son James to be equally divided by Abraham Emmit and son in law Joseph Steel who are guardians of sons.
Executors: friend James Smith and son George.
Witnesses: William Gelaspy, Saml. Carson, Wm. Boyd.

HENDERSON, EDWARD. New London.
February 16, 1731/2. April 7, 1732.
To wife Jane Henderson alias Menarn, my servant James Geary and all other goods to be equally divided among wife and children who are not named.
Executors: brothers John and David Henderson.
Witnesses: Wm. Neill, Robert Greer.

MILLER, HENRY. Upper Providence.
February 14, 1731/2. March 16, 1731/2. B. 23.
To son George the 247 acres of land in Providence which was surveyed for and verbally granted to son John since deceased together with a tract adjacent containing about 100 acres, also my share of the water corn mill, known by name of Providence Mills, also £100 when 21. To son Henry my plantation where I now live in Providence cont about 279 acres, also £50 he to maintain my daughters Dorothy and Sarah while unmarried. To said daughters £120 and household goods to value of £50 each. To friends of Providence Meeting £10. To cousins George Turner, James Turner, Elizabeth Deeble, George Deeble and Jane Deeble £5 each. Remainder to 2 sons and 2 daughters.
Executors: friends Wm. Hammans, Peter Dicks, Geo. Smedley.
Witnesses: Sarah Minshall, Susanna Pyle, Thos. Minshall.

MENDENHALL, MOSES. Kennet, yeoman.
9/27/1731. April 8, 1732. A. 360.
To son Caleb 1/2 of tract of land I now live on at 21. To son Moses the other 1/2 of said tract at 21. To daughter Alice Mendenhall £30 at 18. To daughter Phebe estate until sons are of age.
Executors: brother Joseph and friend Ellis Lewis.
Witnesses: Thos. Chandler, Jane Sheward, Ruth Jones.

MILLER, JAMES. Kennet, yeoman.
1/8/1731/2. April 8, 1732. A. 361.
Provides for wife Rachel including plantation where I now dwell containing 250 acres during life paying to daughter Sarah £40 at 20 also the legacy her grandmother Katherine Fred left to her. To son James 250 acres of land in Sadsbury he paying to daughter Deborah £50 when 20. To son Jesse my plantation where I now dwell at wifes decease.
Executors: wife Rachel and brother in law Benjamin Fred.
Witnesses: John Smith, William Beverly, Barnet McHendy.

BAILY, JOEL. Marlborough.
December 10, 1728. Codicil: 12/9/1731/2. April 8, 1732. A. 363
To son Daniel £8. To son Isaac £4. To son Joel £10. To son Thomas 193 acres of land in Marlborough part of a tract of 400 acres bought of Richard Barnard. To son John 207 acres the remainder of said tract. To son Josiah my new dwelling plantation containing 100 acres paying to son Thomas £15. To daughter Mary and Ann £10 each. To granddaughter Ann Stewart £10.
Executors: sons Thomas and John. Cod. directs son Josiah to pay daughter Mary Harlan £10 and divides the 400 acres equally between Thomas and John.
Witnesses: John Strode, Richard Hays, Jos. Taylor. To cod. Wm. Webb, John Hope, George Carson.

HARLANF SOLOMON. Londongrove.
12/22/1731/2. April 8(12?), 1732. A. 365.
To brother James Harlan my 250 acres of land he keeping mother during life and paying to cousin Dinah Harlan daughter of brother George deceased £5 at 18. Also all personal estate.
Executors: Thos. Speakman and John Allen.

Witnesses: Enoch Hollingworth, John Maris Jr.

TOWNSEND, JAMES. Birmingham,, yeoman.
January 8, 1731/2. April 10, 1732. A. 366.
Provides for wife Hannah. To son James my plantation in Birmingham containing 275 acres.
Executors: wife Hannah and sons in law Wm. Brinton and George Baily. Letters to widow and Baily. Brinton renouncing.
Witnesses: James Nesbit, Harry Young, John Bennet.

CHAMBERLIN, ROBERT. Concord, yeoman.
March 26, 1730. April 12, 1732. A. 367.
Provides for wife Mary including plantation containing 93 acres in Concord during widowhood afterward to son Joseph he paying legacies as follows. To sons John and Robert and daughter Susanna wife of John Pyle £5 each; also to grandson Jacob son of Robert Chamberlin £5; also to said grandson 20 acres of land being the remainder of my tract over and above the 93 acres during life afterward to son Joseph. To son in law Daniel Pyle 1 shilling. To kinswoman Eliza Moore 20 shillings. Remainder in 5 equal shares to sons, John, Robert, daughter Susanna, son Joseph and the 2 daughter of son in law Danl. Pyle, viz Susanna and Mary. Executors: wife Mary, Henry Osbourn and John Taylor to be assistants.
Witnesses: John Goor, Saml. Sharpless, Fughny Ferry.

WILLIS, JOHN. Thornbury.
No date. April 28, 1732. A. 368.
Directs burial at Birmingham. To son John all real estate when of age, wife Mary to possess the same until that time. To daughters Esther and Ann all personal estate when of age.
Executrix: wife Mary.
Witnesses: James Webb, Thos. Price, Joseph Wray.
[Widow married Thomas Smith.]

COOPER, JAMES. Newtown.
October 25, 1731. May 5, 1732. (died November 4, 1731, buried Middletown Presb Ch).
Provides for wife Ann. To son John £20 at 21. To son James the house where he now dwells and 2 acres of land belonging. To daughter Mary Cooper £10. To daughter Ann Tasey 1 shilling. To daughter Martha Dickey 1 shillings. To son Thomas my land in Newtown containing 140 acres.
Executors: wife Ann and son Thomas and friend Richard Iddings, trustees.
Witnesses: John Williamson, John Patterson.

WALTER, JOHN. Sadsbury. Carpenter.
April 19, 1732. May 8, 1732. A. 371.
To wife not named 1/3 of estate real and personal. To son John of remainder. To daughters Mary and Elizabeth Walter the remainder.
Executor: brother and friend Caleb Peirce.
Witnesses: Andrew Moor, John Musgrave, Wm. Walter, Morgan Jones.
[October 12, 1736. Martha Walter,,Wm. Webb and John Pyle appld

guardians of Mary, John and Eliza.]

WHITE, JOSEPH. Nottingham. Carpenter.
March 13, 1731/2. May 18, 1732. A. 371.
To wife Elizabeth the plantation during widowhood, afterward to son Joseph who is to maintain daughter Sarah White during life. To daughter Mary Aldham 5 shillings.
Executors: wife Elizabeth and John Ruddell.
Witnesses: Wm. Lacy, Robt. Patton, Richard Francis.

JENKINS, THOMAS. London, Britain. Weaver.
May 11, 1732. Mary 23, 1732. A. 373.
All estate to be sold and divided among children, viz Sarah, David and Isaac Jenkins if the property is not sufficient to pay the debts directs that 2 sons "shall be put out to service to earn money to pay the remainder of the debt."
Executors: Thos. Edmond of New Castle Co.
Witnesses: David John, Thos. James, John Evans Jr.

GOSS, CHARLES. E. Nottingham.
March 21, 1731/2. June 1, 1732. A. 374.
Father in law Evan Powell to have all estate and take care of wife and children who are not named, also executrix.
Witnesses: Elisha Gatchell Sr, John Boggo.

GIBBONS, JAMES. WESTTOWN.
1/15/1731/2. June 3, 1732. A. 374.
Provides for wife Ann including 100 acres of the land I live on during life, afterward to son James. To eldest son James remaining part of the land I live on which my father gave me being 400 acres. Also 1200 acres near the head of Brandywine and 1/2 of tract of land I bought the right of James Harlan being 500 acres and 1/2 of my share of the Society Mill at Goshen. To son Joseph 400 acres of land adjacent the land I live on bought of Reece Thomas and Anthony Morris, also 100 acres which lies on branch of Conestoga and 1/2 of Harlan tract my share of Mill. To Aaron James and Edward Brinton £5 each. Remainder to Ann, also executrix.
Witnesses: William Brinton, Benj. Mendenhall, John Borras.

PRYOR, SILAS. Kennet, yeoman.
April 14, 1732. June 13, 1732. A. 376.
All estate real and personal to wife Susanna during widowhood. To daughter Joanna wife of Thomas Heald £5 and my great bible. To sons James and Joseph all real estate at wifes decease. Estate entailed to heirs of sons and failing them to heirs of daughter Susanna "so long as wood grows or water runs in and upon this Terestiall Gobb of Earth and water."
Executors: wife Susanna, Ellis Lewis and Jos. Mendenhall, overseers.
Witnesses: Moses Cason, Thomas Parvin.

McGUISTON, DAVID.
April 19, 1732.
Adm. to Andrew Vance.

WILLIS, EDWARD. Birmingham.
April 28, 1732.
Adm. to John Willis, father, widow Katherine renouncing.
Witnesses: Jos. Parker, John Marris.

MERCER, JOSEPH. May 5, 1732.
Adm. to Ann Mercer. [Ann married Daniel Coyle].

BROWN, MESSER.
May 6, 1732.
Adm. to Dinah Brown and Henry Reynolds.

ROBISON, JOHN.
May 30, 1732.
Adm. to Mathew Robison.

BARNS, AARON.
May 31, 1732.
Adm. to James Few.

CAIN, THOMAS.
May 31, 1732.
Adm. to John Cain.

TOWNSEND, AMOS.
June 13, 1732.
Adm. to Mary Townsend. [Acct filed by Mary Yarnall 1752 in which son Thomas and Ann are named].

BUNTING, WILLIAM, of Wellistown. August 2, 1732.
Adm. to John Faroks [married 1724 Mary, daughter of Thos. and Hannah Taylor left 2 children, John born April 1725 and another son.]

LIGHTFOOT, MARGARET. Widow. Darby.
4/14/1732. July 13, 1732. A. 378.
To the Quakers of Darby meeting £5. To the Quakers of Springfield £5. To my brother Thos. Pulford £60. To cousin Elizabeth Hueston and to Hannah Hannams, articles named. To my brother Michael Blunston one great bible. To son in law Saml. Blunston the silver pot that is so called in my husband John Blunston's will. To Sarah Bethel and Hannah Blunston £2 each. To Adam Roads and wife, Saml. Blunston and wife and Ann Gibson 10 shillings each. To Michael Lightfoot and wife and Saml. Lightfoot and wife, Arthur Jones and wife, Joseph Willey and wife, Isaac Starr and wife, John Willy and wife and Jacob Lightfoot, 10 shillings each. To cousins Margaret and Abigail Woodward articles named. To Rachel Shanton, d. To James Hines £2. To cousin Joseph Stidman his bond for £20. To Jacob Simcock £2. To cousins Thomas and James Hewston, sons of James near Brandywine £5 each when 21. Wearing apparel to 5 cousins Margaret and Abigail Woodward, Hannah Jane and Abigail Edge. To John Salkeld and Michael Lightfoot £10 each. To John Smith of Marlborough £20. Remainder at disposal of executors John Smith and Michael Lightfoot.
Witnesses: Saml. Garrett, David Thomas, John Davis.

HOULDSTON or HOULSTON, JOHN. Edgmont, yeoman.
August 1, 1732. August 16, 1732. A. 380.
Provides for wife Sarah. To daughter Sarah a cow. To daughter Ann £12. To son John remainder of lands. To son Benjamin the land devised to wife when he is 21. To daughters Elizabeth and Rebecca £12 each. To daughter Hannah £24 1/2 to go towards bringing her up to 14 years of age.

Executors: wife Sarah and her brother Saml. Phipps and cousin Peter Taylor and son in law, John Quland. Trustees.
Witnesses: Thomas Williamson, Eph. Jackson.

HARLAN, AARON. Kennet, yeoman.
May 5, 1732. October 2, 1732. A. 381.
Provides for wife not named inc real estate until Bon George is 21. To son George when 21 my now dwelling place being the last part of my tract of land on Brandywine, containing about 300 acres. To son Samuel when 21 the west part of said tract as lately surveyed by Zachariah Butcher containing 230 acres. To son Aaron when 21, my plantation in Kennet whereon my father in law now lives. To son Jacob when 21 an equal portion of my estate as either of above named sons. To daughter Charity one gray filly. To daughters Mary and Elizabeth £20 each when 21. Lands to be valued and sons shares to be made equal.
Executors: wife and friend Samuel Hollingsworth and Saml. Pyle and brother Joshua Harlan. Trustees.
Witnesses: Thomas Strode, Geo. Hollingsworth, Dinah Heald.

BAILY, ISAAC. Marlborough, yeoman.
March 6, 1731/2. October 5, 1732. A. 383.
Provides for wife Abigail including plantation till eldest child is 21. To son Isaac 1/2 of the tract I live on. To son Joel the other 1/2 of tract - when they are 21. To the child my wife is now big of, £30 when of age.
Executors: wife Abigail and brother Daniel Baily.
Witnesses: Robert Sharman, Joel Baily, Joshua Johnson.

TOWNSEND, THOMAS. Concord, yeoman.
August 13, 1732. October 20, 1732. A. 384.
To son Nathaniel all my land upon Long Island and in West Chester Co., New York. To 2 youngest sons Thomas and John £600 to be put to interest for them March 1, 1733. To daughter Hannah Underhill £30 besides what she already has. To daughter Sarah Titus £140 when 20. Provides for wife Sarah, sons were all minors.
Executors: wife Sarah and son Nathaniel.
Witnesses: Henry Obourn, John Hannams, Wm. Rattew, John Townsend and Thos. Hollingsworth. Overseers.

JOHNSON, ROBERT. New Garden. Glaizer.
1/26/1732. November 28, 1732. A. 386.
Provides for wife not named. To sons James, Joshua and Robert £20 each. To daughters Abigail and Ann £15 each. To son Benjamin, my plantation whereon I now dwell containing 300 acres, he paying above legacies.
Executors: son Joshua and friend Benjamin Fred.
Witnesses: Saml. Miller, John Willson, Benj. Fredd.

TAYLOR, PHILIP. Thornbury, yeoman.
October 12, 1732. December 13, 1732. A. 387.
Provides for wife Ann including plantation in Thornbury containing 200 acres during widowhood and afterward to son Stephen, he paying to daughter Phebe £50 when 21. To son John my plantation lot of Reece Thomas, Antho. Morris and Ann --- in

Westtown, containing 200 acres, he paying to his sister Phebe £30. To son Philip, my tract of land on West Branch of Brandywine containing 300 acres which I purchased of Richard Clayton and Mary his wife.
Executrix: wife Ann.
Witnesses: Goe Ashbridge, John Yearsly, Benj. Cox.

SELLERS or SELLARS, SAMUEL. Darby, yeoman.
November 1, 1732. December 14, 1732. (died April 22, 1732). A. 389.
To son Samuel 5 shillings having already done well for him. To eldest daughter Sarah Ashmead 1 shilling. To daughter Mary Vernon and Ann Pritchett 1 shilling each. Remainder to wife Anna.
Executors: wife Ann and son Samuel.
Witnesses: Richd. Parker, James Mark, Saml. Bunting.

COWPLAND, JOSHUA. Chester. Cordwainer.
December 12, 1732. December 28, 1732. A. 389.
To my father Wm. Cowpland £6 yearly during life. To my sister Abigail £5. To sister Sarah Stackhouse £10. To brother Caleb Cowpland £10. To brother David all remainder of estate.
Executors: brothers Caleb and David.
Witnesses: John Young, Joseph Parker.

LEWIS, STEPHEN.
August 9, 1732.
Adm. to John Parry, Jr.

PASCHALL, WILLIAM.
August 11, 1732.
Adm. to Hannah Paschall.

THOMAS, WILLIAM.
September 15, 1732.
Adm. to James Thomas and Lewis William.

CHAMBERLIN, JOHN.
September 29, 1732.
Adm. to Lettice Chamberlin.

SPEAKMAN, THOMAS.
October 1, 1732.
Adm. to Ann Speakman.

BARNARD, THOMAS.
October 5, 1732.
Adm. to Sarah Barnard.

TAYLOR, JEREMIAH.
October 5, 1732.
Adm. to Joseph Taylor, father. Mary the widow renouncing.

GRIST, JACOB.
October 14, 1732.
Adm. to Hannah Grist.

BONSALL, OBADIAH.
December 18, 1732.
Adm. to Joseph Bonsall, son. Sarah widow, renouncing.

SCOTT, JOHN.
December 18, 1732.
Adm. to John Scott.

NIXON, THOMAS. Fallowfield.
January 4, 1732/3. January 19, 1732/3. A. 391.
To servant maid Ann Ballar all household goods. Remainder to said Ann's 2 children Thomas and Lydia and James Painston which I have raised from a child I would have put to the shoe making trade. To Wm. Hamilton £2.
Executor: Wm. Hamilton, Jr.
Witnesses: Wm. Hamilton, Mary Halloway, Hannah Travilla.

HUBBARD, JOHN. Ches Co. Weaver.
August 25, 1728. March 3, 1732/3. A. 392.
To my grandchildren issue of only daughter and child deceased 1 shilling each. To wife Mary all other estate real and personal and executrix.
Witnesses: Jacob Buchholts, Jacob Sprint, Margt. Wittersin.
Testator signed in German script.

PARKS, RICHARD. Goshen.
12/10/1732/3. March 29, 1733. A. 393.
To each of my 4 eldest children, viz Thomas, Jennet Huff, Saml. and Richard Parks £1-6-8 being the bequest of their grandfather unto them. To wife Susanna Huff 10 shillings. Remainder of estate to 5 youngest children, viz., Saml., Richard, Susanna, John and Benjamin at 18.
Executors: wife Susanna and son Saml.
Witnesses: Richard Jones, Rees Jones.
[Widow married John Fincher, 1735.]

JACKSON, EPHRAIM. Edgmont, yeoman.
September 11, 1732. March 30, 1733. A. 394.
To wife Rachel £125 and furniture. To sons John and Joseph £10 each. To son Nathaniel all the book debts he oweth me. To son Samuel £10. To son Ephraim £20. To daughter Mary £10 and to her husband 20 shillings. To daughter Rachel £10 and to her husband 20 shillings. To son Nathan £30. To granddaughter Elizabeth and grandson John £5 each when 21. Remainder divided among all children living except Elizabeth and John.
Executors: wife Rachel and friend Wm. Hammons. Proven by consent of all the parties interested.

BARTRAM, ELIZABETH. Darby.
December 5, 1732. May 5, 1733. A. 395.
To brother William Bartram now living at or near Cape Fear £2. All remainder of estate to uncle Wm. Smith also executor.
Witnesses: John Davis, John Shaw, Mary Hughs.

ALLEN, JAMES. W. Nottingham. Cooper.
April 1, 1733. May 11, 1733. A. 396.
To wife Mary all estate during widowhood, afterward divided among all children, viz Ann Harris, John, Morril, James, William, Isaac, Mary and Nathan the last named to have £10 more than the rest.
Executrix: wife Mary.
Witnesses: Thos. Brown, Sarah Hametton, Thos. Rogers.

LEWIS, HENRY. Newtown. Husbandman.
December 22, 1729. May 29, 1722. A. 397.
To son Thomas 5 shillings. To wife Jane and daughter Elinor Goldsmith all personal estate and executors.
Witnesses: Richard Iddings, David Morgan.

PRESTON, JOHN. Thornbury.
May 12, 1733. May 30, 1733. A. 398.
To Mary daughter of Florence Donelson all estate after funeral

expenses are paid also to said Mary £30 sterling under care of my brother John Fell of Green Lane in Pennington Lancashire, Eng. £20 under the care of Adam Squire of Airton near Settle in Yorkshire, to be paid her at 18. Executors: Joseph Eranson and Timothy Ward.
Witnesses: Saml. Bettle, Nathl Ashbrook, Thos. Price.

HUGHS, RICHARD. Newton. Cordwainer.
May 11, 1733. June 16, 1733. A. 399.
Executor to sell all lands and other estate and proceeds to wife for bringing up children and apprenticing them to trades at 14, none named.
Executrix: wife Margaret.
Witnesses: Benj. Hughs, David Wiiliam, John Evans.

BEREY, SAMUEL. Nottingham.
January 8, 1732. August 27, 1733. A. 400.
To my 6 children, viz Thomas, Hannah, Elizabeth, Sarah, John and Margaret £5 each when of age. To wife Margaret all personal estate and executrix.
Witnesses: Henry Reynolds, Roger Kirk.

NOOKS, WILLIAM. Middletown.
June 19, 1733. September 5, 1733. A. 401.
Describes himself as "late of Boars Grove, County of Worcester, Great Britain." To wife Ruth all estate real and personal. To sons Joseph, William, Moses and Thomas 1 shilling each. To daughter Ann, Mary, Sarah, Susanna, Elizabeth and Jane 1 shilling each.
Executors: wife Ruth, friends John Worrall of Edgmont and Philip Yarnall, trustees.
Witnesses: John Edward Goldsmith, Edwd Folwell, Denesse Folwell.

COLLINS, PETER. E. Bradford.
October 9, 1733. October 29, 1733. A. 402.
To wife all estate real and personal during life and after her decease to my brother Daniel Collins or his heirs and if Robert Collins children should come my estate shall be divided among them.
Executors: wife Elizabeth and Richd. Buffington Jr and Geo. Martin. Trustees.
Witnesses: Richd. Buffington, Geo. Martin, Damson Osson.

HANBY, WILLIAM. Nottingham. Farmer.
November 30, 1731. November 21, 1733. A. 403.
To eldest son William all my title claim to 150 acres of land in Northampton Co. Va, given to my brothers Richard, Daniel and me by my fathers will also 40 shillings. To daughter Elizabeth and son John 40 shillings each. Provides for wife Mary including plantation during widowhood afterward to sons Wm. and John.
Executors: wife Mary.
Witnesses: Garret Tool, Wm. Anderson.

MOORE JR, JOHN. Birmingham. Weaver.
October 8, 1733. January 7, 1733/4. A. 404.

To Mary wife of brother Samuel 30 shillings. To nephew Gabriel Moore, one bay mare "running in the woods in Township of Nantmell." Remainder to wife Elizabeth also executrix, brother in law Richard Barry assistant. Witnesses: Jonathan Thatcher, Richard Thatcher, Barth Darby.

LINDLY, JAMES.
January 25, 1732/3.
Adm. to Samuel Nutt.

MAGU, ARCHIBALD.
December 18, 1732.
Adm. to John Scott.

BARBER, JAMES.
February 8, 1732/3.
Adm. to Thomas Hayward.

GARTEN, JOHN.
February 2, 1732/3.
Adm. to James Gibbons, kinsman of widow Rebecca who renounced.

TURNER, JOHN.
March 6, 1732/3.
Adm. to Sarah Turner.

WRIGHT, SAMUEL.
March 10, 1732/3.
Adm. to James McTeer.

GRAY, ELIZABETH.
March 20, 1732/3.
Adm. to George Gray.

ROCKERFIELD, MARTIN.
April 7, 1733.
Adm. to John Rockerfield, son. Mary widow renouncing.

HIND, JAMES.
April 13, 1733.
Adm. to Elizabeth Hind.

ARNOLD, WILLIAM.
April 13, 1733.
Adm. to Anthony Arnold.

COX, JOSEPH.
May 5, 1733.
Adm. to Benjamin Cox.

HUNTER, JONATHAN.
May 11, 1733.
Adm. to Margery Hunter.

MACLERY, JOHN.
May 30, 1733.
Adm. to Henry McTeer.

GORE, JOHN.
August 18, 1733.
Adm. to Margery Gore.

ELDRIDGE, THOMAS.
August 28, 1733.
Adm. to Mary Eldridge.

WILLIAMS, JAMES.
October 1, 1733.
Adm. to Zacharius Williams.

BAKER, JOHN. Goshen, yeoman.
January 26, 1733/4. February 22, 1733/4. A. 405.
Provides for wife Rachel, remainder to 3 children, viz Hannah, Joseph and Mary. Joseph to have a double share as the law directs.
Executors: wife Rebecca and father in law Alex Hunter.
Witnesses: Stephen Beaks, John Collins.
[John Baker and Rachel Hunter married Christ Church, March 4, 1728.]

ELGAR, JOSEPH. Nottingham. Died 11/19/1733.
11/8/1733. March 25, 1734. A. 406.
To wife Mary all real and personal estate during widowhood to

bring up the children. To daughter Margaret born of my former wife Margaret, silk gown and 2 silk petticoats which was her mothers. Remainder equally to all children, viz Margaret, Susanna, Thomas, Mary, Elizabeth, Joseph and the child with whom my wife is now pregnant.
Executrix: wife Mary, John Churchman and Wm. Brown, trustees.
Witnesses: Thos. Rogers, Saml. Brown, John Beckett.

PEARSON, THOMAS. Marple.
October 16, 1730. March 25, 1734. A. 407.
To son John £15. To son in law John West and my daughter Sarah his wife £10. To son in law Nicholas Rogers and my daughter Mary his wife £15. To son in law Peter Thompson and my daughter Margery his wife £15. To son Robert £10 of the money owing by him to me. To 4 sons, viz Robert, Lawrence, Enoch and Abel 5 shillings each. Remainder real and personal to wife Margery.
Executors: Bartholomew Coppock, Saml. Levis Jr.
Witnesses: Rebecca Coppock, Sarah Coppock, Mordecai Massey.

RAYDON, ANDREW. Birmingham. Millwright.
March 10, 1734. April 4, 1734. A. 408.
To eldest daughter Catherine £30 at 16 which will be on the 30th day of 8 month, 1747. To youngest daughter Sarah £30 at 16 which will be on the 1st day of 10 months 1749. To wife Catherine all my lands etc. where I now live also 1/4 of a corn mill in New London, 318 acres of land in Hunterdon Co, New Jersey and all personal estate and executor with friend Wm. Horn.
Witnesses: John Wilson, John Day, Samuel Pyle.

PYLE, NICHOLAS. Concord.
February 24, 1733/4. April 4, 1734. A. 410.
Provides for wife Sarah including use of real estate until eldest son James is 20, said son to be apprenticed to Peter Hatton and youngest son Philip to my brother in law Nicholas Newlins care until he is 20. Real estate not disposed of, daughters are not named.
Executors: brother Saml. Pyle and Peter Hatton, Uncle Ralph Pyle and Henry Pierce, trustees.
Witnesses: Abm. Johnson, Thos. Brown.

LEVIS, SAMUEL. Springfield, yeoman.
October 4, 1728. April 13, 1734. A. 411.
To son Samuels children, viz John, Joseph, William and Samuel 10 shillings each. To son Williams children, viz Samuel and Elizabeth 10 shillings each and to all rest of my grandchildren 10 shillings each. To daughter Eliza Shipley my negro man Jeffry. Remainder to wife Elizabeth during life and after her decease 1/2 to divided between son Saml. and daughter Elizabeth and the other 1/2 to son William and daughter Mary Pennock. Refers to a marriage settlement for wife dated March 5 and 6, 1724/5.
Executors: daughter Eliza Shipley, son in law Jos. Pennock and wife Elizabeth.
Witnesses: John Davis, Rebecca Davis, John Skelton.

YARNALL, PHILIP. Edgmont, yeoman.
August 16, 1733. May 20, 1734. A. 414.
To sons John and Philip 5 shillings each, having had their portions. To son Job all my land in Ridley, he paying £80 to daughter Mary Yarnall, 1/2 at 18. To daughter Sarah Ellis £10 and to her husband Evan Ellis, what he owes me on book. To son Thomas all the land I bought of Jacob Minshall and that which was John Goldings, also £20. To son Nathan the remainder of that tract of land that was Worrilows. To daughter Rebecca Yarnall £80. To son Samuel this plantation I live at subject to provision for wife Dorothy. Mentions "the 2 Dutch children George and Margaret."
Executors: wife Dorothy and son Philip.
Witnesses: Thos. Smedley, John Cheyney, Mathew Hopkin.

POWELL, JOHN. L. Providence, yeoman.
August 19, 1727. July 15, 27, 1734. A. 415.
To son Joseph 5 shillings. To son Thomas 5 shillings. To daughter Mary and Margaret 5 shillings each. To granddaughter Sarah Powell a box iron and haters. To all the rest of my grandchildren a pocket bible. To each of the children of brother Joseph a New Testament. To Susanna daughter of brother Thomas a New Testament. To each of the children of brother in law Samuel Robinett a New Testament. To Owen Thomas, baptist minister in or near New Garden £3 and to the baptist congregation at Birmingham £3. To wife Elizabeth all lands and remainder to moveables also executrix.
Witnesses: John Beckingham, Francis Pullan, Jer. Collet.

PIERCE, GEORGE. E. Marlborough, yeoman.
January 19, 1733/4. July 27, 1734. A. 418.
Provides for wife Ann including all claims due from either of her former husbands. To son Joshua £50 also my share of Society Mill at Concord. To son Caleb 1/3 of d. To son Gainer the remainder 1/3 of said mills also my share in Thornbury School house. To daughter Betty Caldwell £50. To daughter Ann Gibbons £30. To daughter Mary wife of Joseph Brinton £50. To daughter Hannah wife of Edward Brinton £50. To grandson George Peirce son of Gainer £50 when 21, with rev to his 4 sisters, viz Elizabeth, Ann, Sarah and Susanna. Books to 7 children. Household goods to 4 daughters. Remainder to grandchildren.
Executors: wife Ann, sons Joshua and Caleb. Letters to sons, widow renouncing.
Witnesses: Wm. Webb, Thomas Harlan, Samuel Pyle.

MINSHALL, JACOB. Middletown, yeoman.
3/11/1734. August 10, 1734. A. 418.
To eldest son Thomas a piece of land in Middletown containing 70 acres, purchased of John and Thomas Cheyney, also 50 acres of the land where I now live, described and some meadow containing 30 3/4 acres. To wife Sarah use of plantation where I live until son John is 21. To son John the plantation where I live containing 370 acres when 21, subject to provision for wife and paying to daughter Sarah Minshall £40 and to son Moses £30 at 21. (who was indentured to nephew Griffithe Minshall].
Executors: wife Sarah and son Thomas.
Witnesses: Thomas Smedley, Jacob Taylor, Richard Jones.

POWELL, JOHN. Sadsbury.
September 1, 1734. October 1, 1734. A. 420.
To wife not named all personal estate I left in her possession in old England and remainder of estate to son William to be left in possession of my brother Joseph Powell until he is of age.
Executors: brother Joseph.
Witnesses: Andrew Moore, John Clark, James Money.

STEEL, ANDREW. New London.
September 9, 1734. October 1, 1734. A. 421.
To grandson Robt. Steel Jr 15 shillings. To son Robert 15 shillings. To son Peter Highgate 15 shillings. To son James Donell 15 shillings. To son John, all remainder of estate and executor.
Witnesses: James Smith, Robert Smith.

CALLOEHEN, OWEN.
January 7, 1733/4.
Adm. to Saml. Woolason.

MACKEY, JAMES.
January 31, 1733/4.
Adm. to Hugh Cowen and John Mathias, Frances the widow renouncing in favor of her 2 brothers above named.

BULLOCK, AARON.
April 16, 1734.
Adm. to William Andrews of Kennet.

EDGE, JOHN.
May 6, 1734
Adm. to Mary Edge.

HOWELL, EVAN.
June 28, 1734.
Adm. to Sarah Howell.

HAYES, JOSEPH.
July 29, 1734
Adm. to Hannah Hayes.

RATTEW, THOMAS. Aston.
August 9, 1734.
Adm. to John Carter "one of the bigge creditors." Mary the widow renounci: in his favor.

BOND, JOSEPH.
September 21, 1734.
Adm. to Elizabeth Bond.

FEARN, JOSIAH.
September 27, 1734.
Adm. to Rebecca Fearn.

FEW, ISAAC.
October 23, 1734.
Adm. To James Few.
Richard elder son, renouncing.

THOMAS, EVAN.
January 28, 1734/5.
Adm. to Edward Edwards.

HENRY, JAMES. W. Caln. Farmer.
September 3, 1734. November 1, 1734. A. 422.
To wife Ann 1/2 of all estate moveable or immovables. To the child yet unborn, the remainder 1/2 of estate if living at 21, other wise to my 2 brothers. To brother John £2.
Executors: brother Robert and brother in law John Davison.
Witnesses: Andrew Hodge, Robt. Brown.

HOWELL, REECE. Newtown.
5/31/1734. November 26, 1734. A. 422.

To daughter Ann 50 shillings. To son Howell and daughter Mary £10 each.
To son Reece £10. To wife 1/2 of all estate real and personal during
life. To son David the remainder of estate and wife's half at her decease
being about 60 acres of land in Newtown.
Executors: wife Elizabeth and son David.
Witnesses: Lewis Lewis, Evan Lewis, Wm. Lewis.
[Eleanor Davis was a sister to wife of Rees Kowell, see Philadelphia
Certificates.]

HEDGES, JOSEPH. of Manaquiney. Prince George Co. Md.
September 6, 1732. November 29, 1732. A. 423.
To son Solomon a tract of land containing 258 acres lying up Managuncy
Creek on west side. To sons Charles and Joshua each 200 acres of land at
Opeckam and executor to purchase 400 acres at Opeckam for sons Jonas and
Joseph and 130 acres at Manaquiney for son Samuel. To daughter Ruth,
Catharine and Dorcas and son Josiah a mare and colt each. Remainder
equally divided among children and wife who is not named.
Executor: son Solomon.
Witnesses: Chidley Mathews, John Hillard, Thos. Hillard. Will proven in
St Georges Co. Had 2 bonds in Ches Co amt £85.

JAMES, DANIEL. Willistown, yeoman.
December 4, 1733. March 13, 1733/4. A. 424.
All estate real and personal to be sold and proceeds equally divided
between my wife and 2 daughters who are not named. Executors: wife
Susanna and brother Joseph James and brother Geo. Maris.
Witnesses: James Massey, Thomas Massey. Son of Morgan and Elizabeth
James.

THOMAS, DAVID. Newtown.
April 29, 1734. January 13, 1734/5. A. 425.
To son Philip the plantation where I dwell containing 247 acres he paying
to daughter Mary £10 at or before November 16, 1736. To daughter
Elizabeth £10 and to daughters Gwen and Margaret £10 each. To son David
1/2 of a tract of land containing 500 acres in Nantmeal. To son Ezekiel
the other 1/2 of said tract. Household goods to 4 daughters.
Executor: son Philip.
Witnesses: Kenneth Anderson, Francis Noblet, Thos. Otley.

PYLE, WILLIAM. Thornbury, yeoman.
February 5, 1733. January 22, 1734/5. A. 428.
To son William at 21 the plantation where I now live containing 225
acres, subject to privileges to wife Olive and payment of £50 each to
sons Job and Isaac. To daughter Ann wife of John Woodward £40. To
daughters Olive and Phebe £80 at 18 or married. To daughter Mary wife of
Robert Lewis £20. MentionB having deeded to son John 280 acres of land
in Kennet. To sons Job and Isaac, my 455 acres of land in Marlborough.
Remainder to wife Olive.
Executors: wife, son John and friend Thomas West. Letters to son
John, wife being deceased and West renouncing.
Witnesses: John Townsend, Jos. Eavenson, Thomas Gilpin. Cod
February 13, 1733/4. States wife is deceased and gives what was

bequeathed her to 8 children, viz John, Ann, Mary, Olive, William, Job, Isaac and Phebe.

DEVONALD, JOHN. London, Britain.
March 1, 1734/5. April 23, 1735. A. 430.
To son Daniel 5 shillings. To daughters Sarah, Rachel, Mary, Hannah and Judith £7 each. To wife Mary the place on plantation I now dwell on and all moveables during widowhood and afterward sold and divided among daughters.
Executors: wife Mary and elders of Baptist Meeting of Welsh and London Tract to be overseers.
Witnesses: Richard Whitting, John Evan Jr.
[Sarah married John Bolton. Mary married David Evans of White Clay Creek. See Deed book H. 458]

WILLIAM, LEWIS. Whiteland, yeoman.
January 17, 1733/4. June 9, 1735. A. 431.
To wife Lettice and son Joseph all lands and other estate to bring up and educate the rest of the children, who are not named.
Executors: wife and son Joseph.
Witnesses: John Parry, Methusilah David, Roger David. (Widow married Samuel Rees.)

LEWIS, EVAN. Newtown, yeoman.
4/13/1735. Codicil: 5/10/1735. August 26, 1735. A. 432.
Provides for wife Mary. Gives £10 for support of the poor of Newtown meeting. To kinswoman Ellen Lewis £6. to daughter Hannah Pennell £70 and to each of my grandchildren 20 shillings. To daughter Ann Lewis £400. To eldest son Mordecai my plantation whereon I live containing about 700 acres. To son Jonathan my plantation containing 200 acres in Ridley also 259 acres in Whiteland purchased of Daniel Worthington. Mordecai to release to Jonathan all that tract of land in Hatfield Township, which descended to me and my wife from my brother in law Jonathan Hayes. To step father David Powell £5 yearly during life. Jonathan was a minor.
Executors: wife Mary, son Mordecai and brother Lewis Lewis.
Letters to Mordecai and Lewis, Mary being then in Great Britain.
Witnesses: Howell Howell, Wm. Lewis, Richard Jones. Mentions brother in law Simon Maris.

FRANCIS, WILLIAM.
February 20, 1734/5.
Adm. to Margaret Francis.

DUNN, EDWARD.
April 8, 1735.
Adm. to John Sharpless, Jr.

ABOURN, JAMES.
May 12, 1735.
Adm. to Agnes Abourn.

WRIGHT, JACOB.
May 28, 1735.
Adm. to John Chads. Mary the wid renouncing in favor of her brother law John Chads.

TAYLOR, MARTHA.
June 24, 1735.
Adm. to John Taylor.

NUBROUGH, JOHN.
November 27, 1735.
Adm. to Joseph Townsend and Ja Jefferis.

SWAIN, WILLIAM.
December 17, 1735.
Adm. to Elizabeth Swain.

ORAN, JOHN.
February 9, 1735/6.
Adm. to Thomas Moor. Mary the widow renouncing.

PRICE, JAMES. Newtown, yeoman.
January 23, 1734/5. October 1, 1735. A. 435.
To son in law Wm. Thomas Hugh 1 shilling and to his daughter Susanna my grandchild 1 shilling. To daughter Margaret £5. to daughter Tamer £5. To grandson James Thomas £5 at 18. To son in law John Jones and my daughter Jane his wife, remainder of personal estate and real estate during life, afterwards to their son, Price Jones.
Executor: son in law, John Jones.
Witnesses: John and Reece, Lewis Rees.
[James Price departed the 21 day of September in the year 1735, aged 87. St. Davids Church. In memory of the body of Susanna Prise departed this life ye 9 of April the year of our Lord 1733 aged 70 years.]

LEA, HANNAH. Darby. [died July 29, 17351.
November 16, 1734. October 17, 1735. A. 436.
To daughter Hannah Bonsall wearing apparel and household goods. To son John household goods. To daughter Hannah Allen £20. To daughter Mary Pilkington £2. To son Isaac Lea £40. To daughter Hannah Bonsall £40. To son John £40. To grandchildren by my son Joseph Webb deceased and Mary his wife, Hannah. Joseph and Sarah £20 when 21. To my 6 grandchildren by Edward Pilkington and my daughter Mary, viz Thomas, Mary, Hannah, Sarah, Ann and Edward £20 when 21. Remainder to son in law Joseph Bonsall and son John also executors.
Witnesses: Benja. Harvey, Mary Evitt, Jacob Webber.

HUGH, OWEN. Easttown, yeoman.
May 30, 1735. September 4, 1735. A. 438.
To eldest son Evan, second son Hugh and third son Edward each one cow. To daughter Mary Hugh a cow. To youngest son Morgan the plantation where I live and remainder of personal estate also executor.
Witnessed by David Davis, Edward Williams.

COLLINS, JOSEPH. Goshen, yeoman.
May 12, 1732. September 7, 1735. A. 439.
To eldest son John £5. To daughter Sarah wife of Thomas Malin £5. Provides for wife Mary. To sons Joseph and Henry my tract of land whereon I live in Goshen containing 125 acres, also all moveables, subject to wifes life int.
Executor: son Joseph.
Witnesses: Alex Bane, Thomas Evans, Richard Jones.

REYNERS, JOSEPH. Chester. Cordwainer.
September 19, 1735. September 27, 1735. A. 441.
To son Isaac £50 when 21. To son Stephen £50 at 21. To daughters Hannah & Rachel £50 each at 21. Remainder real and personal to wife Mary, executrix. Widow married Samuel Bell. Deed book J.7.

Witnesses: Geo. Ashbridge, Alexa Gandovelt, Joseph Hoskins.

HUTTON, JOSEPH. New Garden.
7/28/1735. November 15, 1735. A. 442.
To wife Mary 1/3 of all estate real and personal. To my children, viz John, Thomas, Joseph, Samuel, William, Benjamin, Nehemiah and Ephraim, the remainder of my estate to be divided in 8 equal shares to them as they attain the age of 21.
Executrix: wife Mary.
Witnesses: Isaac Jackson, Jos. Jackson, Benj. Fredd.

EWING, JOHN. London, Britain. Weaver.
October 17, 1736. November 19, 1735.
To wife Sarah 1/3 of all personal estate to sons Thomas and Joshua each 1/3 of estate. Appoints brothers William Ewing and David Jenkins, guardians of 2 sons.
Executrix: wife Sara.
Witnessed by Andrew Vance, Mathew Warren.

WOOD, WILLIAM. Darby, yeoman.
2/22/1727. November 25, 1735. A. 444.
Dwelling house and plantation in Darby to be sold for bringing up of the children. To wife Mary all estate real and personal for bringing up children who are not named.
Executors: brother George Wood of Darby and wife Mary.
Brothers in law Jacob and Enoch Bonsall, guardians of children.
Witnesses: John Wood, Benj. Lobb, Thos. Worth, Jr.

RICHARDS, JOSEPH. Aston, yeoman.
January 28, 1732/3. January 5, 1735/6. A. 445.
To daughter Susanna Barber £5. To son Edward 1 shilling. To daughter Dinah Linvill 1 shilling. To daughter Elizabeth Johnson £5. To daughter Ruth Worrow £5. To son Joseph all my lands and moveable estate paying above legacies also executor. Will signed by Jos. Richards on November 21 last past and immediately afterward snatched from the hand of Jos. Davenport by Mary the reputed wife of Jos. Richards and thrown onto the fire. Proven by consent of Mary Condrun wife of Richards who admitted the accusation.
Witnessed by Mordecai Woodward, Joseph Davenport, Eliza Peress.

HUTTON, MARY. Widow. New Garden.
11/1/1735/6. January 16, 1735/6. A. 448.
To sister Martha Houlton, wearing apparel. To children, viz John, Thomas, Joseph, Samuel, William, Benjamin, Nehemiah and Ephraim all other estate in equal shares as they come of age. Executors: brothers James Miller and John Hutton. Brother Wm. Miller, trustees.
Witnesses: Nathl. Houlton, Thomas Lindly, Benja. Fredd.

BAKER, JOSEPH. Edgmont.
August 27, 1731. March 10, 1735/6. A. 448.
Provides for wife Mary. To Francis Yarnall and his 3 children 5 shillings each. To son Richard and his 3 children 5 shillings
each. To son Aaron £10. To daughter Ann and her husband James

Sill £10. To daughter Susanna £10. To daughter Jane and her husband Thomas Thomas 5 shillings and their 4 children £3 each. To son Jesse £10. To daughter Sarah and her husband 5 shillings. To son Joseph the plantation. To daughter Rachel £10. To son Nehemiah £10. To son John £10. Legacies to be paid by son Joseph.
Executors: wife Mary and Sons Richard and Aaron.
Witnesses: Evan Howell, Eph. Jackson, Sarah Howell.

WILLIAM, JOHN. Willistown, yeoman.
January 4, 1734/5. February 2, 1735/6. A. 450.
To grandchildren, Erasmus, Lydia, Elizabeth and John children of my daughter Elizabeth and Thomas Lloyd £5 each and to Erasmus all my books and tools. To said daughter Elizabeth the house and land whereon I live during life and afterward to said grandson Erasmus. Remainder to son in law, Thomas Lloyd also executor. Witnesses: Richard Rickeson, Thomas Lewis.
[Thomas and Elizabeth Lloyd made acknowledgement to Haverford Monthly Meeting June 8, 1700.]

CULIN, GEORGE. Ridley, yeoman.
January 13, 1735/6. March 19, 1735/6. A. 451.
To wife Margaret 1/3 of estate real and personal. To eldest son John 5 shillings having had his portion. To daughter Mary Rambo 5 shillings. To son George my meadow on Darby Creek an all my upland. To son Daniel all my estate of land in Ridley on S.W side of Crum Creek with stock. To son Jonas £100 when 21 to be paid by George and Daniel. To 3 daughters, viz Margaret, Ann and Ellen. Remainder of personal estate.
Executors: wife Margaret and son Daniel.
Witnesses: John Crosby, Joseph Carter, Jacob Carter.

BLUNSTON, MICHAEL. Darby, yeoman.
December 22, 1731. Codicil: 4/24/1734. April 1736. B. 1.
Directs the sale of all real estate and provides for wife Phebe. To Samuel Bunting £80 to entertain honest friends and to Sarah his wife £10 and to Elizabeth daughter of brother in law Thomas Bradshaw £10. To friends John Salkeld and Agnes his wife £5. To brother Saml. Blunstons sons of Kirkhallum in Darbyshire, viz Michael and Samuel £6 each. To Samuel Garrett and John Davis for Monthly Meeting in Darby £10. To Sarah and Rebecca daughters of my cousin Sarah Fearn of Darby deceased and Elizabeth Hibberd granddaughter of said cousin £50 to be divided. To my cousin Katherine Rhoads and her 4 daughters Hannah, Sarah, Elizabeth and Mary £50 to be divided. To Sarah daughter of cousin John Blunston deceased £20. To Hannah daughter of John Blunston £20. To Wm. Levis and Elizabeth his sister Children of my brother in law Saml. Levis £10. To Sarah daughter of brother in law Thos. Bradshaw deceased £5. To Elizabeth Bradshaw £30 and furniture which belonged to my former wife her aunt. To Rebecca widow of Isaac Minshall deceased £5. To cousin Saml. Blunston of Conestoga in Lan Co., one pistol. To grandchildren of brother Wm. Blunston deceased the children of his son Wm., deceased one guinea to be divided. To Joseph and Samuel sons of cousin Catherine Rhoads 40

shillings to be divided. To cousin Josiah Fearn 20 shillings. To cousin Adam Rhoads £10.
Executors: cousins Saml. Levis Jr and Saml. Bunting. Codicil gives the int of £50 yearly towards a school, for educating children of Port Friends, also mentions that cousin Katherine Rhoads is deceased and gives her legacy to her son John Rhoads and Elizabeth Hinde, widow, also give £5 to John Hind son of said Elizabeth.
Witnesses: Job Harvey, Benj. Cliff, Nathl. Phillips, George Wood, Wm. Wood, Nathan Garratt.
Samuel Garrett, Jacob Bonsell and Samuel Seller Jr, trustees of money for schooling.

DUTTON, JOHN. Chichester, yeoman.
March 21, 1735/6. April 20, 1736. B. 3.
To sons John, Kinsman, Jacob, Joseph, Robert and to my 2 daughters Hannah wife of Nathaniel Scarlet and Mary wife of Joseph Coeburn 2 shillings each, when of age. Directs conveyance to be made of 130 acres of land in Aston to John Williams and 80 acres in Aston to John Beard. Remainder of estate to wife Elizabeth.
Executors: wife and son John. Letters to the widow, son refusing.
Witnesses: Edward Whitekar, Jo. Parker.

HUNTER, JOHN. Newtown, yeoman.
January 30, 1734. May 19, 1736. B. 4.
Provides for wife Margaret. To son George, son John daughters Marth Cole, Ann Baker 5 shillings each. To granddaughter Margaret Baker £20 at 21. To daughter Elizabeth Steel £20. To daughter Mary Hill £20. To daughter Margaret Hunter £30, household goods. To son Peter £50 at 21. To sons William and James, my plantation in Newtown and remainder of personal estate, also executors. Witnesses: Jos. Hawley, Francis Wayne, Wm. Owen, Saml. Cawley.

LEWIS, MARY. Whiteland.
August 12, 1734. May 25, 1736. B. 4.
Devised the £60 left her by her father now in hands of brother Griffith Lewis as follows. To said brother Griffith 5 shillings to his 3 children, Rebecca, Wm. and Saml. £10 to be divided. To the 3 children of my brother in law Llewellin David of Charlestown, viz Ann, Isaac and Magdalen £10 each. To the 2 children of brother in law David Humphrey, viz Magdalen and Jonathan £19-15.
Executors: brothers in law, Llewellin David and David Humphrey.
Witnesses: David Griffith, David Evans.

PARKER, RICHARD. Darby.
April 28, 1736. June 23, 1736. B. 5.
Provides for wife Martha including tract of 250 acres of land upon a branch of Brandywine. To son Richard my lot of land in City of Philadelphia. To son Joseph 2 lotts of land on N.E. side of Springfield Road also 1/4 of an island called Smiths. To son John the S. W. part of my land in Darby. To daughters Mary and Martha a lot on Springfield Road and £10 each. to son William remainder of land in Darby. Stock when 21.

Executors: wife Martha and friend John Davis of Darby.
Witnesses: Josiah Hibberd, Saml. Sellers, Saml. Bunting.

YOUNG, HARRY.
February 12, 1735/6.
Adm. to Mary Young.

CLAYTON, RICHARD.
March 12, 1735/6.
Adm. to Elizabeth Clayton.

DOUGLASS, JOHN.
March 10, 1735/6.
Adm. to Sarah Douglass.

GEORGE, THOMAS.
March 17, 1735/6.
Adm. to Mary George, sureties
Saml. Scott, Geo. Entriken,
Inv by William Webb and Thomas
Harlem January 31, 1735/6 £60.
1 H.6.

JESSOP, ROBERT.
May 3, 1735/6.
Adm. to Alexander Paxton.

POWELL, EVAN.
May 25, 1736.
Adm. to Sarah Dixon.

MAGEE, RICHARD.
June 22, 1736.
Adm. to Ann Magee.

PYLE, DANIEL.
July 27, 1736.
Adm. to Mary Pyle.

MINSHALL, JOHN. Sadsbury. Cordwainer.
March 6, 1735. August 31, 1735. B. 6.
To friend Anthony Shaw £5. To wife not named, all real and personal estate during life for bringing up my children and after her decease to be equally divided between my daughters except Martha, to her I give all my real estate of land in Appleton in Cheshire, England. She paying £10 to each of her sisters also £20 to my brother Joshua provided he goes to England and settles affairs for her.
Executors: wife and Anthony Shaw of Lancaster. Letters to Hannah, the widow. Shaw renouncing.
Witnesses: John Carnhan, Stephen Cole, William Boyd.

BAKER, JOSEPH. Edgmont, yeoman.
July 15, 1736. August 31, 1736. B. 7.
To my mother Martha Baker the rents of my plantation in Edgmont until brother John is 21 and then I devise said land 200 acres to my brothers Nehemiah and John, subject to the charges in will of my father Joseph Baker, also £10 to be paid my sister Sarah. Remainder to brothers and sisters equally.
Executor: brother Jesse Baker.
Witnesses: Abraham Howell, John Taylor.

BALL, ROGER. Darby, yeoman.
July 15, 1732. September 16, 1736. B. 8.
To son John all my land he paying to his 2 sisters Elizabeth and Hannah £40 each when 21 or married. To daughter Mary Thomas £10. To daughter Hannah Ball £5.
Executors: cousin Saml. Sellers Jr and friend Saml. Bunting.
Witnesses: James Hinde, Jacob Bonsall, Thos. Worth.

HEALD, SAMUEL. Kennet.
March 30, 1736. October 1, 1736. B.9.
To sons William and Samuel all wearing apparel. To son Joseph my saddle. Remainder to wife during life and at her decease to be divided among all children.
Executrix: wife Mary.
Witnesses: Wm. Webb, Joshua Harlan, Abraham Parker.

COEBOURN, THOMAS. Chester.
December 17, 1735. October 1, 1736. B. 9.
To son Joseph a piece of land on Edgmont road next Wm. Jefferis as described containing about 40 acres. To son John £5. To daughter Elizabeth Donavan £8. To daughter Mary Squibb 5 shillings. Give £2-10 to Jacob Howell towards repairing or building a meeting house in Chester. To son Thomas all remainder real and personal, also executor.
Witnesses: Wm. Jefferis, James Sanger, Joseph Davenport.

WHITSITT, GEORGE. Birmingham.
August 7, 1736. October 5, 1736. B. 10.
To Thomas Bullock my ivory headed cane and french razor. To Wm. Dargon, Saml. Piper, Alexander, John and George Pentland and Richard Whittsitt £70. Remainder to wife Rebecca.
Executors: wife and brother Thomas Bullock.
Witnesses: Saml. Hollingsworth, Goe Dilworth, John Furman.

CODWELL, THOMAS. Ches. Co.
March 5, 1735/6. October 13, 1736.
To wife and son Thomas my plantation and farming implements also to wife my servant boy, John Fulton. To son John 20 shillings. To daughter Margaret £2. Remainder divided between wife son Thomas daughters Ann and Rebecca.
Executrix: wife Lillies.
Witnesses: James Smith, Robert McNutt.

BOYLE, JOHN. Fallowfield. Husbandman.
May 23, 1736. June 23, 1736. B. 11.
Provides for wife Agnes. To son Alexander my plantation and all moveables except 2 mares and 50 bushels of wheat to son Wm. To son Hugh and daughter Sarah Fleming 5 shillings each.
Executor: son Alexander, Sarah Dunn, Robert Boyle.

POWELL, EVAN. New Garden, yeoman.
11/2/1734. May 25, 1736. B. 11.
To my 2 grandsons, Evan and Charles Goss £200 each at 21. To the meeting of Quakers in New Garden £10. To Thomas and William sons of Michael Lightfoot of New Garden £5, when 21. To 2 grandsons the right of 100 acres of land in Nottingham which son in law Charles Goss bought. Remainder real and personal to daughter Sarah Dixon. Letters to his daughter Sarah Dixon.
Executor: son in law Joseph Dixon. Letters to his daughter Sarah Dixon. Executor named renouncing.
Witnesses: Thos. Millhous, Francis Hobson, John Sharp.
Overseers: Ellis Lewis, William Miller, at the mill and Michael Lightfoot.

BUFFINGTON, JOHN. W. Bradford, yeoman.
7/24/1736. October 11, 1736. B. 12.
To eldest son John the plantation I now live on purchased of brother Richard containing 188 acres when 21. To wife Sarah use of said Plantation during minority of son and other provision. To son Thomas 50 acres of land adjacent above also £30 at 21. To daughters Mary and Sarah £15 each at 21.
Executors: wife Sarah, brother Richard Eavenson and brother Jeremiah Dean.
Witnesses: Isaac Vernon, Charles Turner, Joseph Wray.

OBORN, HENRY. Concord, yeoman.
7/24/1735. September 28, 1736. B. 13.
To daughter Hannah wife of Ezekiel Harlan £50. To daughter Susanna wife of James Harlan £50. To each of my grandchildren that is to Susanna, Hannah and Ezekiel Harlan, James Power, Ann Oborn and Betty Harlan £5 each at 21. To James Power my tract of land containing 205 acres it joins upon Marlborough line and is of the society land, adjacent land of Magnus Tate. Provides for wife Hannah including use of plantation I now live on in Concord during widowhood, afterward to daughters Hannah and Susanna Harlan.
Executrix: wife Hannah.
Witnesses: John Palmer, John Hannum.

ENGLE, FREDERICK. Middletown, yeoman.
August 3, 1737. September 10, 1737. B. 14.
To sons Frederick and John my plantation with Tanyard when 21. To daughter Mary, Susanna and Ann £60 each at 18. Remainder to wife Ann.

Executors: wife, Joseph Cloud and Edwd. Woodward Sr. Letters to widow Anna Woodward, the other renouncing.
Witnesses: William Hill, Robert Tipping, Henry Camm.
[Frederick Engle, aged 13, son of Paul and Mary, born Germantown, baptized at Christ Church, May 22, 1711.]

PLUMMER, ROBERT. Chester, yeoman.
September 4, 1731. September 24, 1737. B. 14.
Directs sale of real and personal estate, plantation being 100 acres and proceeds to wife Eleanor, for bringing up children.
Executor: Friend Edward Whitaker.
Witnesses: William Askew, Roger Shelly.

KINNISON, EDWARD. Ches. Co.
7/4/1736. December 9, 1736. B. 15.
Directs body to be buried in Goshen burying ground. To wife Mary all estate during life and what remains at her decease to sons Wm. and Charles. To sons Edward and James and daughters Mary and Hannah 1 shilling each.
Executors: friends Thomas Smedley and Thomas James, both of Goshen Mtg.
Witnesses: Richd. Richison/Ruhyon, John Woody. [No doubt Richison but the register made it Ruhyon.]

NEWLIN, JANE. Widow. Concord.
8/5/1736. December 15, 1737. B. 15.
To my 3 sons Joseph, Nicholas and Nathan £5 each the day of their marriage. To daughter Rachel Walter £16. To daughter Elizabeth £5, a bed etc. at her marriage. To daughter Jane £16 at marriage. To daughter Mary £16 at marriage. To daughter Martha £16 at marriage. All above legacies being conditioned upon their marriage with consent of the Monthly meeting to which they belong. To 3 grandchildren 40 shillings each to be paid them at 18 and 21.
Executors: brothers in law Ellis Lewis and John Newlin.
Witnesses: Ralph Eavenson, Grace Eavenson.
Mentions for Nathaniel first of all.

JEFFERIS, THOMAS.
August 31, 1736.
Adm. to Eleanor Jefferis.

TREVILLER, THOMAS.
August 31, 1736.
Adm. to Richard Treviller.

WOODWARD, MORDECAI.
September 13, 1736.
Adm. to Thomas Woodward.

PRITCHETT, EDWARD.
December 1, 1736.
Adm. to Daniel Calvert.

WADE, JOHN.
November 27, 1736.
Adm. to Robert Wade.

MORTON, MATHIAS.
December 9, 1736.
Adm. to Bridgett Morton.

TROAK, JOHN. East Caln.
November 30, 1736.
Adm. to Ann Troak [who married Wm. Mack. Sureties James Jefferis and James Few.]

MOOR, THOMAS.
December 22, 1736.
Adm. to Joseph Cloud and Mary Moor.

SMITH, WILLIAM. Darby, yeoman.
November 19, 1736. December 21, 1736. B. 16.
To son Samuel my plantation in Darby when 21 with reversion to wife and 2 daughters who are not named.
Executors: wife and friend John Davis of Darby.
Witnesses: Isaac Lea, Lewis Thomas, James Maddock.

CARTER, JEREMIAH. Chester, yeoman.
January 17, 1734/5. January 6, 1736/7. B. 17.
To wife Mary my plantation where I now dwell in Chester Township and all other estate during widowhood, afterward the plantation to son Abraham. To sons Edward and Nineveh £5 each. To daughter Sarah Barnard £5 and to her children £10 to be divided.
Executors: wife Mary, sons Abraham and Edward.
Witnesses: Richard Weaver, Eliza Weaver, Mary Weaver.

PRICE, THOMAS. London, Britain, yeoman.
March 22, 1736/7. April 12, 1737. B. 17.
To son William the place he now lives on - on Elk River in Ches. Co. To daughter Kattren Johnson £2 with int, which is due me from her husband Henry Johnson. To daughter Mary Porter the interest of a bond due me which £3 odd. To.son John £20. To daughters Ann,

Elizabeth, Sarah and Martha Price £14 each. To wife Ann and son Rice all my lands and other estate and executors.
Witnesses: Charles Finley, John Evans Jr.

LEWIS, GRIFFITH. Whiteland. Carpenter.
December 20, 1735. October 1, 1737. B. 19.
Provides for wife who is not named. To eldest son William the south side of my plantation. To younger son Samuel the north part of ditto - when said sons are 21. To daughter Rebecca £40 to be paid by sons. In case of death of wife and children, to sister Elizabeth Davies £3. To sister Catherine Humphrey 40 shillings and to sister Mary Lewis 20 shillings and remainder to the use of Goshen Meeting. Friends Goe Ashbridge Jr and Isaac Hains, trustees.
Executrix: wife.
Witnesses: John Cuthbert, David Howell, Nicholas Carter.

GIBY, DAVID. Charlestown.
November 3, 1736. October 5, 1737. B. 19.
To niece Margt Lewis £2. To David Jones son of said Margaret by her first husband, all wearing apparel and £4 at 16 and to Mary Jones daughter of said Margt £2 at 16 and to Thomas Jones son of Margt £2 at 16. Provides for wife Elizabeth. To brothers John and William Giby £5 each as soon as they arrive in Penna. To grandson Thomas Roberts all remainder of estate real and personal and executor.
Witnesses: Wm. Thomas, Evan David, David Emanuel.

WHITE, THOMAS. W. Caln, yeoman.
November 6, 1736. May 3, 1737. B. 20.
To wife Ann 1/3 of all estate and remainder to 3 children Jean, Thomas and John to be equally divided.
Executors: John Love and Samuel Henry and "my brother John White to take account of them both."
Witnesses: William Gregory, Saml. Henry.

PARKE, ROBERT.
February 29, 1736/7.
Adm. to Thomas Parke Jr.

GRAY, ALLEN.
May 11, 1737.
Adm. to Loranna Gray.

REDDICK, ROBERT.
May 18, 1737.
Adm. to Robert McClanahan.

BUNTING, ROBERT.
July 30, 1737.
Adm. to Eleanor Bunting.

ADAMS, HUGH.
August 22, 1737.
Adm. to James Adams.

HARVEY JR, JOSPEH.
November 29, 1737.
Adm. to Susanna Harvey.

GREAG, JOHN.
November 29, 1737.
Adm. to William Boggs.

SLOAN, PATRICK.
August 22, 1737.
Adm. to John Sloan son. Widow Isabel renouncing. Inventory £138.14.4 by Samuel Campbell and Wm. Wilson 25 August 1737.

LEWIS, JANE. Widow. Darby.
May 14, 1737. June 14, 1737. B. 21.
All real and personal estate to be sold by executors of proceeds for bringing up and educating children to be equally divided among them they were not named.
Executors: brother in law, Abraham Levis of Darby and Wm. Lewis of Haverford.
Witnesses: Wm. Kirk, Margaret Haverd, Thomas Worths.

RODES, CHRISTIAN.
March 11, 1736. May 5, 1737. B. 20.
All estate equally divided between my 3 children, viz Jacob, Joseph and Hannah.
Executor: George Bostock.
Witness: Samuel James.

JAMES, MORGAN. Newtown, yeoman.
May 14, 1737. June 17, 1737. B. 21.
Provides for wife Mary, remainder to all children living by my first and second wives, daughter Margaret only named.
Executors: wife Mary and son Joseph, kinsman Saml. Lewis and friend Thos. Thomas of Radnor, trustees.
Witnesses: Lewis Lewis, Michael Thomas, Elinor Jones.

HALL, SAMUEL. Springfield, yeoman.
3/29/1737. July 8, 1737. B. 22.
Provides for wife Mary including rents of plantation during life. To eldest son John all real estate on his mothers decease. To son Thomas and daughter Ann Wall 10 shillings each. Remainder to children and grandchildren who are not named.
Executors: son John and brother in law Aaron Jones.
Witnesses: Joseph Yarnall, Jane Maris, Jenkin Howell.
[widow died June 1, 1750.]

CLAYTON, ABEL. Chichester. Tailor. [Died October 14, 1737.]
9/24/1737. January 6, 1737/8. B. 22.
To wife Easter all real and other estate during life, after her decease to be divided among children. Joseph, Susanna and Margaret.
Executrix: wife Easter.
Witnesses: Thos. Giffing, Jos. Moulder.
[Joseph was about 7, Susanna about 5 and Margaret about 2 at their father's death.]

PHILLIPS, WILLIAM. Marple, yeoman.
February 20, 1737/8. February 20, 1737/8. B. 23.
To son John all wearing apparel. To grandchild William son of James Johnson, one heifer. All remainder to wife Mary.
Executors: wife and friends Charles Linn and Joshua Pennell.
Witnesses: William Johnson, Mary Johnson, Robt. Tipping.

EVANS, JOHN. Willistown. Mason.
December 23, 1735. March 1, 1737/8. B. 24.
To eldest son John my plantation whereon I live in Willistown containing 110 acres subject to provision for wife Ellen and

payment of £40 to youngest son Amos when 21.
Executors: wife Ellen and son John.
Witnesses: George Morgan, Jas. Rowland, Richard Jones.

HIBBERD, JOSEPH.
September 26, 1737.
Adm. to Elizabeth Hibberd.

FINLEY, SAMUEL.
October 29, 1737.
Adm. to Robt. Finley.

BOWES, ALEXANDER.
September 29, 1737.
Adm. to George Connell.

ORAN, JOHN.
October 31, 1737.
Adm. to Joseph Cloud.

BROOM, JOHN.
December 8, 1737.
Adm. to Mary Broom.

STRINGER, JOHN.
December 12, 1737.
Adm. to William Stringer, son, Martha the widow and sons George and Daniel renouncing.

PIKE, JOHN.
January 2, 1737/8.
Adm. to William Jefferis.
Eliza the widow renouncing.

GIBB, SAMUEL.
January 7, 1737/8.
Adm. to John Gibb.

EDMONSTON, ROBERT.
June 9, 1738.
Adm. to Mary Edmonston.

FLOWER, JOHN. Chichester. Weaver.
January 21, 1737/8. March 7, 1737/8. B. 25.
To wife Mary all lands in Chichester all other estate during life. After her decease to sons Richard, John, Thomas and William and daughter Mary Flower, equal shares of estate and to daughter Margaret Flower £20 over and above her 1/6 share.
Executrix: wife Mary.
Witnesses: Richard Edwards, Jemima Edwards, Thos. Giffing.

EVANS JR, JOHN. London, Britain.
[Died April 14, age 38, buried Baptist Church.]
March 15, 1737/8. May 1, 1738. B. 26.
To daughters Mary and Lydia Evans £50 each at 21 or married. To second son Evan Evans 400 acres of land being part of tract of 1,000 acres lately purchased of one Peter Evans, also my Fulling mill houses. To sons George and Peter 600 acres of land, the remainder of said tract when of age. To eldest son John 400 acres of land where I now live with Grist Mill when of age. Provides for wife Jane including rents of above lands during nonage of sons.
Executors: wife Jane and son John. Friends Reynold Howell and Owen Thomas, supervisors.
Witnesses: Richard Whitting, John Jones, Wm. Howell. [Mary Evans married Evan Rice and died January 20, 1752 on Monday. Evan Evans born 1732, died October 22, 1794.]

COOK, NEAL. Nottingham, yeoman.
February 24, 1737/8. May 29, 1738. B. 27.
Provides for wife Ann. To sons John and Daniel 1 shilling sterling each. To son Cornelius 136 acres of land on Back Creek

in Maryland where I formerly lived. To son William 100 acres at the lower end of said tract, paying to my granddaughters Katherine and Elizabeth Cook £5 when of age. To daughter Catherine Wooliston £5. To daughter Mary Ruddell bed. To grand daughter Ann Ruddell, cupboard. To granddaughter Catherine McKeeb a heifer. To Wm. Ruthledge my sorrel mare.
Executrix: wife Ann. Son in law John Ruddell assistant.
Witnesses: Thos. Scott, Wm. Oldham, John Ruddell Jr.

EVAN, JOHN. W. Nottingham.
March 24, 1737/8. June 23, 1738. B. 27.
To sons Robert, James, John 5 shillings each. To daughter Isabel wife to David Evans 5 shillings. To daughters Margaret and Mary Evans 5 shillings each. To wife Jane all land and moveables estate to be disposed of among my children as she pleases with the consent of her brother Joseph Moore or in his absence of her brother in law, John Moor.
Executrix: wife Jane.
Witnesses: Thomas Williams, Alex McKee.

CLAYTON, ELIZABETH. Widow. Chichester.
December 31, 1737. August 19, 1738. B. 28.
To granddaughter Grace Clayton, bed. To son Thomas Clayton all remainder of estate also executor.
Witnesses: John Garret, Moses Cox, John Riley.

WELDON, JOHN. Aston.
July 15, 1738. September 19, 1738. B. 28.
To wife Margaret household goods. To sons John and Joseph 1 shilling each. To son Benjamin articles named. Remainder real and personal to be sold and equally divided between wife, son Benjamin, daughter Elizabeth South.
Executors: son Benjamin and friend Jos. Richards.
Witnesses: Humphrey Scarlet Jr, Geo. Deeble, Andrew Collins.

FREE, ABRAHAM. Newtown. Cooper.
September 4, 1738. October 2, 1738. B. 29.
Provides for wife Anne including plantation whereon I live in Newtown during widowhood. Executors to sell land in Philadelphia County containing about 250 acres and other land and moveables and proceeds, divided among children, viz John, William, Abraham, Mary and Martha Free, sons to have £10 each more than daughters.
Executors: wife Anne and friend Mordecai Lewis of Newtown.
Witnesses: Lewis Lewis, Reeces Howell, Jabez Lewis.

HALL, SAMUEL. Kennet. Weaver.
October 3, 1738. October 24, 1738. B. 30.
To wife Elizabeth 1/3 of estate real and personal. To daughter Mary wife of Robert Whitacre 20 shillings. To daughter Sarah wife of David Baily 20 shillings. To daughter Phebe wife of Calvin Cooper 20 shillings. To daughter Elizabeth wife of Robt. Whiteside 20 shillings. To daughters Hannah, Dinah, Susanna and Margaret 30 shillings and cow each. Remainder of estate real and personal to 4 sons, George, Samuel, James and Charles.
Executors: William Cooper, Robert Lewis.

Witnesses: Samuel Jackson, John Clark, John Watson.

THOMAS, EVAN. Easttown, yeoman.
August 23, 1738. October 2, 1738. B. 31.
To grandson David Thomas the land on which I dwell when 21 with rev to grandson William Thomas. To my 3 daughters Ann Jones, Jane Yarnall, Gwen Griffey 2-6 shillings each. To grandson Abel Griffey my young mare. To grandchildren Ann, Nathan, Isaac, Joshua and Caleb Yarnall, 10 sheep. To daughter in law Elizabeth Thomas, mare and cow.
Executor: William Thomas.
Witnesses: Mordecai Bevan, Mary Lewis, Grace Reese. Mentions granddaughter Mary Thomas.

JONES, DAVID. Caln. Wheelwright.
July 9, 1738. October 2, 1738. B. 31.
Authorizes executors to raise money and secure patent for land I now live on which is near 300 acres and has been surveyed to me by warrant. To wife Elizabeth all estate real and personal during widowhood, afterward to be equally divided between son David and son in law Charles Arthur. Mentions that said son in law may pretend a demand against my estate on account of a small legacy left him by his father Charles Arthur whose widow I married and have appointed executor of this will.
Executrix: wife Elizabeth, friends David Davis and Aubrey Roberts, trustees.
Witnesses: Evan Wadkin, Moses Weait. Test signed D I.

TURNER, SARAH. Widow. Middletown.
March 29, 1737. December 28, 1738. B. 32.
Directs burial by husband in Friends grave yard at Middletown. To the children of John Talbot deceased, Joseph, Benjamin, John, Elizabeth, Sarah and Hannah 1 shilling each. To Thomas Hail and John Chapman 1 shilling each. To Joseph Vernon Jr, my arm chair. Remainder to friend Lydia wife of Joseph Vernon.
Executor: Joseph Vernon.
Witnesses: Thos. Vernon, Silvanus Bassett, Nathl. Vernon.

SPRAY, CHRISTOPHER. Darby, yeoman.
January 17, 1736/7. October 2, 1738. B. 33.
Provides for wife Sarah including real estate during life afterwards to be Bold and equally divided among children, viz Thomas, Mary, Jane, Rebecca, Elizabeth, Phebe and grandson James Spray.
Executors: friends Saml. Lewis of Haverford and Abm. Lewis of Darby.
Witnesses: Saml. Garrett, Nathan Garrett, Thos. Worth.

MILLEMAN, PETER.
August 7, 1738.
Adm. to Abraham Dilbeck. Gasper, eldest son, renouncing.

MORTON, DAVID.
November 11, 1738.
Adm. to Eleanor Morton.

BETTY, WILLIAM.
October 26, 1738.
Adm. to William Patten.

THOMAS, WATKIN.
October 2, 1738.
Adm. to Elizabeth Thomas.

HAYES, THOMAS.
January 20, 1738/9.
Adm. to Mary Hayes.

SPRUCE JR, JOHN.
January 23, 1738/9.
Adm. to John Spruce, father.
Lydia the widow renouncing.

CARNAHAM, JOHN.
March 6, 1738/9.
Adm. to Jane Carnahan.

GUEST, HENRY.
March 14, 1738/9.
Adm. to John Guest.

ALLISON, THOMAS. London, Britain.
December 3, 1737. January 19, 1737/8. Not rec.
To 2 eldest sons Andrew and William and to daughter Annas Allison 10 shillings each. To wife Isabella 1/3 of personal estate and use of real estate during widowhood to raise up and educate children, afterwards plantation to sons, James and Robert. Remainder to sons, James, Robert, John and daughters Margaret, Christiana and Mary Allison.
Executors: wife Isabella and son James.
Witnesses: James Adams, Peter Highet, George Gray. Alexander White Ches. Co. and Joseph Steel, Cecil Co., overseers.

CAMM, JOHN. U. Providence.
September 7, 1736. A. 458.
To wife Mary and son Henry all estate real and personal to dispose of as they see fit, also executors.
Witnesses: Charles Crossley, Isaac Williams, Richd. Haslum.

JACKSON, ROBERT. Uwchlan, yeoman.
February 24, 1738/9. March 16, 1738/9. B. 33.
To wife Margaret all lands during widowhoods afterward to be sold and equally divided between sons Joseph, Jacob and Benjamin and daughters Jane McGloughlin and Barbara Jackson.
Executors: Cadwallader Jones and Aubrey Roberts.
Witnesses: Oliver Colbertson, Ann Colbertson.

EVANS, ROGER. London, Britain. Carpenter.
January 3, 1738/9. February 6, 1738/9. B. 34.
To daughter Eleanor wife of Morgan Jones and daughter Lettis wife of Thomas Morgan 5 shillings each. To wife Mary all lands and moveable estate during widowhood afterward to above named 2 daughters and possible posthumous child.
Executrix: wife Mary, friends John Jones and Wm. Sample, overseers.
Witnesses: Charles Finley, John Finley, Thomas Crosby.

JEFFERIS, ROBERT. E. Bradford.
August 4, 1738. April 19, 1739. B. 35.
To sons James and William 5 shillings each. To sons Robert and Benjamin 5 shillings each. To daughter Patience Batterton El. To daughter Charity Cope and son George £2-10 each. To daughters

Jane, Ann and Mary £2 each. To sons Thomas and John 20 shillings each.
To son Richard £20 at 21. Provides for wife Anne.
Executors: wife and Joseph Webb.
Witnesses: Jos. Taylor, Bej. Taylor, Wm. Lowry.

SAVAGE, THOMAS. Coventry.
February 24, 1738/9. June 6, 1739. B. 37.
To my mother Ann Nutt £20. To brother Samuel Savage all personal estate not otherwise devised. To sister Ruth Potts £20. To sister Rebecca Nutt £20. To brother Jos. Savage £100. To my aunt Esther Hockley, riding horse. to brother Samuel my plantation in Nantmell Township, he paying above legacies of £160.
Executor: Samuel Savage.
Witnesses: Hugh Roberts, Edward Morgan, Wm. Detters.

SMITH, JOHN. Darby, yeoman.
June 19, 1739. June 30, 1739. B. 38.
To my 3 aunts Mary Garrett, Sarah Sellers and Martha Parker the household goods left me by my father. To cousins Saml. Sellers and Isaac Garrett my implements of the weaving trade. Executors to sell plantation in Darby and other estate. To sister Anne Davis £50 and to her children, Samuel, Jane, Bethel and Mary Davis £10 each at 21. To brother Saml. Bethel £20 and to his children 40 shillings each. To my 3 aunts above named £20 each and to their children 40 shillings each. To my uncle Saml. Sellers £20. Leaves £50 in trust the int to be for educating children of poor friends of Darby meeting in care of John Griffith, Thos. Pearson and Saml. Bunting.
Executors: uncle Saml. Sellers and friend Lewis Thomas of Darby.
Witnesses: Thos. Pearson, John Griffith, Samuel Bunting.

BONSALL, JACOB. Darby, yeoman.
July 2, 1739. July 30, 1739. b. 39.
To oldest son Abraham my old house and 49 acres of land. To eldest daughter Mary Bonsall 20. To son Thomas the 50 acres of land I purchased of Nicholas Ireland when 21. To son Jacob 48 acres of land when 21 also the book of Martyrs. To son Moses 49 acres of land at 21. To son Jesse 49 acres of land at 21. To daughter Lydia Bonsall £20 at 18. To above 5 sons my meadow at Kingsess near my brother Benjamin. Remainder divided among all children.
Executors: son Abraham and brother Benjamin.
Witnesses: John Hallowell, John Ball, James Mark.

RICHARD, THOMAS. Tredyffins.
May 18, 1739. May 29, 1739. B. 40.
Bequeths £5 for repairing the fence about the graveyard Presbyterian Church in Tredyffrin. To my kinsman Rees John of Charlestown £10 household goods. To children of friend James David of Whiteland, viz Mary, Margaret, Ann, Lettice, Dinah and Sampson £E1 each. To friend George James £l. To Morgan David £1-10. To friend John Rowland Sr £1-10. To friend Joel Evans now at New Haven in New England £3. To Lettice wife of Saml. Morris £l. To Wm. Thomas now living with John Jerman in Radnor £1. To Morris John of Tredyffrin £1. To Jenkin David Shoemaker £1. To David

Thomas, shoemaker £1. Remainder to friends David Evans and John Parry who are also executors.
Llewelly Parry, James David, Thomas Lloyd.

RAWSON, JOHN. Chichester, yeoman.
September 24, 1736. October 11, 1739. B. 41.
To son John my plantation whereon I live containing about 106 acres when 21. To daughter Mary £10 at 18 or married. To daughter Martha £10 at 18 or married. To daughter Lydia £10 at 18 or married. To wife Margaret remainder of personal estate and use of real estate until John is 21 and provision for life.
Executors: son John and friend Richard Bezer.
Witnesses: Richard Edwards, Margaret Riley, John Riley. Widow married Martin Reardon.

SHARMAN, ROBERT. E. Marlborough, yeoman.
September 8, 1739. October 1, 1739. B. 42.
To wife Judith all real and personal estate until children come of age. To son Robert the plantation whereon I dwell containing about 280 acres. To wife and daughters, viz Elizabeth, Ann, Sarah, Judith and Eleanor all remainder of estate.
Executors: friends Benj. Fredd and James Miller.
Witnesses: Richard Ryan, Wm. Sharp, Anthony Delworth.
Letters adm. to Judith the widow. Executors named renouncing.

GUEST, HENRY.
March 14, 1738/9.
Adm. to John Guest.

SLACK, JOHN. Bermingham.
March 14, 1738/9.
Adm. to Robert Hannum.

BELL, WILLIAM. Londongrove.
April 4, 1739.
Adm. to John Bell.

MORRISON, WILLIAM. Nantmeal.
April 9, 1789.
Adm. to Rebecca Morrison.

ROADES, JOHN. Darby.
May 1, 1739.
Adm. to Elizabeth Roades.

LERRETT, EDWARD.
May 29, 1739.
Adm. to Susanna Lerrett.

PALMER, MARGARET.
May 31, 1739.
Adm. to Robt. Richardson.

NUTT, SAMUEL. Coventry.
June 6, 1739.
Adm. to Rebecca Nutt.

WARD, TIMOTHY.
June 28, 1739.
Adm. to Hannah Ward.

PORTER, ANDREW.
August 28, 1739.
Adm. to James Porter.

INGRAM, GEORGE.
September 4, 1739.
Adm. to Joseph Fawcett.

HARPER, SAMUEL. Londongrove.
October 2, 1739.
Adm. to Wm. Barnett.

RUDDERFORD, SAMUEL. E. Nottingham.
October 9, 1739.
Adm. to Wm. Erwin.

FERGUSON, CHARLES.
October 15, 1739.
Adm. to Wm. Ferguson.

ELLAM, JOHN.
October 15, 1739.
Adm. to Aaron Mendenhall.

PAULL, JOHN. Nottingham.
October 25, 1739.
Adm. to Margaret Paull.

HOSKINS, RUTH. Widow. Chester Boro.
July 3, 1739. October 8, 1739. B. 43.
To granddaughter Ruth Mather, daughter of son in law John Mather the house and lot where Aubrey Bevan now lives in Chester known by the name of the Pennsylvania Arms. To son in law John Mather, the house and lotts of land which I purchased of Wm. Hurteen in Chester, he paying £40, to 3 grandchildren, viz John, Ruth and Mary Hoskins the children of my son Stephen when 21. To grandson Joseph Mather, my negro woman Maria and her child Caesar. To daughter in law Sarah Hoskins, bed. To sister Abigail Bell, wearing apparel. To son Joseph Hoskins my silver tankard. Remainder real and personal to son in law John Mather, also executor.
Witnesses: Joseph Parker, Jas. Houston, James Mather.

TREHEARN or TREHERN, WILLIAM. Chester.
May 22, 1736. October 16, 1739. B. 44.
To my good servant and wife's goddaughter Garterce Griffith one corner lot of ground on Philadelphia Road at wifes decease. To wife Catherine all other real and personal estate also executrix. Witnesses: Jacob Lightfoot, Wm. Robison, Richd. Barry.
[Widow conveyed land in Chester which Wm. T had bought of Arthur and Mary Shiell to John Rees her sister's son.]

SALKELD, JOHN. Chester.
February 25, 1733/4. Codicil: 3/29/1739. November 28, 1739. B. 44.
To son Joseph the house and 100 acres of the plantation where I dwell. To wife Agnes the remainder of said plantation also a house and lot during life and after her decease to sons Wm. and David. To sons Wm. and David my 200 acres of land in W Caln. Also £60 each at 21. To son Thomas the house and lot where my son in law Anthony Shaw now dwells in Chester also the 20 acres of land recently purchased of Tobias Hendricks. To daughter Agnes Salkeld, house and 5 acres of land also £100. To daughter Jane Salkeld £200 at 21. To son John £5. To daughter Mary wife of Anthony Shaw £5. Remainder to wife Agnes also executrix. Son John and cousin Joseph Parker, overseers. Cod revokes the legacies to daughter Agnes as "I have ordered my daughter Agnes portion to be paid otherways."
Witnesses: Elisha Gatchell, Jacob Howell, Henry Reynolds.

WAYNE, ANTHONY. Easttown.
June 13, 1739. December 13, 1739. B. 45.
To sons Francis, Gabriel and Isaac daughters Anne, Mary and Sarah 1 shilling each. To grandson William Wayne 1 shilling. To grandson Abraham Wayne 1 shilling. To wife Hannah all household goods and £15 per year. To son John £125 as it becomes due from Isaac Wayne.
Executor: son John.
Witnesses: James Famson, Robert Gay, Humphrey Wayne, Isaac Wayne.

ERWIN, JAMES. Londonderry, yeoman.
September 24, 1739. October 1, 1739. B. 46.
To son William and the rest of my children all my lands and other estate except £8 to my cousin William Watson.
Executors: Wm. Watson and Thos. McKim. Letters to Watson, the other renouncing.
Witnesses: Wm. Armstrong, Thos. Peirsey. [Testator signed Irwin.]

CLOUD, JOSEPH. Concord.
August 20, 1739. October 19, 1739. B. 47.
To son Joseph one bond of £10 due from him to me. To daughter Mary Kerlin 1 shillings. To daughter Anne Vernon 1 shilling. To wife Mary £2 per annum to be paid by son Joseph and other provision for life.
Executrix: wife Mary.
Witnesses: Jeremiah Cloud, Richard Rundels.

TURNER, WILLIAM. Birmingham, yeoman.
B/1/1739. October 30, 1739. B. 48.
To wife's granddaughter Jane Lowdon £15 at death of wife. To wife Eleanor all remainder of estate real and personal.
Executors: wife and Wm. Seal.
Witnesses: Abm. Darlington, Thos. McCall, Wm. McCall.

BUNTING, ROBERT. Fallowfield.
October 9, 1739. October 19, 1739. B. 48.
To wife Mary all land and moveables during widowhood except as follows. To son John 20 bushels of wheat. To daughter Margaret 3 sheep. To daughter Eleanor 3 bushels of wheat, 2 cows, 4 sheep. To son William the 1/2 of the place at wifes decease. To daughter Mary Stock.
Executrix: wife Mary.
Witnesses: Hugh Boyle, Wm. Simson.

WALKER, GABRIEL. Londonderry, yeoman.
October 2, 1739. October 31, 1739. B. 49.
To daughters Jane and Mary 5 shillings each. To son John £57. to son Joseph 15 shillings. To daughter Robecca £20, mare and saddle. To son James 5 shillings. To wife Mary my plantation with all stock and other estate. If son Nathaniel stays with his mother until her death the estate shall be equally distributed betwixt him and his brothers Andrew and Isaac.
Executors: wife Mary and son James.
Witnesses: Robert Brown, Joseph Walker.

EAVENSON, RICHARD. Thornbury.
8/30/1739. November 19, 1739. B. 49.
Provides for wife not named. To son Nathaniel the plantation I now live on containing 352 acres in Thornbury and Westtown when 21, also the lot of land in the Valley where Jacob Taylor liveth being part of the 100 acres I bought of Jacob Wright. Refers to a tract of 100 acres leased to John Stanton for 999 years being a part of the Society land on Brandywine Creek, gives to wife during life and afterward to daughter Mary, also said daughter £100 at 21. Remainder to wife son. Nathaniel and daughter Mary.

Gives to son Richard Eavenson, "if he recover from the illness he is now ins," a desk and the dutch boy named Hance Adam Smith now living with him.
Executors: brothers Ralph Eavenson and John Newlin.
Witnesses: John Townsend, Edith Newlin, Kath. Eavenson.

GILPIN, JOSEPH. Birmingham, yeoman.
8/29/1739. December 5, 1739. B. 51.
To wife Hannah my tract of land in New Garden containing about 195 acres with all personal estate not otherwise disposed of during life. To son Samuel £60 also £5 to his son Joseph. To son Joseph £10. To son Moses £50. To daughter Esther Gilpin £20. To grandson Joseph Seal £5. To grandson Joseph Mendenhall £5. To grandson Joseph Peirce £5. To grandson Joseph Cook £5. To son George, clock and great Bible, Sewalls history. To daughter Rachel Peirce £15. To son in law Jos. Mendenhall £5. Remainder to daughters, viz Hannah Seal, Ruth Mendenhall, Lydia Dean, Sarah Cook " Mary Taylor & Esther Gilpin, after wifes decease.
Executors: wife Hannah, son George & son in law Jos. Mendenhall.
Letters to widow and son in law. Son Geo. renouncing.
Witnesses: Jeremiah Dean, Nathaniel Ring.

CORNELIUSF STEPHEN. Londonderry.
July 8. 1738. December 21, 1739. B. 52.
To wife Windey Frett of all estate of land and moveables. To son Stephen the other of d. To sons John and Charles £5 each. To son Andrew £1. To son Easton £10. To daughters Charity and Catherine £1 each.
Executors: wife and son Stephen.
Witnesses: David Porter, James Porter, John Glenn.

BUFFINGTON, THOMAS. E. Caln, yeoman.
November 30, 1739. December 22, 1739. B. 52.
Provides for wife not named. To sons Richard and William 5 shillings each. To daughters Rebecca Atherton and Ruth Feree 5 shillings each. To daughters Betty and Susanna Buffington 5 shillings each. To daughters Rachel James and Anne Morgan 5 shillings each. Remainder real and personal to be sold and at disposal of wife for bringing up children.
Executors: wife and Samuel James. Letters to wife. James renouncing.
Witnesses: Peter Whitacre, John Henderson, James Cunningham. He also mentions son Thomas.

WILCOCKSENF GEORGE.
October 25, 1739.
Adm. to Elizabeth Wilcocksen.

HOWARD, SAMUEL.
November 23, 1739.
Adm. to James Howard.

QUINN, WILLIAM.
November 24, 1739.
Adm. to Owen Evans.

BURCK, BARTHOLOMEW.
December 10, 1739.
Adm. to Samuel White.

SINCLAIR, ROBERT. Nottingham.
December 26, 1739.
Adm. to Mary Sinclair.

LAMPLUGH, JACOB. Chichester. Died January 3rd.
December 27, 1739. January 21, 1739/40. B. 53.
To son Samuel the plantation adj between Thomas Howell and John Druit, he paying the £100 which Richard Bezer is bound when he is 21. Provides for wife Mary including house and lot I now live in during life and after her decease to son William, he paying to son John £20 at 21.
Executors: John Welson, Richard Edwards, John Riley.

LEET, EDWARD. E. Marlborough. Gardener.
September 29, 1739. February 5, 1739/40. B. 53.
To wife Mary all goods, bonds, notes, cash, also executrix. Witnesses: James Miller, William Sharp, Henry Munday.

JOHNSON, THOMAS. Chichester.
January 27, 1739/40. February 7, 1739/40. B. 54.
To wife Sarah all personal estate "except that she should marry to the disadvantage of my children."
Executors: Robert McCleman and Wm. Peters.
Witnesses: William Wilson, William Donache.

PARK, ARTHUR. Fallowfield.
January 5, 1739/40. February 21, 1739/40. B. 55.
Provides for wife Mary and sister Jean Park. To son in law Wm. Noblett and his wife £25 and £10 each to his 2 daughters, Anne and Margaret Noblett, when of age. To brother Samuel £13. To brother David's daughter Ann Park a heifer. To Dinah Woods one heifer and her freedom dues. To my 2 grandsons Arthur Park Jr and Arthur Park Sr £10 each when 21. Directs that remainder of money due proprietaries be paid and patent secured for plantation he lives on and orders son John to make a deed to son Joseph for the tract of land he now lives on lying along the Susquehanna River. To sons Joseph and John, the remainder of estate in equal shares.
Executors: sons Joseph and John.
Witnesses: John Park, Thomas Carnwath.
[He directed that his sons Joseph and John should officiate as executors in their father's stead over the children of their brother Samuel. Mary Park, widow of Arthur endorsed the will January 29, 1739/40 and was willing her sons Joseph and John should execute it - same witnesses as to the will. She made her mark.]

EDWARDS, OWEN. London, Britain. Blacksmith.
March 14, 1738/9. February 25, 1739/40. B. 55.
To daughter Margaret wife of David William £2, and to said William my saddle. To son Edward 5 shillings. To daughter Sessil married to John James £2. To daughter Elizabeth wife of Abel James [and gone to Carolina] 5 shillings. To son Thomas Owen, all my lands and other estate also executor.
Witnesses: Thomas Jones, James Allison, Owen Thomas.

SHORTLIDGE, JAMES. W. Bradford. Weaver.
January 12, 1739/40. March 5, 1739/40. B. 50.
To wife Hannah all estate, bonds, bill and implements of weaving trade for educating and bringing up my children, who are not named.
Executors: brother in law Wm. Woodward and wife Hannah. No record of letters.
Witnesses: George Entriken, David Fling, Thos. Worth.

JACK, SAMUEL. Sadsbury. Blacksmith.
January 27, 1739/40. March 17, 1739/40. B. 57.
Provides for wife Jane, including use of plantation, stock during widowhood. She to keep my 6 youngest children, viz Thomas, Jane, John, Mary, Elizabeth and Anne and instruct them in learning. To son William 5 shillings. To daughter Margaret her freedom. To daughter Ann £1-10.
Executors: cousin Patrick Jack and brother Joseph White.
Witnesses: James Boyd, Thomas Carnwath.

TAYLOR, PETER. Upper Providence.
February 27, 1739/40. March 25, 1740. B. 57.
Provides for wife Elizabeth. To son Nathan, the plantation I now live on with stock. To son Mordecai £5 besides what he had before. To daughter Sarah £2 besides what she has received. To daughter Margaret £15. To son Peter £15 when 21. To son John £15 at 21. To son Joseph £15 at 21. To daughter Elizabeth £15 at 18. Remainder to wife and son Nathan.
Executors: wife Elizabeth and son Mordecai.
Witnesses: Henry Camm, Peter Trego, Aaron Minshall.

MENDENHALL, BENJAMIN. Concord, yeoman.
September 20, 1736. April 14, 1740. B. 58.
Provides for wife Ann. To son Benjamin £20. To son Joseph £14 and clock. To son Robert my farming utensils also servant lad named King Roberts. To daughter Hannah wife of Thomas Marshall £60. To daughter Anne wife of John Bartram £60. To grandson Caleb Mendenhall son of Moses deceased £5. To each of my grandchild 20 shillings. To son in law Thos. Marshall £5. Remainder to sons Benj. and Joseph and daughters Hannah and Anne.
Executors: wife Anne and son in law Thos. Marshall.
Witnesses: John Taylor, Elizabeth Taylor, Isaac Taylor.

DAVID, EVAN. Haverford. Laborer.
February 14, 1739/40. May 8, 1740. B. 59.
To friend David Lawrence of Haverford £20. To friend Rachel Lawrence of ditto £8. To Wm. Lawrence of ditto £7. To Daniel Lawrence of ditto £6. To Sarah daughter of Thomas Lawrence of ditto £6. To friend John Shelton of Newtown £4. To Jacob Jones of Newtown £5. To Ann wife of Rees Price of Merion 20 shillings and 20 shillings for repair of Friends burying yard in Haverford. All remainder to friend Thos. Lawrence of Haverford also executor.
Witnesses: John Brown, Richard Griffith, John Davis.

EVANS, JOHN. London, Britain, yeoman being ancient.
September 12, 1738. May 27, 1740. B. 60.
To grandson John Evans £25 when of age. To grandchild Evan Evans £25 when of age. To grandchildren George and Peter Evans £35 each when 21. To granddaughters Mary and Lydia Evans £25 each and all household goods when of age or married. To daughter in law Jane Evans the remainder of purchase money due me from the estate when Peter Mathers now dwells, also the rents of tract now in tenure of Patrick Hamilton until grandsons Evan, George and Peter are 21 and then to be sold and proceeds distributed among them. To friend Owen Thomas £3. To John Robinson suit of clothes and 5 shillings each to Saml. Rankin and John Oliver.
Executrix: daughter in law, Jane Evans, friend Reynolds Howell, supervisor and trustee.
Witnesses: John Jones and John Rankin.

VERNON, JACOB. Thornbury, yeoman.
12/7/1739/ June 5, 1740. B. 61.
To son Jacob 150 acres of land to be surveyed off at the south end of the tract whereon I dwell after decease of wife Anne. To wife Anne the message whereon I live with the 150 acres purchased of Richard Arnold and 100 acres part of my tract of 500 acres her heirs and assigns. To son Abraham 10 shillings. To daughter Hannah wife of John Brinton £10. To daughter Sarah Vernon £100. To daughter Mary Vernon £100 at 21. To daughter Anne Vernon £100 at 21. Remainder to wife.
Executors: wife Anne and friend Caleb Peirce.
Witnesses: Thomas Gilpin, John Newlin, Thos. Marshall.

TAYLOR JR, JOSEPH. Kennet. Wheelwright and blacksmith.
July 30, 1740. August 23, 1740. B. 62.
Directs sale of 2 lotts of ground at Newport, New Castle Co., purchased of Saml. Marshall and share in Copper mine in township of Lebanon, Lanc Co. To wife, plantation in Kennet whereon I live during widowhood, to maintain and bring up my 4 children, viz John, Susanna, Elizabeth and Joseph till they are of age and after her decease to be divided among said children. To sons John and Joseph 1/7 of tract of land on Pequea Creek in Lan Co. whereon there is a lead mine. To Wm. Baxter son of my wife by her former husband £5 at 21.
Executors: wife Catharine and Edward Brinton. Letters to the widow. Brinton renouncing.
Witnesses: Isaac Vernon, Richd. Taylor, Thos. Worrall.

BOGGS, JAMES.
January 3, 1739/40.
Adm. to John Boggs.

CUNNEGAN, THOMAS.
February 5, 1739/40.
Adm. to John Steel.

BROOMFIELD, ROBERT.
February 22, 1739/40.
Adm. to James Shields and Geo. Stuart.

EVANS, JOHN.
March 21, 1739/40.
Adm. to Margaret Evans.

SCARLETT, SHADRACK. London Grove.
March 26, 1740.
Adm. to Nathl. Scarlett and John Allen.

LAWRENCE, MARY.
March 31, 1740.
Adm. to John Lawrence.

WILCOCKSON, ELIZABETH.
April 17, 1740.
Adm. to Philip Yarnall.

FLEMING, WILLIAM. Sadsbury.
June 5, 1740.
Adm. to Mary Fleming.

FLEMING, MARY.
August 11, 1740.
Adm. to James Fleming.

SAVAGE, JOSEPH, of Upper Providence 1737, of Coventy 1739.
August 20, 1740.
Adm. to Samuel Savage.
Suretees Henry Hockly, Samuel Brogden. [Looks like Brodond. No renunciation, no inventory.]

RICHARDSON, ANNE. New Londonderry.
April 9, 1740. August 27, 1740. B. 63.
To son John 5 shillings. Remainder divided between the rest of my children that is, Lettice, Mary and Thomas, the son to have 50 shillings beforehand.
Executors: Thos. Charlton Sr and Henry Charlton Sr. Letters to Thomas, the other renouncing.
Witnesses: Thomas Bradshaw, Margaret Bradshaw.

ARCHER, JOHN. Ridley.
November 9, 1738. September 19, 1740. B. 64.
Provides for wife Gertrude or Gartrad. To sons Gunner and John Archer the plantations they now possess to each of them. To son Adam 103 acres. To daughters Eleanor and Elizabeth, household goods and all gold and silver. To grandson John Morton 20 shillings. To grandchildren John and Mary Waldrum 5 shillings each. To granddaughter Christian Archer £5 at 21. To son Jacob all remainder of estate real and personal, also executor.
Witnesses: Jos. Harvey, Benj. Taylor, Enoch Elliott.

PARRY, JOHN. Haverford. Gent.
July 14, 1740. October 2, 1740. B. 65.
To daughter Mary wife of Jacob Hall £60. To daughters Susanna, Margaret, Hannah, Sarah and Martha Parry £150 each. To son Rowland the plantation where I dwell in Haverford containing about 380 acres, subject to wifes 1/3 int. To wife Hannah and son in law Jacob Hall, kinsman John Parry and friend, Wm. Lewis et al, tract of land in Charlestown purchased of wm. Allen called Monor of Bilton, to be sold for payments of debts. To brother David, wearing apparel and to his 2 children 20 shillings each. To sisters Enunals children 20 shillings each. Remainder to wife Hannah and son Rowland.
Executors: wife Hannah, son in law Jacob Hall, kinsman John Parry and Wm. Lewis.
Witnesses: Robert Jones, Jenkin Davis, Jo. Parker.

HEALD, JOHN. Kennet, yeoman.
8/14/1740. November 13, 1740. B. 67.
Provides for wife Martha including use of plantation where I live till son John is 21. To son Thomas £2 with £10 annually as my

executors shall see him have occasion if it. To son John my plantation where I live containing 200 acres and farming implements at 21. To daughters Mary Passmore, Martha Wilson £40 each. To daughter Elizabeth Key 5 shillings and use of £30 in trust. To daughter Phebe Yearsley £40. To above 4 daughters my int in a tract of land on west of Susquehanna containing 200 acres and some houses on lotts in Newport on Christiana River, to be equally divided, they paying to the 5 children of son Thomas, viz Hannah, Susanna, Joseph, James and Lydia Heald 40 shillings each.
Executors: wife Martha and son John. Friends Wm. Levis, Joseph Mendenhall, Robert Lewis and Thos. Carleton, trustees.
Witnesses: Thos. McCullough, Danl. McFarson, Valentine Davis.

LOWNES, GEORGE. Springfield, yeoman.
August 8, 1740. December 5, 1740. B. 69.
To son George the tract of land where he now lives containing about 80 acres. To son Benanuel this plantation where I dwell containing 150 acres, also farming utensils. To daughter Esther wife of Saml. Odgen £50 also use of £50 in trust for her children. To daughter Ann wife of George Maris Jr int of £100 in trust for her children. To daughter Mary household good. To grandson Richard Maris £5 at 21. Remainder to be sold and proceeds divided among all children.
Executor: son Benanuel.
Witnesses: James Lownes, John West, John Gleaves.

EWING, JAMES. L. Providence.
December 14, 1739. November 28, 1740. B. 70.
To wife Margaret all real estate during life and at her decease to my heirs generally that is, to children of daughter Elizabeth wife of Robt. McClellan 1/4 part. To daughter Margaret wife of William Linsey 1/4. To daughter Jane 1/4 and remaining part to Rebecca wife of John Cohoon. To granddaughter Elizabeth McClelland £16. To grandson James Ewing son of Wm. £4. To sons Wm. and Thomas 1 shilling each.
Executors: sons in law Robert McClelland and Wm. Linsey.
Witnesses: John Bradish, John McClellan, Wm. McClellan.

COEBURN, WILLIAM. Chester, yeoman.
February 2, 1733. January 12, 1740/1. B. 71.
To wife Sarah the plantation where I now dwell and all personal estate. To son Samuel 5 shillings and all the debts he rightly should have paid me and to each of his children 1 shilling. To son in law Anthony Baldwin and his children 1 shilling each. To son in law John Miniard and his children 1 shilling each.
Executors: Caleb Harrison of Middletown and kinsman Robert Squibb of Chester, weaver.
Witnesses: Thos. Woodward, Thomas Martin, Jos. Swaffer.

MARSHALL, THOMAS. Concord, yeoman.
No date. February 27, 1740/1. B. 72.
Provides for wife Hannah inc profits of real estate until son Benjamin is 21, when he shall take his half and when Thomas is 21 he shall have the other 1/2 of plantation paying to his brother

John £70 when 21. To daughter Ann Hickman £35. To daughter Martha Marshall £50. To daughters Hannah and Mary £50 each also provides for a possible child to be born. Land at Newport, New Castle Co to be sold and all remainder of estate divided among wife and children above named.
Executors: brothers in law Jos. and Robt. Mendenhall.
Witnesses: Henry Peirce, Peter Hatton, Thos. Mitchell.

YARNALL, JOB. Ridley, yeoman.
November 6, 1740. March 3, 1740/1. B. 73.
To wife Rebecca my tract of land purchased of Wm. Shipley containing about 100 acres, she paying debts. To son James 100 acres of my plantation he paying to his sisters Sarah and Susanna £20 each. To said 2 daughters the remainder of my plantation of 250 acres in Ridley.
Executors: wife Rebecca and James Lownes Jr, Moyamensing.
Witnesses: Thos. Tatnall, John Lewis, David Brooks.

GARRETT, GEORGE. Whiteland. Weaver.
July 29, 1739. March 25, 1741. B. 74.
To sons Thomas and George a tract of land in Goshen as described to be divided. To son William my plantation in Whiteland and all other lands he providing for wife Anne during life. To daughters Anne Collins, Eleanor Meredith and Elizabeth Collins 1 shilling each. To son John EB at int until he is 21.
Executrix: wife Anne.
Witnesses: John Jerman, Mary Haines, Jere. Potts.

PATTERSON, JAMES. Nottingham.
January 6, 1740/1. March 26, 1741. B. 76.
To wife Anne all estate for support of herself and bringing up and schooling of our children, during widowhood, afterward to my children, viz Margaret, Mary, Anne, Samuel, Rebecca and James, an equal share of what remains. Sons to have £10 each more than daughters.
Executrix: wife Anne.
Witnesses: Wm. Maffitt, Mathew Armstrong, Saml. Maffitt.

STEEN, JOHN. E. Nottingham.
March 7, 1740/1. April 30, 1741. B. 77.
Provides for wife Margaret. To son in law Samuel Hathorn my right of my plantation in improvements he paying £80 for use of wife and children Mary and Martha. Remainder to said wife and daughters with rev to daughter Agnes Hathorn.
Executors: Friends Daniel McClellan and Saml. Hathorn.
Witnesses: Robert Brown, John Marlin.

NICHOLSON, WILLIAM.
August 26, 1740.
Adm. to Mary Nicholson.

MORRIS, TERRENCE.
November 17, 1740.
Adm. to William Levis.

DRUITT, JOHN.
November 18, 1740.
Adm. to Elizabeth Druitt.
[He left issue, John and Mary Derritt. Widow married John Moore of Brandywine Hundred before October 2, 1744: daughter of Charles Rawson of

Brandywine Hundred. She had a
1/3 interest in a small estate.]
HAYWARD, JAMES.
January 3, 1740/1.
Adm. to Mary Hayward.
FINNEY, LAZARUS.
January 21, 1740/1.
Adm. to Catherine Finney.

BROWN, JOHN.
March 7, 1740/1.
Adm. to Joseph Brown.

BROWN, WILLIAM.
March 25, 1741.
Adm. to Elizabeth Brown.

PRESSOLL, VALENTIN.
Mary 2, 1741.
Adm. to Robert Grace.

NEWLIN, ELIZABETH. Concord. Single woman.
March 5, 1740. May 8, 1741. B. 78.
To brothers Nathaniel and Joseph 1 shilling each. To brothers Nicholas
and Nathan £1 each. To sister Rachel Walter's eldest daughter
Elizabeth bed. Remainder to sisters Rachel, Mary and 1/4 shares.
Executors: Uncle John Newlin, and brother in law Wm. Walter.
Witnesses: Thomas Hall, Wm. Hughes, Wm. Lowry.

SINKLER, MARY. E. Nottingham. Widow of Robert.
April 14, 1741. May 12, 1741. B. 79.
To Mary my eldest daughter and Elizabeth second daughter, articles
named. Directs that the land at Opeckin in Virginia be secured at cost
of estate and be kept until sons Aaron and William come to age and be
equally divided between them. Remainder divided among all children who
are not named "but if son Aaron shall not come to the possession of
that estate in London or Scotland in monies or lands then he shall
have a double share of what is to be divided."
Executors: John White and Joshua Brown.
Witnesses: John Coppock, Wm. White, John White Jr.

BUFFINGTON, RICHARD. W. Bradford, yeoman.
April 3, 1741. May 12, 1741. B. 80.
To son John daughter Frances wife of Saml. Osborn and daughter Phebe
wife of John Wall 5 shillings each. Executors to sell all real estate.
To sons Richard, Samuel, Henry, Peter, Nathan, Jeremiah, Isaac and
Joseph £23 at 21, also £23 to the child my wife is now breeding of.
Saml. and Henry to be put to trades after my deceased.
Executors: Saml. Grubb, son John and wife Phebe.
Witnesses: John Freeman, Henry Grubb, Cathrine Davis.

WILLIAMS, ZACHARIUS. Sadsbury, yeoman.
July 28, 1739. May 16, 1741. B. 81.
To wife Anna 1/3 of estate. To sons Amos and James my plantation
I now enjoy, when 21, they paying £10 each to - daughter Rachel
Williams when she is of age. To brother Wm. Marsh my saddle.
Executors: brother Amos and wife Anna.
Witnesses: Henry Marsh, Gravener Marsh, Josiah Kerr.
[James, Amos and Zachariah probably brothers whose mother had married
Wm. Grimson prior to 1720.]

HOUSTON, SAMUEL. E. Nottingham. Farmer.
September 19, 1739. May 27, 1741. B. 82.
To wife Esther all real and personal estate during life, she paying £3 yearly to my mother Martha Houston during life and at her decease. Personal estate to Robert, Christopher and James Houston, Anne Walker, Margaret Linn, Jennet Linn and Martha Linn to be equally divided. The plantation called Philips Bottom and Philips hill with the improvements be returned to Christopher and James Houston free of charges they paying to Robt. Houston and others above named £10 each.
Executrix: wife Esther, and Hugh Linn and Saml. Thompson, overseers.
Witnesses: John Thompson, Mathew Thompson, Robt. Loughrig. There is nothing to show the relationship of above legatees to the testator.
Acct filed by Henry and Esther Glesford. September 1, 1742.

SIDWELL, HUGH. W. Nottingham.
October 24. 1740. June 2, 1741. B. 84.
To wife Anne my right to the plantation on which I live and another piece of land as described during widowhood. To eldest son Henry his choice either of the place my brothers live upon and the place I first settled or 1/3 of my tract on River Shenandoah in Orange Co, Va., said tract containing 650 acres. To son Abraham the second choice of above tracts. To sons Hugh and Isaac the other two thirds of the tract at Shanandore. To son Richard the remainder of tract in Nottingham left by my father to brother John and me also 150 acres at Opeckon in Orange Co, Va. To son Jacob the remainder of said tract. To youngest son Joseph the land bequeathed to wife at expiration of her estate or at 21. To daughters Anne and Mary £40 each when 21. Remainder to 7 sons, viz Henry, Richard, Hugh, Abraham, Isaac, Jacob and Joseph.
Executors: wife Anne and friend Henry Reynolds of Nottingham.
Letters to widow. Reynolds renouncing.
Witnesses: George McCord, John Gartil.

ORSON, WILLIAM. Sadsbury, yeoman.
June 6, 1741. June 19, 1741. B. 85.
Provides for father during life and directs that brother George be bound to a trade and after fathers decease all estate to be sold and divided between, Joseph Powell, Thos. Edmunds, John Davis, Tamson Orson and my sister Ann Orson, Saml. McNees and Geo. Orson and Rachel Orson.
Executors: brothers Joseph Powell and Thomas Edmunds.
Witnesses: Jos. McDowell, Solomon Griffith, Josiah Ker.

LEPER, GIEN. New London, yeoman.
June 30, 1741. July 28, 1741. B. 86.
Provides for wife Isabel. To Rev Francis Allison £5. To cousin Gayen Leper son to cousin James Leper 100 acres of the tract I have in Nottingham, when of age. To cousin Andrew Leper 200 acres of land being the remaining part of said tract. To Blanch Leper alias Patrick £10. Gives to wife Isabel 1/2 of all the clothes that belonged to my son Alexander. Remainder to sister Jane McElduff and cousin James and Andrew Leper.

Executor: John Steel of New London.
Witnesses: James Donnel, John Taylor, Wm. Connen.

BAKER, ADAM. Whiteland, yeoman.
3/17/1741. August 6, 1741. B. 87.
Provides for wife Margaret. To daughter Sarah Guest my plantation whereon I live containing about 100 acres also to said daughter and her husband Thos. Guest all farming utensils, stock, they paying to daughter Mary Davis £40. Give 30 shillings for use of the poor of people called Quakers. Mentions servant lads John Hitching and Wm. Bradley.
Executors: Thos. and Sarah Guest.
Witnesses: Saml. John, Wm. Owen, Richard Jones.

JACKSON, BARBARA. E. Bradford. Spinster.
November 1, 1740. August 21, 1741. B. 89.
To Jane Nosset a petticoat. To brother Joseph Jackson a silk handkerchief. To brother Benjamin one bible. To sister Jane McLaughlin remainder of wearing apparel. To my brother John Evan all my proportion of the money left by my father Robert Jacksons will.
Executor: John Evans.
Witnesses: William Bennett, David Donegan.
Original shows a bequest to brother Jacob Jackson of a silk handkerchief.

PILE, RALPH. Ches Co.
January 1, 1739. September 1, 1741. B. 89.
Provides for wife Mary. Gives int of £20 for use of a minister of the church of England to preach 3 sermons yearly in the township of Concord and int of £20 for schooling of a poor mans child who shall be a resident of Concord or Birmingham and a member of the Church of England. To grandson Ralph Pile 200 acres of land in Birmingham when 21. To grandson Joseph Pile £80 at 21. To my granddaughters £50 each at 18. To daughter in law Betsy [in original] Pyle £10. To Sarah Goodwin 20 shillings.
Executor: son William.
Witnesses: Anna Backhouse, Elizabet Lewelyn, Mary Pyle.

BISHOP JR, SAMUEL. Nantmeal.
August 31, 1741. September 16, 1741. B. 91.
To wife Esther 1/3 of all estate and to the child she is now with 1/2 of remainder and the other 1/2 to my brother John Bishop.
Executors: John Peersall and Wm. Darlinton.
Witnesses: Thomas Vernon, Elizabeth Moor, Ealse Bishop.
[Samuel Bishop and Hester Trantar, Christ Church, April 24, 1739.]

HALLIDAY, WILLIAM. New Garden.
4/1/1741. October 1, 1741. B. 91.
To daughter Rachel Moore 6 wains cot chairs. To daughter Margaret Miller £5. To daughter Deborah Linley my big pott I brought from Ireland. To daughter in law Mabel Halliday one cow. To son Robert my plantation where I dwell containing 200 acres and remainder of personal estate, he paying above legacies.

Executor: son Robert.
Witnesses: Mathew Miller, Thos. Hutton, Benj. Fred.

FOSTER, FRANCIS.
May 12, 1741.
Adm. to Mary Foster.

DEAN, JEREMIAH.
May 12, 1741.
Adm. to Hannah Dean.

McCOY, ANN.
August 25, 1741.
Adm. to John Porter.

MONTGOMERY, HUGH.
August 25, 1741.
Adm. to Hugh Miller.

WILLIAMS, GRIFFITH.
September 2, 1741.
Adm. to Jane Williams.

GROGAN, HUGH.
September 14, 1741.
Adm. to Bryan McGee.

EBERNATHY, JAMES.
September 14, 1741, died September 11th.
Adm. to Abraham Marshall.

REES, CATHARINE.
September 18, 1741.
Adm. to John Rees.

WILLIAMS, HUGH. Vincent.
August 27, 1741. October 1, 1741. B. 92.
To daughter Mary 1 shilling. To daughter Studney 1 shilling. To the children of son Evan, viz Hugh, Sara, Hannah and Mordecai £40 to be divided when of age. Remainder to son Evan, also executor. Witnesses: Francis Boulton, Philip Thomas, John Pugh.

JERMAN, ELIZABETH. Widow of Thos., Tredyffrin.
September 12, 1741. October 1, 1741. B. 93.
To each of my grandchildren by my son in law James Anderson £10 as they come of age amounting to £80. To my grandson Patrick Anderson one cow. To daughter Mary Walker one cow. To daughter Elizabeth Anderson, wearing apparel. To granddaughter Margaret Walker, bed. To granddaughter Sarah Walker 2 ewes.
Executor: son in law Enoch Walker and friends Robt. Jones of Merion and Thomas Thomas of Radnor, trustees.
Witnesses: Stephen Evans, Samuel Hodge, John Potts.

HUBBERT, ALICE. Widow. Whiteland.
September 8, 1741. October 1, 1741. B. 93.
To friend Morris Griffith of Willistown £10. To Lewis son of Jos. Williams of Whiteland £15. To friend Geo. James of Tredyffrin all remainder of estate also executor.
Witnesses: Benj. Williams, Anne Jenkin, David Emanuel.

OWENS, ELIZABETH. Widow. Willistown.
Being ancient. May 5, 1741. October 1, 1741. B. 94.
To son Thomas £4. To daughter Eleanor Vernon 5 shillings. Remainder to daughter Catherine and her husband Benoni Griffith also executors.
Witnesses: Thomas John, Nathan Griffith, Ricd Jones.

WHITELY, JOHN. W. Nottingham. Clothier.
September 18, 1741. October 1, 1741. B. 95.

To my father James Whitely in Ireland £20. To brother Robert Whitely £10. To brothers Edward and William £5 each. To my uncle John Whitely £5. To sisters Margaret and Frances Whitely £5 each. To Timothy, William, Elizabeth, Deborah, Rebecca and Samuel Kirk of Nottingham 20 shillings each. To Deborah Rogers of said township 20 shilling. To the poor of W. Nottingham £3.
Executors: Roger Kirk and Thomas Rogers.
Witnesses: James Johnson, Messer Brown, Jas. Johnson, Jr.

MORRIS, JONATHAN. Marple, yeoman.
September 12, 1741. October 1, 1741. B. 96.
Provides for wife Katherine. To youngest son Samuel my plantation whereon I live when 21, paying to his sister Phebe and Hannah £20 each. To eldest son Jonathan remainder of land east of Radnor road, when of age, paying to his sister Mary £20.
Executors: wife and brother in law Francis Yarnall.
Witnesses: Mordecai Morris, John Morris, Mirick Davis.

JERMAN, MARY. Widow. W. Nantmeal.
September 24, 1741. October 8, 1741. B. 97.
To Jeremiah Potts £10. To grandson Hezekiah Evans £10. To grandchildren Obadiah, Hannah and Rebecca Evans £5 each. To my granddaughter, the daughter of Mary and Jeremy Peirsal, my bed. To my children, viz John Jerman, Griffith Evans, Philip Rogers and Jeremiah Peirsal 10 shillings each.
Executors: David Thomas and Jermiah Peirsall. Letter to Thomas the other renouncing.
Witnesses: Rebecca Morrison, Israel Seymour.

NEED, JOSEPH. Darby, yeoman.
[Died June 15, 1741, aged 93 years 6 months.]
December 28, 1740. August 26, 1741. B. 98.
To son in law John Davis and Rebecca his wife my plantation they paying £6 per year during life to my daughter Ann Fred, also my ground rents in Phila. To son in law Nicholas Fred £5. To daughter Ann's son John £20 and to her daughters Mary, Sarah and Cathrine and her son Joseph £20 each. To my daughter Rebeccals 8 children, viz Joseph, Lewis, Rebecca, Ann, Hannah, John, Mary and Sarah £20 each.
Executors: son in law John Davis and grandson Joseph Davis.
Witnesses: Josiah Hibberd, Jacob Hibberd, Joshua Weaver.

HARLAN, MARY. Widow. Bradford.
September 6, 1741. October 20, 1741. B. 99.
To sons Michael, Joel and George £5 each. To daughter Hannah furniture. Remainder to all children.
Executors: sons John and Robert Stuart.
Witnesses: Ezekiel Harlan, Josiah Baily.

WEBB, DANIEL. Kennet, yeoman.
October 11, 1741. October 20, 1741. B. 99.
Provides for wife Mary inc profits of real estate until son Daniel is of age, for breeding up and schooling of children. To son Daniel my plantation with the land bought of John Hopes paying legacies as follows. To his sister Elizabeth £20 when 21.

To sons George, Ezekiel, Joshua and daughter Mary £20 each. Executors:
wife Mary, friend Thomas Harlan and brother in law Ezekiel Harlan.
Letters to widow and Ezekiel Harlan. Witnesses: Wm. Webb, James Few,
Jacob Bennett. [Mentions that his brother William had erected a dam on
a corner of his land.]

FINLEY, ROBERT. W. Nottingham.
October 10, 1739. November 24, 1741. B. 101.
To wife Sarah £10. To son Robert £10, large bible, gun. Remainder to wife
and every one of my children in equal shares, children not named. Refers
to his son John Johnson and daughter Mary. Executrix: wife Sarah and Wm.
Finley of Chestnut Level and Saml. Anderson of W. Nottingham, trustees.
Witnesses: John Dick, John Johnson.

ADAMS, JAMES. Londonderry.
December 2, 1740. October 27, 1741. B. 101.
Appoints John Bleakly executor and directs him to return all estate to
brothers and sisters in Ireland to be equally divided among them, except
brother Wm. Adams who is to have but 5
shillings. Refers to the bonds notes left with Wm. and John Neil.
Letters C. T. A. to Wm. Neil, Bleakly renouncing.
Witnesses: Wm. Neil, John Neil, James Geery.

POWELL, ELIZABETH. Widow of John Powell. N. Providence. May 1740.
December 7, 1741. B. 102.
To sons Joseph and Thomas Powell and daughter Mary wife of Enoch Jenkins
my plantation in N. Providence containing 150 acres they paying to my
daughter Margaret Davis the 1/4 of the rent of said land every year
during her life. Remainder to said 4 children who are also executors.
Witnesses: Robt. Stevenson, John Moor, John Beeke.

BISHOP, SAMUEL. W. Caln, yeoman.
November 28, 1741. December 14, 1741. B. 103.
To son Joseph 5 shillings. To daughters Susanna, Hannah, Sarah, Alice,
Lydia, Mary, son John, daughter Priscilla, son Charles and daughter
Rose 1 shilling each. All remainder of estate real and personal to
wife Alice not named also executrix.
Witnesses: Jason Cloud, Geo. Jefferis, John McNabb.

KENDALL, THOMAS. Sprinfield. Plaistere.
December 9, 1741. December 21, 1741. B. 104.
To son Thomas the plantation where I now live in Springfield
containing about 166 acres. To son John the plantation in Bucks Co,
containing 190 acres, also that tract in Bucks Co, surveyed to me by
warrant containing 310 acres adj the 190 acres. To my 3 grandchildren
Thomas, Margaret and Hannah Woodward children of Jesse Woodward by
daughter Jane £3 each when of age. To daughter Mary Hall £10. To
daughter Ellin Kendall £20 and other provision while unmarried.
Remainder to son Thomas also executor.
Witnesses: Thos. Cummings, John Dutton, Alice Cummings.

McCUIN, JOHN.
September 25, 1741.
Adm. to Sarah McCuin and David Allen.

KELLER, OWEN.
October 1, 1741.
Adm. to Thomas Wiley.

McCLELLAN, ROBERT.
October 2, 1741.
Adm. to Elizabeth McClellan.

REYNOLDS, WILLIAM.
October 20, 1741.
Adm. to Nathaniel Jenkins.

FRINSTER, JOHN.
October 23, 1741.
Adm. to Wm. Snadden.

WILLSON, ARTHUR.
November 19, 1741.
Adm. to James Willson.

HINDMAN, JOHN.
November 24, 1741.
Adm. to James Buchanan.

NOX, WILLIAM.
November 25, 1741.
Adm. to Catherine Nox.

DAWSON, JAMES.
November 25, 1741.
Adm. to Elizabeth Dawson.

ANDERSON, MARGARET.
November 25, 1741.
Adm. to Hugh Vogan.

CONNOLLY, CONSTANTINE.
December 16, 1741.
Adm. to Edmund Connelly.

DENNER, JAMES.
December 25, 1741.
Adm. to Andrew Makomson.

JENKIN, JOHN. Vencent. Tailor.
January 19, 1741/2. February 17, 1741/2. B. 105.
To wife Elizabeth all estate.
Executors: wife and Thomas Morgan.
Witnesses: Evan David, Mathew Reading, Jane Williams.

EDWARDS, RICHARD. Nantmeal. Husbandman.
11/21/1741/2. February 24, 1741/2. B. 105.
To daughters Lettice and Mary £3 each. To daughter Susanna £5. To daughters Hannah and Elizabeth £15 each. To daughter Jane £30. All remainder of estate and moveables to wife Mary. Executors: wife Mary & brothers son John Edwards. Letters to Mary.
Witnesses: John James, Timothy Kirk, Wm. Williams.

ELLIS, HUMPHREY. Haverford.
9/8/1731. March 17, 1741/2. B. 106.
To sons Humphrey and Jeremiah 10 shillings each. To daughter Rachel 10 shillings. To daughter Eleanor £5. To granddaughters Perthiana and Sarah 5 shillings each. Remainder inc land and plantation to son Subilynus and daughters Margaret and Mary subject to maintenance of wife Jane during life.
Executors: sons Subilnus and Jeremiah.
Witnesses: Amos Lewis, Enoch Lewis, Thos. Vaughan.

SAVAGE, SAMUEL. E. Nantmeal.
September 22, 1741. May 26, 1742. B. 107.
Provides for wife Anne, inc 2 plantations during life. To son Samuel when 21 my part of Warwick Furnace. To son Samuel and

daughters Anna, Martha, Ruth and Mary my 2 plantations in Nantmeal and Coventry at their mother's death, also to said 4 daughters £50 each at 18.
Executrix: wife Anna. John Taylor, Henry Hawkly and John Potts to assist her. Mentions brother Thomas.
Witnesses: William Jones, Robert Hogg, James Speary. [See deed book T. 275.]

PUSEY, ELIZABETH. W. Marlborough.
10/9/1740. May 31, 1742. B. 109.
To son John Pusey 1/2 rent due me from my husbands real estate and £10. To son Joshua the other 1/2 of said rent. To son William £80. To grandson John Baily £20. Remainder to 4 daughters, viz Elizabeth Baldwin, Jane Pennock, Mary and Hannah Pusey.
Executors: sons John and William.
Witnesses: John Strode, George Carson, Jeremiah Barnard.

THOMAS, DAVID.
May 17, 1742. May 31, 1742. B. 109.
To wife Anne 1/3 of estate during life. To my mother Elizabeth Chandler 1/3 of estate during life. To daughter Mary Thomas 1/3 ditto when 18. To brother Thomas Thomas son Solomon £5. To brother Philips son David my land if daughter Mary dies under 18.
Executors: brother Philip and cousin David Thomas.
Witnesses: Jonathan Davis, Philip Thomas, Elizabeth Davis.
[Mary Thomas married William Gilkey.]

PALMER, JOHN. Concord.
February 22, 1739/40. July 16, 1742. B. 110.
Provides for wife Mary inc use of real estate during life. To son John the real estate at his mothers deceased paying the following legacies. To each of my daughters, viz Catherine Skears, Alice Buffington, Margery Kerlin, Ann Trimble and Mary Trimble £10.
Executors: wife Mary and son John.
Witnesses: John Norrey, Jos. Armstrong, John Anderson.

DAVIS, DAVID. Uwchlan, yeoman.
March 10, 1738/9. August 9, 1742. B. 111.
To son in law Philip Davis and daughter Elizabeth Davis all estate real and personal they to provide for wife Margaret and son Thomas Davis during their lives. To daughters Mary Wadkin and Sarah Phipps £5 each after wifes decease.
Executors: Philip and Elizabeth Davis.
Witnesses: Jonathan Roberts, Awbrey Roberts.

EVANS, HANNAH. Widow. Goshen.
6/29/1740. August 31, 1742. B. 112.
To daughter Jane and son in law David Davis £15 and all furniture. To son John Jones £10. To daughter Lowry Evans £10. To daughter Sarah Cowpland £5. To daughter Margaret Ashbridge £10. To son Edward Jones £5. Remainder of money to eldest son Richard Jones. To granddaughter Margaret Mather articles named. To daughter Jane Davis, wearing apparel.
Executors: son Richard Jones and son in law David Davis.
Witnesses: Ress Jones, Thomas Brinton, Benj. Jackson.

BIZALLION, PETER. E. Caln, yeoman (ancient).
January 9, 1741/2. August 31, 1742. B. 113.
To the poor at discretion of executor £5. To wife Martha all real and
personal estate also executrix [names 8 negroes among his estate].
Witnesses: William Pim, Robert Miller, George Larow, Wm. Harlan.

GARDNER, JAMES.
January 4, 1741/2.
Adm. to John and James Gardner.

WELLDON, JOHN. of Chichester.
February 10, 1741/2.
Adm. to Elizabeth Welldon.
[Married Edward Brogdon. Deed book
F. 361.]

LOUGHLIN, TERRENCE.
February 16, 1741/2.
Adm. to James Miller.

McGARR, MICHAEL.
April 2, 1742.
Adm. to Isaac Wickersham.

GRAGE, WILLIAM.
April 3, 1742.
Adm. to Martha Grage.

CALDWELL, JAMES.
May 19, 1742.
Adm. to William McKnight.

WICKERSHAM, JOHN.
May 25, 1742.
Adm. to Isaac Wickersham.

HARRIS, ROBERT.
February 16, 1741/2.
Adm. to James Harris.

MILLER, JOSEPH.
May 25, 1742.
Adm. to Jane Miller.

WRIGHT, JOHN.
May 27, 1742.
Adm. to William Neill.

PUMMELL, HENRY.
May 27, 1742.
Adm. to William Jones.

THORNBURY, THOMAS. W.
Bradford.
May 31, 1742.
Adm. to Elizabeth Thornbury.

SHARP, JOHN.
August 4, 1742.
Adm. to Ezekiel Harlan.

TURNER, WILLIAM. Chester.
August 18, 1742.
Adm. to Eliza Turner and Geo.
Ashbridge.

OBRYAN, HENRY.
August 21, 1742.
Adm. to Thomas Vernon.

BRUCE, JAMES.
August 31, 1742.
Adm. to Deborah Bruce.

MILLER, GAYEN. Kennett, yeoman.
3/31/1742. August 31, 1742. B. 114.
To son William £5. To 4 sons, viz Robert, Patrick, Samuel and
Benjamin £5 each. To my 2 daughters, viz Sarah wife of Joshua
Johnson and Elizabeth wife of Joseph Dickinson £5 each. To son
James 4 children, viz Sarah, Deborah, James and Jesse 10
shillings each. To daughter Mary's 3 children, viz, Saml., James
and Mary 10 shillings each. To son Benjamin part of a tract of
land by Pequea Creek in Lancaster Co now in his possession. To
son John the remainder of said tract, estimated to be 250 acres.
To son Josephs widow Jane Miller and her 2 children, Samuel and
Rebecca £6. To son George 1/2 of plantation where I dwell and the

other 1/2 at wifes decease. To wife Margaret all remainder of estate real and personal.
Executors: wife Margaret, son William and cousin Jas. Miller.
Witnesses: Rachel Miller, George Miller, David Bradford.

HANNUM, MARGERY. Widow. Concord.
July 19, 1737. September 10, 1742. B. 115.
To sister Mary Palmer £5. To daughter Margery Baldwin articles named. To son John Hannum the int of what money he now owes me. To daughter Mary Smith gold ring. To daughter Elizabeth Bronun, do. To granddaughter Mary Broom £5. To granddaughter Sarah Scott £2-10. To grandson James Hannum, great Bible. To grandson John Way a colt, he paying to his cousin Robert son of Jacob Way £3. To son Robert Hannum £20. Remainder to 5 daughters, viz Mary, Elizabeth, Margery, Sarah and Ann.
Executor: son Robert.
Witnesses: Mary Brownhill, Henry Peirce.

HAINES, JACOB. W. Nottingham.
3/24/1742. September 13, 1742. B. 116.
To eldest son Joshua and youngest son Stephen my land at Pequea to be equally divided. Provides for wife [not named]. Remainder of personal estate to children, Prudence, Jacob, Jeremiah, Mary and Sarah Haines. To sons Jacob and Jeremiah my plantation in W. Nottingham containing 490 acres.
Executors: wife Mary and Joshua Brown.
Witnesses: Jeremiah Brown, Joseph Haines, Henry Reynolds.

FUREY, HUGH. New London.
September 14, 1742. September 18, 1742. B. 116.
To wife Elizabeth 1/3 of estate real and personal. To sons and daughters, Wlliam, Thomas, Mary, Catherine and Margaret 5 shillings each. Remainder equally divided among the rest of my children.
Executrix: wife Elizabeth.
Witnesses: Arthur Latimore, James Moot, James Latimore.

JONES, JACOB. Newtown, yeoman.
5/28/1742. October 1, 1742. B. 117.
Executors to sell tract of land whereon I live in Newtown containing 200 acres. To wife Ellen 1/3 of estate. Remainder to all children, daughter Esther to £3 in advance, the minor children Abram and Mary being named.
Executors: wife Ellen and eldest son John.
Witnesses: Saml. Lewis, John Fawkes, Mordecai Morris.

SEAL, WILLIAM. Birmingham, yeoman. 7/8/1742. October 1, 1742. B. 118.
Provides for wife Hannah. To son Joseph my plantation where I live in Birmingham he paying to his 3 brothers £20 each. To sons William, Joshua and Caleb my lotts of land in Wilmington, when they are of age. To daughters Rachel and Hannah Seal £30 each. Executors: wife Hannah and friends Abm. Darlington and Jos. Mendenhall.
Witnesses: Jos. Chambers, Rachel Peirce, Abm. Darlington Jr.

TRANTER, RICHARD. W. Bradford, yeoman.
September 19, 1742. October 5, 1742. B. 119.
To son Richard all wearing apparel at 18(21?). To daughter Esther
Bishop my iron hackle. Remainder of estate to wife Priscilla, to
enable her to bring up my youngest son Samuel.
Executrix: wife Priscilla.
Witnesses: Thos. Parke, Samuel Patteson, George Jefferis.

TAYLOR, JACOB. Edgmont. Wheelwright.
September 22, 1742. November 3, 1742. B. 120.
To friend Mary wife of Joseph Pratt 20 shilling, remainder of estate
to Alice and Ann Pratt the 2 youngest daughters of Joseph Pratt. To my
brother in law Philip Norbury wearing apparel. To Elizabeth wife of
said Norbury a gown that was my deceased wifes Deborah.
Executor: Joseph Pratt.
witnesses: James Sill, Simon Hampton, Josiah Lewis.

HICKMAN, BENJAMIN. Westtown, yeoman.
(died December 7th). December 4, 1742. December 11, 1742. B. 121. To
son Benjamin my plantation in Westtown. Remainder equally to my 6
children, viz Mary Hunt, Elizabeth Vernon, John and Francis Hickman,
Ann Cheyney and Hannah James.
Executors: friend Caleb Peirce and son Francis.
Witnesses: Sarah Pyle, Henry Peirce.

PATTEN, WILLIAM. W. Marlborough. Farmer.
September 5, 1742. December 29, 1742. B. 122.
To eldest son James 5 shillings and wearing apparel. To grandson John,
son of James Patten £10. To second son Robert my tract of land at Moss
Creek in Lancaster Co. To my 3 grandchildren Wm., Elizabeth and John
Graham my eldest daughter Jane's children £6 to be divided. To son
William my plantation in W. Marlborough with stock. To daughter
Elizabeth Brandon £10. Directs sale of lotts in Wilmington. Remainder
to son James and daughters Jane Graham and Elizabeth Brandon.
Executors: son William and friend Joseph Sharp Sr. Letters to son the
other renouncing.
Witnesses: James Forguson, David Forguson, Richd. Ryan.

ELLIS, LYDIA. Widow. Easttown. Being aged.
November 25, 1742. December 29, 1742. B. 123.
To daughter Rebecca wife of Richard George of Radnor all household
goods, her daughter Lydia George being mentioned. To grandson Ellis
son of said Rebecca £6 at 21 and 40 shillings each to her other sons
when 21. To children of daughter Bridget wife of John David of Radnor
30 shillings each when 21. To the children of daughter Elizabeth Price
deceased 10 shillings to sons and 20 shillings to her daughters. To
children of son Joseph 10 shillings each. To children of son Benjamin
10 shillings each. Mentions son Evan Ellis and his daughter. To nurse
Susanna Skelton 2 ewes.
Executor: son Benjamin Ellis.
Witnesses: Susanna Skelton, Thos. Thomas, Mirick Davis.

WASHBORN, SAMUEL. Nantmell. Clerk.
August 30, 1742. December 31, 1742. B. 124.
To mother Sarah Washborn 40 shillings. To brothers John, Nicholas and Richard Washborn 1 shilling each. To sister Jane Washborn 10 shillings. To friend Matildith Shepard all remainder of estate and after her decease to Ann Action of white lady Auston in England, her daughter.
Executors: friends Alexander Buller of Philadelphia and Hen Hockley.
Witnesses: Saml. Savage, John Bound, John Martin.

BENNETT, JACOB.
September 21, 1742.
Adm. to Esther Bennett.

McTEAR, HENRY.
October 1, 1742.
Adm. to Margaret McTear.

SUMMERS, THOMAS.
October 1, 1742.
Adm. to Robert Kirkum.

THOMAS, JAMES.
October 1, 1742.
Adm. To Margaret Thomas.

CONNER, JAMES. Sadsbury.
October 8, 1742.
Adm. to Mary Conner.

LAMPLUGH, NATHANIEL.
October 12, 1742.
Adm. to Jacob Lamplugh.

YOUNG, JOHN.
October 20, 1742.
Adm. to Henry Camm.

RASAMOND, NATHAN.
October 20, 1742.
Adm. to Thomas Pennell.

RHOADS, BENJAMIN.
October 21, 1742.
Adm. to Catherine Rhoads.

JOHNSON, HUGH.
December 21, 1742.
Adm. To David Johnson.

BOYCE, JOSEPH. Ridley.
November 9, 1742. January 1, 1742. B. 125.
To wife Phebe 1/3 of estate. To 2 sons Joseph and John when John is 21 my plantation in Ridley whereon I live. To my 2 daughters Mary and Margaret Boyce £10 each.
Executrix: wife Phebe.
Witnesses: Aaron Hibberd, John Lewis, Stephen Gardner.

TIPPING, ROBERT. Newtown, yeoman.
January 20, 1742/3. January 27, 1742/3. B. 126.
To friend William Reilly all the lands, tenements now in my possession. To kinsman John Atkinson of London £30.
Executor: Wm. Reilly.
Witnesses: William Fling, John Smith, Jane Anderson.

SALKELD, WILLIAM. Chester. Blacksmith.
11/6/1742/3. February 21, 1742/3. B. 126.
To daughter Agnes Salkeld my share of tract of land in Caln Twp which my father devised to myself and brother David with reversion to brother John's son John Salkeld. Remainder of estate real and personal to wife Mary for the bringing up and educating my daughter till she is 18.
Executors: wife Mary and brother John Salkeld. Letters to Mary

the other renouncing.
Witnessed by Agnes Salkeld, Moses Minshall. Mentions mother Agnes
Salkeld.

WIDOWS, JAMES. Aston.
August 4, 1742. March 5, 1742/3. B. 127.
To Elizabeth Owen born in my house £5 when 18. Remainder to friend
Henry Peirce for his care in my last sickness also executor.
Witnesses: Dennis Higgins, Elizabeth Pike.

FLEMING, ROBERT. Londonderry.
September 25, 1741. March 14, 1742/3. B. 128.
Provides for wife [not named]. To son David £40 and benefit of the
plantation until his son Robert is 18 when it is to be his that is
grandson Roberts. To granddaughter Jane and grandson John £5 each. To
grandson Robert £10. To granddaughter yet unbaptized £5.
Executors: wife and son David and friends John Fleming and Stephen
Coughron to be overseer.
Witnesses: John Fleming, Stephen Coughron, James White.

GARRAT, MARY. Widow. Darby. Died 12/11/1742/3.
12/4/1742/3. March 14, 1742/3. B. 129.
To sons John and Joshua bed each. To son William £15 when of age. To
daughter Mary articles named. To daughter Hannah £20 when 21. To the
meeting at Darby £1-10. Remainder to sons and daughters, viz John,
Elizabeth, Isaac, Martha, Joshua, Mary, Hannah and William.
Executors: son John and son in law Isaac Pearson.
Witnesses: John Paschall, Joseph Levis, Jos. Parker.

BOGGS, JAMES. Whiteland, yeoman.
January 22, 1742/3. March 15, 1742/3. B. 130.
To youngest son Alexander all estate moveable and immovables except as
hereafter devised. To son William one cow. To John's son one heifer.
To son Joseph one cow. To Margaret Johnson 3 sheep. To Josephs
daughter Margaret 2 sheep. To Williams eldest son 2 sheep. To son John
1 shilling.
Executor: son Alexander.
Witnesses: Wm. Johnston, Joseph Boggs, Alex Walker.

DAVIS, HUGH. Uwchland, yeoman.
11/19/1742/3. February 22, 1742/3. B. 131.
To wife Ann £6 yearly as mentioned in a certain agreement between me
and Henry Atherton dated June 30, 1734 also the profits of place where
we live. To Mary wife of Hugh Pugh, Sarah wife of Thos. Thomas, Dinah
daughter of Richard Richards and Hugh son of Richard Richards. To
Elizabeth widow of John Davis, Edward son of Jona. Jones of Merion.
Ruth wife of David Jones of Radnor. Articles named. To the 4 meetings
Uwchland, Radnor, Haverford and Merion all remainder of estate in
equal shares for use of the poor.
Executors: friends Cadwallader Jones and Hugh Pugh.
Witnesses: Thomas Thomas, Richard Thomas Jr, Richard Richards.

GATLIVE, CHARLES. Uwchlan.
December 12, 1742. March 14, 1742/3. B. 132.
To wife Margaret my plantation in Uwchlan containing 83 1/3 acres. To son James 1/2 of the tract of land on which I live containing 200 acres. To eldest son Rees, the other 1/2 of said land. To my 2 daughters Elizabeth and Mary Gatlive all my goods, chattels debts..
Executor: son Rees, Thos. Downing and Saml. John Sr, overseers.
Witnesses: John Rigg, Jonathan Pugh, Henry Atherton. Letter adm. to Thos. Downing during minority of executor named.

HAYES, RICHARD. W. Marlborough.
December 9, 1742. March 18, 1742/3. B. 133.
Provides for wife Mary including dwelling plantation until son Henry is 21. To son Henry when 21, my dwelling plantation the part bought of Danl. Davis excepted he paying to my daughter Margaret £30. To daughter Mary £30 and to sons George, Jonathan and Jesse £40 each when they are 21.
Executors: wife Mary and brothers Wm. and Joseph Hayes.
Witnesses: John Strode, John Hall, Thos. Maguire.

WHITTING, RICHARD. London, Britain, yeoman.
January 18, 1742/3. March 24, 1742/3. B. 134.
To daughters Elizabeth and Anne £20 and a cow each. To daughter Mary £10 when 12. To son John the tract of land I now live upon containing 200 acres when 21, paying £8 yearly to his mother during life and to son Benjamin £30 and to son Thomas £20 when they are 21. To wife Hannah all remainder of estate also executor. Richard Thomas and Hugh Evans, overseers.
Witnesses: John James, David William, Owen Thomas.

SWAIN, ELIZABETH.
February 7, 1742/3.
Adm. to William Swain.

MOORE, JOHN.
March 15, 1742/3.
Adm. to John Taylor.

TEMPLIN, WILLIAM.
February 15, 1742/3.
Adm. to Jos. Edwards and John Jones.

GRIMES, CATHERINE.
March 22, 1742/3.
Adm. to Michael Lynch.

THOMPSON, JOHN.
March 25, 1742/3.
Adm. to Andrew Alexander.

ALLISON, ALEXANDER. Nottingham, yeoman.
September 22, 1744. April 25, 1743. B. 135.
To daughter Martha 1 shilling. I also acquit my son in law James Bohamen all debts due from him to me. To daughter Mary £40. To daughter Rebecca 1 shilling. To daughter Elizabeth 1 shilling. To 2 sons, viz David and Alexander, my 2 plantations, viz the one I live on and one on Christiana Creek in New Castle Co.
Executors: sons David and Alexander.
Witnesses: John Kees, Saml. Ingram, Robt. Hynman.

JENKIN, DAVID. Uwchland, yeoman.
March 17, 1742/3. May 2, 1743. B. 136.
Provides for wife Gwin. To daughter Mary wife of William Bayle £20. To son John all lands and remainder of personal estate also executor.
Test signed .
Witnesses: John Morgan, Evan Jenkin, John Rigg.
[William Bayle and Mary Davis married May 17, 1736. Christ Ch., Philadelphia.]

PATTISON, ROBERT.
November 10, 1742. May 30, 1743. B. 137.
To wife Mary £12. To sons Mole and James daughters Margaret and Agnes and son Robert, remainder of estate.
Executors: wife Mary and James Mole.
Witnesses: Robert Mordah, Robert Shippard.

WHITE, ALEXANDER. Farmer. [London Britain].
May 10, 1741. May 27, 1743. B. 138.
To wife Jean 1/2 of all moveable estate. To daughter Susana White 5 shillings she having got her part when married. To daughter Agnes Cross 5 shillings. To son Alexander 5 shillings and to his son Joseph £4. To daughter Ilender Gutey 5 shillings and to her son Alexander Gutey £3. To son John the plantation from the main road north to Christiana. To daughter Mary Ranken 5 shillings and to her son Alexander 100 acres of land called Plom Pount Fork. To daughter Elizabeth Jamson 5 shillings. To daughter Martha Steel 5 shillings "having got her part before only 8 acres about your house." To son David the plantation I now live upon from the main road south only 8 acres belonging to son in law James Steels house, also the plantation called Raccoon Point.
Executrix: wife Jane.
Witnesses: James Steel, Moses Alexander, Moses Steel.

ELLIS, EVAN. Easttown. Merchant.
April 24, 1743. August 30, 1743. B. 139.
"Intending to proceed on a voyage from hence to the West Indies." To wife my upper plantation on Newtown Road during life afterward to daughter Lydia Ellis. To said daughter Lydia at 21 my lower plantation with reversion if she die without issue to the children of my brothers and sisters. Remainder to wife Sarah also executrix. Brothers Bejamin Ellis and John Yarnall and friends Geo. Ashbridge and Cadwallader Evans, trustees.
Witnesses: John Marran, Thomas McKean, Wm. Ramsey.

MENDENHALL, BENJAMIN. Concord.
2/26/1743. October 1, 1743. B. 141
Provides for wife Lydia. To son Samuel 1/2 of the tract of land I now live on paying to his sisters Martha and Lydia Mendenhall £30 each when 20. To son Joshua the other 1/2 of my land when 21, paying to his Lydia £10 when 20. To daughters Mary and Hannah Mendenhall £45 each.
Executors to sell tract of land in Caln.
Executors: wife Lydia and friend Thomas Gilpin.
Witnesses: Thos. Carleton, John Buckingham, Alice Buckingham.

YARNALL, DOROTHY. Edgmont.
3/9/1743. October 1, 1743. B. 143.
To son Thomas Yarnall £20. To son Nathan Yarnall £5. To daughter Rebecca Jones £20. To daughters Sarah Ellis, Rebecca Jones and Mary Milinor all household goods. Remainder to all children, viz John, Philip, Thomas, Nathan and Samuel Yarnall and 3 daughter above named.
Executors: sons John and Philip Yarnall.
Witnesses: Joshua Hoopes, William Lang.

McCLELLAN, SAMUEL. Ches. Co.
January 5, 1742/3. November 1, 1743. B. 143.
Provides for wife Martha. To son James £20. Remainder to wife.
Executors: wife Martha, and Gilbert Bughanon.
Witnesses: David Porter, Nathaniel Walker, John Glen.

McNEILE, ARCHIBALD.
April 6, 1743.
Adm. to Elizabeth Mc Neile.

SHUAN, SARAH.
May 6, 1743.
Adm. to Saml. Hollingworth.

ABRAHAM, JOSEPH.
May 23, 1743.
Adm. to Richard Barry.

BARRETT, ARTHUR.
June 1, 1743.
Adm. to Hannah Barrett.

DAVIS, LEWIS.
July 29, 1743.
Adm. to John Davis.

COLLIER, JOSEPH.
August 1, 1743.
Adm. to Mordecai Thompson.

TAYLOR, THOMAS. of Haverford.
August 13, 1743.
Adm. to Phebe Taylor.

NEELY, ROBERT.
October 1, 1743.
Adm. to John Neely.

CARR, JOHN.
October 1, 1743.
Adm. to William Rowan.

DUCKER, JOHN.
October 8, 1743.
Adm. to Daniel Boyle.

READ, JOHN.
October 19, 1743.
Adm. to Margaret Read.

ROGERS, PHILIP.
October 31, 1743.
Adm. to Elizabeth Rogers.

BROWN, ROBERT.
November 4, 1743.
Adm. to Sarah Brown.

GATLIVE, CHARLES.
November 16, 1743.
Adm. to Thomas Downing.

HASTINGS, DAVID.
December 21, 1743.
Adm. to Jennet Hastings.

LOVE, SAMUEL.
December 27, 1743.
Adm. to James Cochran.

BELL, THOMAS.
December 30, 1743.
Adm. to John Taylor.

HEDGES, CHARLES. Londonderry, yeoman.
October 12, 1743. November 8, 1743. B. 144.
To son Andrew £50 towards the payment for the place sold him whereon we lived. To sons John and Joseph £16 each. To daughter Mary Bishop £16. To son Peter £10. To son John oldest Bon a colt. To Ezekiel son of Peter Hedges, a colt.
Executors: sons John and Andrew.
Witnesses: Christopher Springer, Wm. Cleneay, John Gordon.

CARLTON, THOMAS. Londonderry.
September 6, 1742. November 8, 1743. B. 145.
To son John 1 shilling and to sons Thomas and Arthur 1 shilling each. To daughter Isabella Perry and Ann Geatenby 1 shilling each. To daughters Jane, Elinor, Mary, Letice and Alice Charlton £20 each. Remainder of money and personal estate to wife Allice and son Poynton Charlton also executors.
Witnesses: Thomas Charlton, Henry Charlton.

THOMPSON, ALEXANDER. New London.
November 5, 1743. November 18, 1743. B. 146.
To wife Mary 1/3 of all estate real and personal. To son John 5 shillings. To daughter Mary McDonald and her husband John McDonald a cow and sheep. To grandson Alexander McDonald all remainder of estate at wifes deceased with reversion to his brother Isaac.
Executors: son in law John McDonald of Miln Creek, New Castle Co and John Ross. Letter to Ross the other renouncing.
Witnesses: David Wiley, Geo. Correy, Robt. McDowell.

HORNE, WILLIAM. Birmingham, yeoman.
12/28/1742/3. November 25, 1743. B. 147.
To friend William Horne of Darby £50, etc. To William Horne my brother's son that lives with me £50 when of age. To my cousin Grace Clayton that now lives with me £50. To cousin Thomas Hopes of Kennet my clock. To wife Elizabeth all estate real and personal during life the legacies to be paid after her decease.
Executors: wife Elizabeth and kinsman John Chads.
Witnesses: Benjamin Ring, Bathsheba Ring, Geo. Deeble.

RUSSEL, JACOB. Late Sussex Co, Del.
12/27/1742/3. December 2, 1743. B. 148.
To my mother [not named], cow and calf. To brother Joseph Russel my mare. To sister Sarah Russel my plantation in Sussex containing about 34 acres also my undivided right of a tract of land in same, etc.
Executor: brother Joseph.
Witnesses: Elizabeth Rhoads, Charles Bevan, Henry Lewis.

WHITE, JOHN. W. Nottingham, yeoman.
August 30, 1743. December 29, 1743. B. 148.
To brother Thomas White wearing apparel. To wife Catherine my plantation and all moveables also executrix.
Witnesses: Thomas Stockton, Frances Stockton, John Poak.

IRWIN, WILLIAM. E. Nottingham. Farmer.
September 17, 1743. January 13, 1743/4. B. 149.
To wife Mary 1/3 of estate "as the law directs." To son Thomas the plantation bought of Wm. Peterson and 1/3 personal estate. To son Samuel the plantation bought of Robert Wilson and 1/3 personal estate. To son William £40 when 19. To daughter Martha £25 when of age or married. Directs sons Thomas and Samuel "to such trades as suits their genius and constitution." To brother Thomas wearing apparel.
Executors: David Linn and Robert Mackey.
Witnesses: James Rammels, David Irwin, Mammas Lambe.

LEWIS, MORDECAI. Newtown, yeoman.
September 29, 1743. January 25, 1743/4. B. 150.
Provides for wife Ellen including plantation whereon I now live during widowhood. She keeping my daughter Mary until she is 11 years of age. To said daughter Mary all lands messuages in Edgmont and elsewhere with reversion to brother Jonathan Lewis. To said brother my land in Hattenfield Philadelphia Co. To cousin Evan Pennell son of Joshua my 2 lotts in Wilmington, Delaware. To Newtown Meeting £10 for use of poor. To sister Hannah wife of Joshua Pennell mare and colt. Mentions his mother Mary Waln and Uncle Lewis Lewis.
Executors: brother in law William Lewis of Haverford and cousin Wm. Lewis of Newtown.
Witnesses: Joshua Pennell, Reece Howell, M. Davies.

MILLER, MARGARET. Widow of Gayen. Kennett.
January 11, 1743/4. January 26, 1743/4. B. 152.
To son George Miller all estate except as other wise devised. To granddaughters Margaret Dickenson and Margaret daughter of William Miller articles named. To sons Patrick, Benjamin and John Miller and Joseph Dickenson £5 each.
Executor: son George.
Witnesses: Stephen White, Mary Jackson, Jos. McDowell.

HARLAN, RUTH. Widow. Kennet.
January 10, 1743/4. February 12, 1743/4. B. 153.
To sons Ezekiel, Joseph and Benjamin Harlan 5 shillings each. To daughter Mary widow of Daniel Webb £5. To daughter Elizabeth White and daughter Ruth wife of Daniel Leonard wearing apparel also to daughter Ruth the house and 14 acres of land where I now dwell during life and afterward to son Benjamin. Son Benjamin to be put apprentice to brother in law Charles Turner of Birmingham to learn to trade of Cordwainer.
Executor: son Ezekiel and son in law Wm. Harlan of W. Mar, overseers.
Witnesses: Jos. Taylor, John Walker, Thos. Worrall.

CRESWELL, WILLIAM. Derry. Farmer.
September 8, 1741. February 24, 1743/4. B. 154.
To wife Mary £60. To son James EBO. To son William £40. To son Samuel £60. To son Robert £40. To son Abraham £40. To daughter Susanna wife of John Dunwoody £1.
Executors: son James, John Smith of Nottingham and David Greswell

of Cecil Co. Letters to son James and John Smith. Witnesses: James
Smith, Abraham Smith.

GARRATT, SAMUEL. Darby, yeoman.
November 30, 1743/4. March 8, 1743/4. B. 154.
To granddaughter Mary Oldman £5. To my 3 daughters, viz Mary Eldridge,
Hannah Lewis and Jane Garratt 2/3 of estate to be equally divided.
Remainder to 4 sons, viz Samuel, Nathan, Joseph and Thomas.
Executors: son Nathan and Thomas.
Witnesses: John Garratt, Margaret Hestermarry, Benj. Pearson.
Sons Joseph and Samuel and sons in law Obadiah Eldridge and Wm. Lewis,
trustees.

WHARREY, DAVID. E. Nottingham.
July 12, 1743. March 27, 1744. B. 155.
Provides for wife who is not named. To 2 sons James and David my
plantation and other effects to be equally dis they paying to my
son in law John Lusk £3. Letters C. T. A. to sons.
Witnesses: Samuel Dickey, Patrick Hanigen.

BULLER, JOHN. W. Caln, yeoman.
March 22, 1743/4. March 29, 1744. B. 156.
To my kinsman Richard Buller 5 shillings. To Jane daughter of Wm.
Brinton Jr and wife of Joseph Walter £20. To Thomas son of said
Wm. Brinton £20. Remainder both Real and Personal to my kinsmen
Thomas Booth and Elizabeth his wife also executors.
Witnesses: Thomas Gilpin, Isaac Taylor.

EAVENSON, RALPH. Concord.
March 24, 1744. April 9, 1744. B. 157.
To son Jacob the plantation formerly George Lees except 50 acres of
the east end, he providing for his mother Grace during her widowhood.
To son Joseph the plantation I now live on and the 50 acres above
mentioned subject to provision for his mother. To daughter Phebe
Eavenson and grandson Enoch Woodward my lot in Wilmington. To daughter
Hannah Woodward 20 shillings.
Executors: wife and son Joseph.
Witnesses: Jos. Eavenson, John Palmer, John Cheyney.

SMITH, MARY. Birmingham.
August 22, 1743. Codicil: September 3, 1743. October 1, 1743. B. 140.
To son John the plantation his father left when he is 21, also stock.
To my grandson John Broom £20 when of age. Remainder equally to
daughters Ann Willis and Hester Broom.
Executors: brother Wm. Webb of Kennett and James Broom of Wilmington,
Delaware. Cod gives to Ann Smith daughter of my now husband Thomas
Smith £10 out of the estate of my former husband John Willis.
Witnesses: Saml. Hollingsworth, Joseph Way.

HUNT, JOSEPH. Darby. Weaver.
August 31, 1743. September 22, 1743. B. 141.
To wife who is not named all estate real and personal during

widowhood if she marry the house and lot given me by my father to my said father James Hunt and mother Elizabeth Hunt, my brother John Hunt and sisters Elizabeth Marshall, Hannah Elliot and Mary Hunt. To wife that lott of ground given me by father Job Harvey. Executors: wife and brother John Hunt. Letters to Mary and John Hunt.
Witnesses: John Marshall, John Paschall, Hannah Bonsall.

THOMAS, RICHARD. Whiteland, yeoman.
12/12/1743/4. April 25, 1744. B. 158.
Provides for wife Grace. To daughter Hannah £30 besides what she has already received. To daughter Mary £100 at 27 unless she marry sooner. To daughter Grace £100 at 27. To daughter Elizabeth £100 at 27. To my sister Mary in Wales and her children 10 shillings each if she come to this county and demand it. Remainder to son Richard also executor.
Witnessed by Hugh Pugh, William Beale.

HULBERT, JOHN.
May 10, 1744.
Adm. to Mordecai Howell.

HACKNEY, JOSEPH.
May 30, 1744.
Adm. to Charity Hackney.

HARLAN, JOSHUA. Kennett, yeoman.
June 18, 1744. Codicil: June 22. July 13, 1744. B. 164.
Provides for wife Mary. To son Joseph his choice of plantation as described. To son Joshua the other part of plantation my 1/3 part of the corn mill also 1/3 of sawmill ground to be sold and money applied for use of sons, Samuel and Caleb until they are 25. To Samuel Pyle 1/3 of saw mill and ground. To John Packer 1/3 of do. To my 3 daughters, viz Deborah wife of Thomas Evans, Sarah and Rebecca Harlan remainder of personal estate.
Executor: son Joseph.
Witnesses: Wm. Webb, Saml. Pyle, Rebecca Webb. Mentions brother James.

TAYLOR, JOSEPH. Kennet.
May 9, 1744. July 13, 1744. B. 162.
To the children of son Joseph deceased and his wife Catharine, viz John, Susanna, Elizabeth and Joseph £100 to be divided at 21. To sons Richard and Benjamin £100. To grandson Jeremiah son of Jeremiah deceased £150 when 21. To Joseph Taylor son of my daughter in law Mary Smart formerly wife of son Jeremiah deceased 5 shillings when 21. To daughter Hannah wife of Wm. Temple £250. To daughter Sarah wife of John Jones a tract of land containing 26 acres in E. Bradford, purchased of John Collier during life afterwards sold and divided among her children, viz William, Edward, John, Hannah, Benjamin and Lydia.
Executor: son Benjamin. Friend Edward Brinton and Jona. Rumford, trustees.
Witnesses: Thomas Worrall, Saml. Savill, Samuel Taylor.

GORSUCH, WILLIAM. U. Providence. Sadler.
6/2/1744. August 22, 1744. B. 163.
Provides for wife Rebecca. Remainder of estate to be sold and divided among children, viz John, Thomas, Ebenezer, Hannah, Lydia and Mary Gorsuch. Orders the sale of that part of his estate in Queen Anne County, Md.
Executrix: wife Rebecca and friend Caled Cowpland. Letters to the widow the other renouncing.
Witnesses: Henry Camm, Nathan Taylor, Thos. Pennell.

DENESTON, JAMES. Nottingham.
January 8, 1742/3. September 6, 1744.
To be buried in grave yard at Nottingham where wife Margaret was buried. To wife Martha her thirds during widowhood. To daughter Elizabeth 2 rings. To son James the cattle and clothier tools. To eldest daughter Mary Cashwell 5 shillings. To second daughter Isabella Cashwell 5 shillings.
Executors: wife Martha and John Betty.
Witnesses: Martha Deniston, John Betty, Wm. Douglass.

MILLISON, JOHN. Goshen, yeoman.
August 25, 1744. September 12, 1744. B. 165.
Provides for wife Mary. To son James 5 shillings. To daughter Ann wife of Thomas Wade living in Chester 5 shillings. To daughter Hannah wife of George Slone in Lancaster Co 15 shillings and a colt. To son Jonathan the land I now live on purchased of heirs of Nathaniel Newlin, Clement Plumstead and John Taylor containing 90 acres with 40 odd acres purchased of Clement Plumsted and Saml. Powell and about 90 acres adj purchased of John Taylor and remainder of personal estate also executor.
Witnesses: John Taylor, John Townsend, Wm. Rettew.

MARSH, WILLIAM. Sadsbury.
August 10, 1744. October 1, 1744. B. 166.
Provides for wife Sarah. To son William 150 acres of the south side of my plantation. To son Gravner 150 acres of land now in his possession. To son Henry 200 acres of land now in his possession. To sons James and John £20 each when of age. To 3 youngest daughters, viz Deborah, Susanna and Rachel Marsh £5 each. To daughters Mary, Sarah, Eleanor, Lydia and Elizabeth Marsh 5 shillings each.
Executors: sons William and Gravner and son Henry, overseers.
Witnesses: Daniel Ker, John Hetherinton.

FARR, RICHARD. Edgmont, yeoman.
5/14/1743. October 8, 1744. B. 167.
Provides for wife Alice inc plantation where I now live during life afterward to brother Edward Farr he paying legacies. To daughter in law Sarah Warner 50 shillings. To daughter in law Hannah Mattson 50 shillings. To brother Wm. Farr 20 shillings.
Executors: wife Alice and friend Joseph Pratt.
Witnesses: Wm. Griffith Sr, Thos. Goodwin, Cadwallader Evans.

PASSMORE, WILLIAM. Kennet, yeoman.
7/24/1744. October 13, 1744. B. 168.

To 2 sons Humphrey and Enoch my plantation where I now live containing about 400 acres when 21. To sons Joseph and George my tract of land on West side of Susquehanna when 21. To daughter Lydia, Hannah and Phebe Passmore my land in Bradywine Hundred containing about 50 acres, also my interest in 140 acres adj above and houses and lotts in Newport and 20 acres in Kennet. To daughters Mary and Susanna Passmore, my land in Christiana Hundred containing about 197 acres when 18.
Executors: Robert Lewis, Wm. Levis and Samuel Levis Jr.
Witnesses: Thos. Carleton, Jacob Chandler, Jos. Mendenhall.

ROBINSON, JOHN. E. Nottingham.
April 15, 1744. October 29, 1744. B. 169.
To wife Martha the full right of my land during life and remainder of goods to be at her discretion. To children, viz John, Aaron, Mary, Ruth, Martha and Miriam 5 shillings each.
Executrix: wife Martha and Wm. Bean (who renounced).
Witnesses: William Bean, Alexander Yung.
[Martha was daughter of Aaron Coppock.]

ROSS, THOMAS. London, Britain, yeoman.
April 5, 1744. October 31, 1744. B. 170.
Provides for wife Jane. To daughter Margaret wife of Thos. Jordan 10 shillings. To daughter Eleanor wife of John Reed £25. To grandson John Jordan and Thomas Jordan, articles named. Thos. Jordan and wife to occupy plantation until grandson John Jordan is of age.
Executors: wife and Thos. Jordon.
Witnesses: John Alexander, Patrick Miller.

TAYLOR, RICHARD. Kennett, yeoman.
August 21, 1744. November 17, 1744. B. 171.
Provides for wife Eleanor including plantation in Kennett during widowhood or until sons are 21. To sons John and Joseph when 21 the above plantation they paying legacies to daughters Sarah and Hannah and another child yet unborn.
Executrix: wife Eleanor. John Marshall and Saml. Seller, overseers.
Witnesses: John Brinton, John Jones, Jos. Harlan.
March 27, 1747. By inter marriage of Eleanor the widow to Thomas Huston her executorship terminated and letters were granted to John Marshall and Saml. Sellers.

CLOUD, JOHN. Brandywine Hundred.
March 19, 1743/4. December 10, 1744. B. 172.
To son Edward £40 which he owes me. To daughter Ann 5 shillings. To daughter Susanna Bird 5 shillings. To son John all remainder of estate also executor.
Witnesses: Adam Buckley, John Buckley.

LOGAN, JAMES. Londonderry.
October 29, 1744. December 12, 1744. B. 173.
To wife Anne 1/3 of all estate. To daughters Katherine, Jane and Ann and son James each 1/6 of estate.
Executors: wife Ann and Jos. Donnell. Robt. Smith and Wm. Porter,

overseers.
Witnesses: William Smith, William Porter.

WAY, EDWARD.
August 5, 1744.
Adm. to Jane Way.

HAYWARD, ADAM.
September 7, 1744.
Adm. to Jennett Hayward.

TREECE, THOMAS.
August 15, 1744.
Adm. to Anne Treece.

KEYSER, NICHOLAS.
October 16, 1744.
Adm. to William Moore.

HENDERSON, JOHN.
August 28, 1744.
Adm. to Anne Henderson.

FOREMAN, JOHN.
December 21, 1744.
Adm. to Susanna Foreman.

HIBBERD, JOSIAH.
September 4, 1744.
Adm. to Anne, John, Benj. and
Jacob Hibberd.

HALE, WILLIAM.
December 25, 1744.
Adm. to Frances Hale.

COLE, STEPHEN. Chester borough, yeoman.
December 26, 1744. January 17, 1744/5. B. 173.
Provides for wife Martha. To son Stephen my lott of land in Chester containing about 12 acres when 21 also £10. To sons John, James, William and Mark and daughter Elizabeth Cole, 5 lotts of ground in Chester when of age.
Executors: wife Martha and friends Thos. Cummings and Res Richd. Backhous.
Witnesses: John Mather, James Mather.
[Some of the sons went to Fayetteville, NC about 1758.]

MORGAN, JOHN. Uwchlan. Taylor.
7/3/1744. January 23, 1744/5. B. 175.
To only daughter Sarah Morgan 1/2 of estate. To son Jacob the other 1/2 of estate. [He was under 12 years of age].
Executors: James Rees and Samuel James.
Witnesses: Griffith John, John Jenken.

GRAHAM, WILLIAM. Londonderry, yeoman.
November 25, 1743. February 25, 1744/5. B. 175.
Provides for wife Anne. To son James the plantation where I live with stock, when 21 paying legacies. To daughter Cathrine £20. To daughter Agnes £20. To daughters Anne and Frances £20 each when of age. TO Bon John £20 at 21. Refers to mother in law Agnes Adams.
Executors: wife Anne, son James and George Curry.
Witnesses: Robert Caldwell, Wm. Finney, Robert Adams.

PALMER, MARY. Widow. Concord.
March 28, 1744. March 18, 1744/5. B. 177.
Directs £10 to be laid out in buying bibles for grandchildren. To daughter Eals Buffington my saddle. To daughter Catherine Seares, pewter dish. Remainder to children, viz John Palmer, Catherine Seares, Ealse Buffington, Margery Kerlin, Ann Trimble and Mary

Trimble.
Executors: son John and son in law Wm. Trimble.
Witnesses: John Roberts, John Chamberlin, John Anderson.

ROADES, ADAM. Darby.
8/15/1740. March 26, 1745. B. 177.
To son Joseph 200 acres with buildings, being part of the plantation where I dwell paying to son Adam £5. To daughter Elizabeth Kirk remainder of plantation paying to Adam £5. To son Adam 165 acres of land in Easttown. To son Samuel my plantation in Blockley, Philadelphia Co. To daughter Hannah Thomas £20. To daughter Sarah Nickinson £10. To daughter Elizabeth Kirk £20. To daughter Mary Roades £50. To granddaughter Katharine Thomas 10 shillings. To granddaughter Katherine Kirk 10 shillings. To grand daughter Katherine Roades 10 shillings. To brother Jacob Roades 40 shillings yearly during life.
Executors: son Samuel and son in law John Nickinson. Son Adam and son in law Wm. Kirk, overseers.
Witnesses: George Wood, Thos. Pearson, Benj. Pearson.

WHAREY, MARGARET.
January 4, 1744/5.
Adm. to Margaret Charter.

BENNETT, JOHN.
January 14, 1744/5.
Adm. to Sarah and John Bennett and Nathanl Pennock.
Sureties Abra. Darlington, Daniel Corbit Jr.
Inventory By Abra. Darlington and Edward Brinton.

WALTER, THOMAS.
February 2, 1744/5.
Adm. to Samuel Bettle. Ann Walter the widow renouncing.
Acct file 1746 charges for 2 coffins and two graves estate insolvent.

PARSONS, JOSEPH.
February 7, 1744/5.
Adm. to Robert Pearson.

HARVEY, BENJAMIN.
Darby.
February 9, 1744/5.
Adm. to Mary Harvey.

EAVENSON, JACOB.
February 12, 1744/5.
Adm. to Joseph Eavenson.

GILBERT, THOMAS.
March 5, 1744/5.
Adm. to Samuel Lamplugh.

BRINTON, THOMAS.
March 25, 1745.
Adm. to Joseph Walter.

TREGO, JAMES.
April 20, 1745.
Adm. to Elizabeth and James Trego.

EAVENSON, JOSEPH. Concord, yeoman.
March 12, 1744/5. April 23, 1745. B. 179.
To mother Grace Eavenson during life the plantation left me by my father Ralph Eavenson during life, afterward to my sister Phebe Guess also that plantation left by my father to my brother Jacob Eavenson. To kinswoman Mary Arnold £5. To kinsman Enoch Woodward £1. Remainder to mother.
Executors: mother Grace Eavenson and brother in law James Guess.
Witnesses: Henry Pierce, Josiah Arnold, John Cheyney.

SIMPSON, GEORGE. Chester borough.
12/18/1743/4. May 1, 1745. B. 179.
Provides for wife Ruth. To son Zebulon the house and lott where I now
live after wifes deceased. Remainder to son Zebulon also executor.
Witnesses: Thos. Cummings, Dinah Russell.

GIBBONS, JAMES. Westtown, yeoman.
November 20, 1744. May 2, 1745. B. 180.
Provides for wife Jane, including plantation where I now live until
eldest son James is 21. To son James the said plantation which my
grandfather John Gibbons by deed, October 4, 1708 conveyed to my
father James Gibbons and which he devised to me containing 500 acres,
also to said son my part of Goshen Society Mill. To younger sons,
William and Thomas my tract of land in Nantmell containing 1200 acres,
patented March 4, 1733. To only daughter Jane Gibbons £400 at 18
unless she marries by other means than the rules of the people called
Quakers, then she shall have only 10 shillings.
Executors: wife Jane and friends Caleb Peirce, Jos. Brinton, Edwd.
Brinton and Richard Jones, overseers.
Witnesses: David Davis, Jane Davis, John Cheyney.

THOMSON, AARON. U. Providence. Tailor.
November 9, 1744. May 31, 1745. B. 182.
All estate real and personal to be sold. To wife Jane 1/3 part and
remainder equally divided between sons Daniel and Joshua at 21, they
to be apprenticed at 14.
Executors: brother Joshua Thompson and friend Wm. Malin.
Witnesses: David Malin, Thomas Pennell.

CHARLTON, HENRY. Londonderry.
July 18, 1744. July 30, 1745. B. 182.
To sons John, Edward and Henry Charlton 1 shilling each. To son in law
John Charlton 1 shilling. To daughter Lettice Charlton £20, provided
she marries with consent of my executors. All remainder of estate to
wife Isabella and son Thomas also executors.
Witnesses: John Gordon, Jane Charlton.
Also leaves to wife "the orphan child called Mary Richardson."

SHELLEY, ROGER. Chichester, yeoman.
May 4, 1745. August 5, 1745. B. 183.
Provides for wife Elizabeth. To daughter Esther Larkin 20 acres of
land adj to Jos. Parker. To son Nathan 15 acres of land adj the above.
To daughter Sarah Cassell 10 acres of land adj above. To daughter
Rebecca Roads £10. To daughter Lydia Shelley £10. To son and heir
James Shelly the remainder of lands when 21.
Executors: wife Elizabeth and son James.
Letters to the widow. James being under 14 years of age.
Witnesses: Moses Key, John Larkin, John Riley.

THOMSON, MOSES. Marple. Husbandman.
July 31, 1745. August 12, 1745. B. 184.
To wife Mary 1/3 of estate and remainder equally divided among

children none of whom are named all young.
Executors: wife Mary and brother Joseph Sheldon.
Witnesses: Joshua Thomson, Joshua Thomson Jr.

MARIS, RICHARD. Springfield, yeoman.
October 25, 1742. August 14, 1745. B. 184.
Provides for wife Elizabeth including 2 tracts of land during life also plantation now in tenure of Robert Caldwell to contain 250 acres absolutely. To eldest son Jonathan the part of my land on north side of Darby road containing about 300 acres. To youngest son Joseph, the plantation where I now dwell in Springfield containing 300 acres. To daughter Elizabeth Bartram 150 acres of land in Marple. Remainder of land to Jonathan. Executrix: wife Elizabeth. Cousin Bartholomew Coppock and Kinsman Mordecai Lewis, trustees.
Witnesses: Thos. Taylor, Thomas Shipley, Ellin Lewis. Mentions land in tenure of John Earl and of Wm. McAfee.

WILLIS, JOHN. Thornbury, yeoman.
March 28, 1745. August 16, 1745. B. 186.
Provides for wife Esther including plantation I now live on containing about 270 acres during life. To son Benjamin the plantation at his mothers death. To son Henry 1 shilling. To daughter Mary wife of John Wall 1 shilling. To Jos. Webb, husband of daughter Ann in her lifetime 1 shilling. To son John's son John 1 shilling. To daughter Esther wife of Stephen Foulk 1 shilling. To the surviving children of son Edward 3 shillings. To daughter Sarah wife of Thomas Ward 1 shilling.
Executrix: wife Esther.
Witnesses: Samuel Bettle, Joseph Brinton Jr.

CLOUD, MORDECAI. Of or near Bradford, yeoman.
6/23/1745. August 27, 1745. B. 187.
To wife Abigail the plantation on east side of the road from Trimbles Mill to Marlborough containing 200 acres during life also the plantation I now live on until son Mordecai is 21. To son Mordecai the aforesaid plantation on west side of said road containing 350 acres when 21. To son Abner, the plantation of east side of the road on his mothers decease. To daughter Betty £40 at 21 or married. To daughter Sarah £50 at 21 or married. To daughter Susannah £50 at 21 or married. To daughter Elizabeth £50 at 21 or married. To son Joseph £60 when 21.
Executrix: wife Abigail.
witnesses: Jeremiah Cloud, Jere. Cloud Jr, Joseph Davis.

LEEPER, ISABELLA. Widow [of Gavin Guyan]. New London.
October 9, 1742. August 27, 1745. B. 187.
To my cousin Mary Piper, all estate real and personal execpting so much as she shall give unto her cousin Jean daughter of David Sumerill "which it is my will that she do."
Executors: Mary Piper and David Sumeril. Letters to Mary.
Witnesses: Abra. Emmit, Alexander Morison. Wm. Gamble.

REECE, DAVID. Newtown, yeoman.
6/6/1745. September 17, 1745. B. 188.

Provides for wife Jane. Remainder real and personal to be sold and
equally divided between 2 children, viz John and Joseph, who are to be
put to trades.
Executors: wife Jane and brother Caleb Reece.
Witnesses: Thomas Massey, David Reece Sr, Wm. Lewis, father Thos.
Reece, father in law Francis Yarnall, trustees.

HENDERSON, JOHN. Sadsbury.
August 29, 1745. September 21, 1745. B. 189.
To brother Daniel Henderson 1/2 of plantation "whereon he and me
dwells." To cousin David Henderson the remainder 1/2 of said
plantation when 21 he paying to executors £80 with reversion to his
brothers Mathew and Joseph successively. To the issue of my sister Ann
wife of John Potter £20. To Joseph Talford £15. To nephew Wm.
Henderson £15. To nephew Michael Henderson £10. To Richd. Nickalson
£5. To my cousin Saml. Ramsey £5. To the Presbyterian Congregation of
Upper Octorara £10. To my sister Isabel wife of above said Daniel
Henderson £15.
Executors: brother Danl. Henderson and brother in law John Potter.
Witnesses: James Boyd, John Boyd, James Boyd.

CHEYNEY, JOHN. Thornbury, yeoman.
September 8, 1744. October 1, 1745. B. 190.
Provies for wife not named including use of real estate until sons are
of age. To daughter Mary £50 at 18 to be paid by sons. To sons Thomas,
John, Joseph and Richard all lands when they are of age.
Executors: wife Ann and brother John Hickman.
Witnesses: James Gibbons, Joshua Hoopes, Cadwallader Evans.

GRAHAM. DANIEL.
May 2, 1745.
Adm. to Walter Stewart.

THORNBURY, ROBERT. W.
Bradford.
August 3, 1745.
Adm. to Susanna Thornbury.

WEBSTE, WILLIAM. Chester.
August 8, 1745.
Adm. to Thomas Webster.

PEDRICK, PHILIP. Chichester.
August 22, 1745.
Adm. to Edward Russell and
Jos. Cobowen.

CREIGHTON, JOHN.
August 23, 1745.
Adm. to Wm.
Creighton.

WALL, ABSALOM.
August 27, 1745.
Adm. to John Wall.

GRIFFITH, WILLIAM.
September 17, 1745.
Adm. to Wm. Griffith.

MARRS, GEORGE.
September 26, 1745.
Adm. to John Read.

JEFFERIS, JAMES. E. Bradford, yeoman.
August 19, 1745. November 17, 1745. B. 192.
To eldest son James my plantation on opposite side of Brandywine
in E. Bradford where I now dwell bought at three purchases
containing about 220 acres when of age. To younger son Emmor, my

land bought at several purchases adjoining the piece where I dwell, about 266 acres after wifes decease. To daughter Abigail £100 at 20 or married. To John Carter my wifes son by her former husband my right to 200 acres surveyed to me in West Bradford adjoining Robert Wilsons and near the Great Valley. Provides for wife Elizabeth.
Executors: wife and Thomas Worth.
Witnesses: Wm. Kargin, Rebecca Coope, Christopher Hicks.
[He lived at the Carter homestead on west side of creek.]

THOMAS, WILLIAM. Darby. Innholder.
December 5, 1743. December 9, 1745. B. 193.
To wife the messuage in Darby where I now live and all other estate.
Executors: wife Sarah and friends Joseph Bonsall and Isaac Pearson.
Letters to Sarah Thomas.
Wintesses: Thos. Pearson, John Pearson, Benj. Harvey.

STEEL, NINIAN. New London, yeoman.
September 28, 1745. December 17, 1745. B. 193.
To wife Mary 1/2 of estate. To children, viz Robert, Martha, Samuel, Susana, Ninian, William and the child my wife is now with each 1/7 of remainder of estate.
Executors: James Allen and Wm. Alexander.
Witnesses: Samuel Steel, John Steel.

KILPATRICK, WILLIAM. Birmingham.
August 24, 1745. December 26, 1745. B. 194.
To my cousin Robert Kilpatrick my loom and tackling and wearing apparel. To brothers James and Samuel and sister Anne Kilpatrick and cousin Sarah Lasley remainder of effects.
Executor: cousin Robert Kilpatrick.
Witnesses: Walter Denny, Saml. Hollingsworth.

HAYES, HENRY. E. Marlborough. Husbandman.
April 1, 1745. December 30, 1745. B. 195.
To wife Isabella £200 "if she delivers that paper to my executors which I signed to her before marriage." To son John £20. To son William 1 shilling. TO Bon Stephen £10. To daughters Mary and Joanna 1 shilling each. Remainder of real and personal estate to daughters Margaret, Elizabeth, Anne, Rachel, Ruth and Lydia. Margaret to have £20 more than the others.
Executors: sons Joseph and James.
Witnesses: Jonathan Jackson, George Carson.

TURNER, ELEANOR. Birmingham. Widow.
10/16/1745. January 21, 1745/6. B. 196.
To granddaughter Jane Lowden £16. To grandchildren, viz Henry, Anne, John, Mary, Joseph and Eleanor, children of John and Sarah Harvey £10 each.
Executor: friend Abm. Darlington.
Witnesses: Moses Pyle, Robert Pyle, Wm. Seal.

STUART, GEORGE.
September 27, 1745.
Adm. to Wm. McCullough.

CASSELL, ANDREW.
October 1, 1745.
Adm. to Moses Wait.

GILPIN, ISAAC.
October 1, 1745.
Adm. to Mary Gilpin.

PATTERSON, WILLIAM.
October 1, 1745.
Adm. to Wm. Manson.

HUGHES, THOMAS.
October 8, 1745.
Adm. to Elizabeth Hughes.

TAYLOR, JOHN.
October 17, 1745.
Adm. to Mary Taylor.

DEVONALD, MARY.
October 21, 1745.
Adm. to Hannah Devonald.

CONSTABLE, THOMAS.
November 2, 1745.
Adm. to Thomas Moore Jr.

HARLAN, THOMAS. Kennett, yeoman.
August 19, 1745. February 27, 1745/6. B. 196.
Provides for wife Mary. To daughter Abigail Wilson £20 if she be now living. To son Thomas the plantation where I live. To daughters Lydia, Anne and Susanna £30 each when 18. Mentions father in law Robert Carter. Directs that a tract of 200 acres in Nantmeal recently purchased of Elizabeth Ring alias McNeill be reconveyed to her.
Executors: cousin Wm. Webb and son Thomas.
Witnesses: Richard Flower, Owen Evans, John Nickols.
[To son Isaac 5 shillings.]

SCARLET, HUMPHREY. Chichester, yeoman.
September 16, 1745. March 27, 1746. B. 197.
Provides for wife Anne including all estate during life. To eldest son John 5 shillings. To sons Nathaniel and Humphrey £30 each. To grandchildren Shadrach, Anne, Else and Phebe Scarlet 1 shilling each when 21. To son in law Richard Cox 1 shilling. To son Nathaniel and son in law Thomas Hall the plantation where I now dwell containing 135 acres to be sold after wifes decease and proceeds divided as follows 2/3 to daughters, viz Mary Hall, Susanna Brown and Rebecca Brown and 1/3 to 3 sons above named.
Executors: son Nathl. and Thomas Hall.
Witnesses: John Brown, Edward Whiteker, Susanna Whiteker.

ROBB, WILLIAM. Londongrove.
December 19, 1744. April 1, 1746. B. 198.
To son George 20 shillings. To daughter Mary and Margaret and son Robert 5 shillings each. Remainder real and personal to son William and wife Sarah who are also executors.
Witnesses: Archibald Young Jr, Wm. Boyd.

JACKSON, SAMUEL.
November 9, 1745.
Adm. to Mary Jackson.

TAYLOR, ISAAC.
November 16, 1745.

Adm. to John Taylor.

TOWNSEND, JAMES
December 11, 1745.
Adm. to Sarah Townsend.

BONSALL, THOMAS.
December 16, 1745.
Adm. to Esther and Abraham Bonsall.

DUTTON, JONATHAN.
January 8, 1745/6.
Adm. to Richard Dutton.

JACKSON, THOMAS.
January 23, 1745/6.
Adm. to Lydia Jackson.

BUFFINGTON, SAMUEL.
February 6, 1745/6.
Adm. to Samuel Grubb.

TAYLOR, JACOB. Whiteland. Blacksmith. February 26, 1745/6.
Adm. to John Taylor.
[Surety Josiah Lewis bond £300 adm. accounts show total estate 385-16-8. Expenses and commissions £144-13-6. Paid Amos Davies for his wife and childs coffins £2-3-0. Paid Robert William for digging two graves £0-16-0. Account dated 20 August, 1749. Filed 10.]

ROWLAND, JOHN. Whiteland, yeoman.
April 4, 1745. April 30, 1746. B. 198.
To my grandchild the surviving issue of son James deceased in South Carolina £15. To daughter Catherine wife of Thomas Williams £20. To daughter Anne wife of Morris James £20. To son John £20. To son William £20. To wife Letitia all household goods also my right and title to 100 acres of land in Tredyffrin with fulling mill, by virtue of bargain and sale from Samuel Lilly also my right and interest in the real and personal estate of brother James Rowland deceased.
Executors: wife Letitia and sons John and William.
Witnesses: Thomas Hubart, Thomas Lloyed, M. Davis.

ROBINSON, RICHARD. W. Bradford. Farmer.
April 16, 1746. May 27, 1746. B. 199.
To son Ralph £5 also provides for a child yet unborn. Remainder to Mary who is also executrix.
Witnesses: John Buffington, Saml. Savill.

PYLE, WILLIAM. Birmingham.
January 8, 1745/6. June 12, 1746. B. 200.
Provides for wife Betty. To eldest son Ralph at 21 £250 besides what is given by his grandfathers will. To son Joseph tract of land in W. Marlborough containing 350 acres when 21. To son John when 21 the plantation on which I live in Birmingham containing 250 acres. To son William £500 at 21. To daughters Eleanor, Mary and Sarah Pyle £150 each at 21.
Executors: wife Betty and son Ralph.
Witnesses: Saml. Hollingsworth, John Chads, Elizabeth Chads, Samuel Pyle.

MORGAN, GEORGE. U. Providence, yeoman.
August 1, 1746. August 6, 1746. B. 202.
To the friends of Goshen and Newtown Meetings £5 each. To my 2 daughters, Elizabeth wife of John Rowels of Carolina and Susanna wife of Henry Philips of Chester Co, and granddaughter Gennet

Morris, all remainder of estate real and personal. Executors: friends Geo. Ashbridge Jr and Ellis Williams. Lettters to Ashbridge the other renouncing.
Witnesses: John Wm.son (Williamson), Abraham Hoopes, John Pritchet.

BENSON, ROBERT. Uwchlan, yeoman.
July 3, 1746. August 12, 1746. B. 203.
To wife Katherine and daughter Ann Benson the income of all estate real and personal during their lives and after their decease to son William he paying legacies. To son John £20. To son James £25. To grandsons John, William and James Nowlan, £5 each and to daughter Hannah Nowlan 5 shillings.
Executors: sons John and William.
Witnesses: Richard Willis, Awbrey Roberts, Ruth Roberts.

BROWN, ANDREW. Nantmead. Chester Co.
February 6, 1745/6. August 18, 1746. B. 203.
To wife not named all estate during widowhood afterwards to sons Charles, John and Michael. "As for sons Joseph, Samuel and Andrew, I give them my clothes for their part." Letters C.T.A. To widow Jennet Brown.
Witnesses: Robert McConahee, Janet McConahee, James Barnhill.

MILLS, JOHN.
February 28, 1745/6.
Adm. to Jane Mills.

CRUDDERS, CHARLES.
March 25, 1746.
Adm. to Margaret Crudders.

WOOD, THOMAS.
April 1, 1746.
Adm. to Mary and Wm. Woods.

COLLIER, JOHN.
April 5, 1746.
Adm. to Mary and James Collier.

PIERCE, GAINER.
April 21, 1746.
Adm. to Sarah Peirce.

GOHEEN, JOHN.
June 21, 1746.
Adm. to Anne Goheen.

HARPER, MOSES. East Bradford.
July 15, 1746.
Adm. to Elizabeth Harper.
[Sureties Edward E Seed and Joseph Buffington. Inventory by Thos. Worth, Anthony Arnold, Wm. Bennett, £96-14-1. Elizabeth Jefferies signed account October 3, 1750. Balance for children £18-3-9.]

HAMILTON, JOHN.
July 22, 1746.
Adm. to Alexander Russell.

DAVID, JAMES. Whiteland, yeoman.
June 13, 1746. August 26, 1746. B. 204.
To daughter Mary £5. To daughters Margaret, Ann and Lettice £30 each. To daughter Dinah £30 at 21. To son Sampson all lands, with stock when 21. Provides for wife Elizabeth who with Morris Griffith are executors. Letters to widow. Griffith renouncing.
Witnesses: John David, David Davies, Saml. Evans.

ABRAMS, SARAH. Widow. Radnor.
October 24, 1743. September 9, 1746. B. 205.
Directs eldest son James Abrams to pay £83.18 with interest as hereafter directed, referring to an indenture dated December 1, 1716, which through ignorance and over persuasion she was induced to sign which indent was calculated to defraud the rest of children. To son Noah £5. To daughter Elizabeth Martin £5. To granddaughter Blanch Gunter £25 in lieu of wages. To grand daughter Margaret Lawrence 20 shillings. To granddaughter Sarah Abram £5 when 18 [prob daughter of Noah]. To grandson Joseph Abram 20 shillings. To friend David Meredith 20 shillings. To son Enoch £61 the remainder of above sum of £83.18.
Executor: son Enoch Abram.
Witnesses: Edwd. Jones, Richard Richards, John Moore.

LINN, CHARLES. U. Providence. Weaver. Died September 13, 1746.
September 12, 1746. September 20, 1746. B. 206.
To son Charles tract of land in U. Providence containing 33 acres. To grandson Hugh eldest son of Charles 350 at 21. To son Hugh 1/2 of looms and mare he paying to John Linn 1/2 her price. To son Charles the other 1/2 of Looms, he paying to Martha Linn £1-5 when of age. To granddaughter Margaret Linn, pewter dish. To granddaughter Jennett one pewter dish.
Executors: sons Hugh and Charles.
Witnesses: Hugh Trimble, Joseph Sleigh, Jorg McNight, rec as McMichael.

SEAL, JOSEPH. Birmingham.
7/17/1746. September 29, 1746. B. 207.
To brother William Seal my plantation I live on in Birmingham at 21 subject to provision for mother under the will of deceased father. To brothers Joshua and Caleb remainder of personal estate.
Executors: brother in law John Bennett and Jos. Mendenhall.
Witnesses: Mary McClintock, Mary Mercer, Ann Caye.

SEAL, HANNAH. Widow. Birmingham.
July 17, 1746. September 29, 1746. B. 208.
To daughters Rachel Seal and Hannah Bennett and son Joseph articles named. Remainder sold and divided between 5 children, viz., William, Joshua, Caleb, Rachel and Hannah Bennett.
Executors: daughter Rachel Seal and Jos. Mendenhall. Letters to Mendenhall the other being deceased.
Witnesses: John Bennett, Mary McClintock, Eliza Darlington.

BROWN, WILLIAM. W. Nottingham.
October 23, 1743. Codicil: October 28, 1744. October 1, 1746. B. 209.
To son Thomas £10 which he is indebted to me. Gives negro woman Terry her freedom and articles named. Remainder to son Samuel also executor.
Witnesses: John Gartril, Thos. Berrey, James Johnson.

CLINTON, ARCHIBALD. London, Britain, yeoman.
September 5, 1746. October 1, 1746. B. 210.

Provides for wife Sarah. To son William the plantation on which I live at value of £100. To son James, daughter Mary, son John and daughter Sarah each an equal share of estate. To daughter Elizabeth 1 shilling. To daughter Hannah 10 shillings.
Executors: wife Sarah, son William and Arthur Lattimer.
Witnesses: Wm. McCulloch, Fra. Alison, Andrew Willson.

ARNOLD, ANTHONY. E. Bradford, yeoman.
September 18, 1746. October 1, 1746. B. 211.
To John Arnold son of brother Richard £30 when 21. To daughter in law Sarah Buffington £30 at 18. To daughter Hannah the plantation where I dwell containing about 140 acres in E. Bradford and Westtown at 18. To Thos. Buffington a colt. To Mary Morgan and Sarah Buffington my wifes daughters by a former husband, my wifes wearing apparel.
Executors: friends Jos. Evenson and Jos. Chamberlin.
Witnesses: Saml. Osborne, Thos. Worth, Richard Thatcher.

SHARPLESS, JAMES. N. Providence, yeoman.
5/28/1734. October 13, 1746. B. 211.
To wife Mary all estate real and personal she paying to each of my children Lydia, Mary, James, Rachel, Sarah, David and Esther 5 shillings each and as for those that are yet unmarried.
Executors: wife Mary and Samuel Levis.
Witnesses: Thos. Vernon, Joseph Vernon, John Needham.

HODGEN, ROBERT.
September 23, 1746.
Adm. to Jane Eakin.

WOODWARD, EDWARD.
October 18, 1746.
Adm. to Sarah Woodward.

ALLEN, JAMES.
September 30, 1746.
Adm. to Agnes Allen.

HEWST JOSEPH.
October 27, 1746.
Adm. to Margaret Hews.

THOMAS, MARGARET.
October 8, 1746.
Adm. to Thomas Thomas.

HENRICKSON, JOHN.
November 16, 1746.
Adm. to Maudlin Hendrickson and Geo. Culin.

WALKER, ALEXANDER. Goshen. Wheelwright.
September 26, 1746. November 10, 1746. B. 212.
To son James of Christiana Hundred, wheelwright tools. To son in law John Boggs who married daughter Margaret 5 shillings. To son in law Joseph Boggs who married daughter Jane all remainder of personal estate also executor.
Witnesses: David Buchanan, Robt. McLaughlin, Joseph Wray.

CHANDLER, WILLIAM. Londongrove.
6/30/1745. December 16, 1746. B. 213.
To son John my house and land cont about 100 acres he paying to daughter Anne £15 at 21. To son Thomas £10 at 21. To son Moses £20 at 21. To daughter Mary £15 also articles named. To son William £15.
Executor: son William.

Witnesses: Thos. Carleton, Joshua Pusey, Joshua Mendenhall.

PASSMORE, JOHN. W. Marlborough.
July 14, 1743. December 16, 1746. B. 213.
To sons, viz William, John and George 1 shilling each. To son Augustine £30. To son Samuel £30. To daughter Eleanor Carson 1 shilling and to her 3 children, viz John, Mary and George Carson £5 each. To daughter Mary Pusey £30. To wife Mary all remainder of estate real and personal during widowhood.
Executors: son George and Samuel. Letter to Geo. Saml. renouncing.
Witnesses: John Hoode, Ezekiel Harlan, Hannah Harlan.

SHARP, JOSEPH. Londongrove. Tanner.
4/21/1746. January 3, 1746/7. B. 214.
To son Joseph £10. To daughter Elizabeth wife of Jeremiah Douglas the tenant right of 125 acres adj my plantation and £100 toward the purchase of said land. To daughter Abigail Sharp the tenant right of 350 acres of London land in Salsbury Township, Lancaster Co and £250 when 18. To son Samuel the plantation whereon I live containing 300 acres in Londongrove and New Garden and £50 when 21, his uncle Saml. Pyle to bring him up and educate him. To granddaughter Mary daughter of Jos. Sharp £20 at 18. To granddaughter Mary Duglas £20 at 18. To granddaughter Elizabeth Duglas £20 at 18. To grandson Joseph Duglas £20 at 21. Remainder divided among 4 children above named. Executors: brother in law Saml. Pyle, physician and his son Nicholas Pyle. Letters to Nicholas, [tanner]. "The other having desired to consider of it."
Witnesses: Henry Dobson, Wm. Gray, John Dobson.

EAVENSON, GRACE. Concord.
November 11, 1746. January 29, 1746/7. B. 215.
To Mary daughter of brother Thomas Arnold £5. To grandson Enoch Woodward £5. To Stephen Hurly £2-10 when 21. To Elizabeth Boss £2-10 at 18. To grandson Joseph Gess £5. To all my brothers and sisters children a new Bible. To daughter Phebe Gess remainder of estate.
Executors: son in law James Gess and John Palmer.
Witnesses: Wm. Trimble, Jos. Eavenson, Jos. Chamberlin.

BUTCHER, ISABELLA. Birmingham.
March 11, 1743/4. January 31, 1746/7. B. 216.
To daughter Susanna Simonson bed, furniture. Remainder to grand children, viz Elizabeth, Mary and Peter Terrett, Stephen and William Simonson in equal shares. Mentions son in law Edward Terrett.
Executor: son in law Henry Simonson.
Witnesses: Saml. Hollingsworth, Jos. Gilpin, Robert Stevens.

LUSK, WILLIAM.
No date. February 24, 1746/7. B. 217.
To wife Sarah and son David my plantation during her widowhood. To sons James, Samuel, John, William and Hugh 1 shilling each. To daughter Mary 1 shilling. To daughters Martha and Sarah a horse

and saddle each. Son David to have the place if wife marries.
Executors: wife Sarah and brother John Lusk.
Witnesses: John Buzars, Thomas McCluer.

RUSSELL, ALEXANDER. E. Bradford, yeoman.
January 31, 1746/7. February 24, 1746/7. B. 217.
To my daughters, viz Isabel and Elizabeth Russell all estate to be divided when 21.
Executor: friend Wm. Jefferis
Witnesses: John Carrell, JameL Collier.

SEAL, RACHEL. Birmingham.
7/17/1746. February 25, 1746/7. B. 218.
Mentions brother Joseph Seal, sister Hannah Bennet and brothers William, Joshua and Caleb Seal, also aunt Lydia Dean and cousin Lydia Dean. To mother a side saddle.
Executors: brother Joseph Seal and brother in law John Bennett.
Letters to Bennett the other being deceased.
Witnesses: Jos. Mendenhall, Elizabeth Darlington.

SCARLET, HUMPHREY. Chichester, yeoman.
January 9, 1746/7. March 10, 1746/7. B. 218.
To my brother John Scarlets son John 1 shilling. To wife Mary all remainder of estate real and personal especially £30 in the hands of my father Humphrey Scarlets executors.
Executrix: wife Mary.
Witnesses: Richd. Edwards, Mary Riley, John Riley.

ELLIOTT, SAMUEL. Sadsbury. Millwright.
September 15, 1746. March 17, 1746/7. B. 219.
To brother Benjamin Elliott £5 which he owes me. To brother Abraham Elliott £5 that my father in law owes me. Remainder to brother Joseph Elliott also executor.
Witnesses: William Boyd, Henry Marsh.

CALDWELL, ROBERT. Aston.
February 17, 1746/7. April 2, 1747. B. 219.
Provides for wife Margaret including the plantation where I now dwell during widowhood, afterward to my 3 children, viz Jane, Elizabeth and Margaret Caldwell.
Executors: wife Margaret and eldest daughter Jane Caldwell.
Witnesses: Hugh Linn, Charles Conner, Henry Caldwell.

BROWN, THOMAS. W. Nottingham.
2/3/1745. May 12, 1747. B. 220.
Provides for wife Ellen including plantation where I now live except 25 acres until son John comes of age. To son Nathan the 100 acres of land already conveyed to him by deed, also 25 acres off the north end of place where I live. To son John when 21 the remainder of plantation where I live. To sons Thomas and Eleazer my 231 acres of land in Little Britain in Lancaster Co to be equally divided. To daughter Rebecca Long £10. Remainder to 3 daughters Rachel, Anne and Elizabeth Brown.
Executors: wife Ellen and son Nathan.
Witnesses: Joseph Brown, John Gartril, Henry Reynolds.

SULLIVAN, DARBY.
November 20, 1746.
Adm. to John Strode.

HEWES, WILLIAM.
November 24, 1746.
Adm. to Mary Hewes.

LONG, ALLEN.
December 5, 1746.
Adm. to Rebecca Long.

MENDENHALL, CALEB.
December 8, 1746.
Adm. to Anne Mendenhall.

CLOUD, JOEL.
December 15, 1746.
Adm. to Esther Cloud.

PYLE, SUSANNA.
December 15, 1746.
Adm. to George Turner.

O'SHANACH, OWEN.
December 24, 1746.
Adm. to Daniel Culin.

REYNOLDS, JAMES.
February 6, 1746/7.
Adm. to Margaret Reynolds.

GRIFFITH, HENRY.
February 19, 1746/7.
Adm. to Thomas Griffith.

WEST, THOMAS.
February 21, 1746/7.
Adm. to Susanna West.

DAVIS, ANNE.
February 24, 1746/7.
Adm. to Benjamin Jackson.

THOMPSON, JOSEPH.
March 6, 1746/7.
Adm. to James Miller.

ASKEW, LAZARUS.
March 19, 1746/7.
Adm. to Mabell Askew.

HOLSTEN, BENJAMIN.
March 30, 1747.
Adm. to John Holsten.

HOPTON, JOHN.
April 30, 1747.
Adm. to John Hopton.

LACKEY, ALEXANDER.
May 1, 1747.
Adm. to James Cochran and John Taylor.

LEVIS, WILLIAM. Kennett.
2/9/1747. May 27, 1747. B.221.
Provides for wife Elizabeth including 100 acres of land in Kennett where Walter Clark lived during life after her decease to my 3 daughters, viz Sarah, Mary and Lydia Levis. To son Samuel the plantation where I dwell except a part run off for son William, also stock, paying to 4 daughters Elizabeth James, Sarah, Mary and Lydia Levis £50 each. To son William 2 tracts of land in Kennett one being the west side of my plantation containing 134 acres and a piece of land with sawmill adjoining paying to 4 daughters, £10 each, remainder to 3 unmarried daughters.
Executors: wife Elizabeth and sons Saml. and Wm.
Witnesses: Wm. Pennock, Gabriel Clark, Elizabeth Pryor.
Mentions brother Samuel Levis.

POSTON, JOHN. Fallowfield.
December 8, 1745. June 8, 1747. B. 222.
To eldest son Robert the settlement he now lives on. To son John my real estate he paying to son Anthony £30. To daughter Ann "I give according to her behavior" 5 shillings. Provides for wife

Martha.
Executors: wife and son John.
Witnesses: John Devor, Martha Dun.

TATNALL, THOMAS. Darby. Gent.
July 7, 1747. July 25, 1747.
Provides for wife Anne. To daughter Elizabeth Tatnall, messuage where I dwell containing about 500 acres in Darby and Ridley also remainder of Island called Carpenters which is not conveyed to my son in law John Blakely containing about 400 acres in Kingsess with rev to brother Edward Tatnall he paying £300 to brother Jonathan Tatnalls 3 children. To use of poor in Ridley £10. To Joshua son of Thomas Treese late deceased £40 when 21. Remainder to daughter Elizabeth also executrix.
Friends Thomas Cummings and Jos. Parker, overseers. Witnesses: John Houlton, Jacob Carter, Benjamin Davis.

HUNTER, MONGEY. Chester Township. Taylor.
July 29, 1747. July 31, 1747. B. 224.
To my friend Mary McGhee articles named if she marries with her parents consent. To Susanna McGhee articles named. To friend John Neely 1 shilling. To friend Wm. Neely 1 shilling. To friend James Rowan 1 shilling. To my brother Matthew Long 1 shilling. To friend Richard Venable remainder of goods; also executor.
Witnesses: Andrew Jack, William Dening, David Reed.

PARRY JOHN. Tredyffrin.
July 22, 1747. August 15, 1747. B. 224.
To each of my sisters, viz Lettice, Elizabeth, Margaret, Mary and Esther £5. To my cousins Margaret Davis and Margaret Williams £10 "for their extraordinary good behavior while they lived with me." To cousin Rowland Parry my watch. To cousin Hannah Parry my english house Bible. To cousin Tobitha Parry an english Bible. To prentice bound girl Abigail O'Neal one year of her time. To negro man Harry his freedom at 35 and 2 acres of land. To servant Henry McCormock one year of his time. Remainder of estate real and personal to my brother David Parry also executor.
Witnesses: Isaac Davis, Jos. Bartholomew, John Griffith.

CRAMPTON, SUSANNA. Londongrove.
July 13, 1747. August 10, 1747. B. 225.
To brother James Crampton and friend Margaret Cook all my personal estate.
Executors: brother James and friend John Cook Jr.
Witnesses: John Cook Sr, Micajah Speakman.

VERNON, JOSEPH. N. Providence, yeoman.
5/8/1739. August 20, 1747. B. 226.
Provides for wife Lydia. To only son Joseph all remainder of estate real and personal also executor. Brother Jacob Vernon, brother in law Caleb Harrison and friend Peter Dicks to aid and assist.
Witnesses: Thos. Vernon, John Needham, Wm. Gorsuch.

STEEL, JOHN. New London.

August 7, 1747. August 18, 1747. B. 226.
To wife Jennet 1/3 of all estate during life. Remainder in equal shares among children, viz James, Elizabeth, William and Francis Steel eldest son James to have the plantation at appraisement.
Executors: wife Jennett and son James. Friend and brother Peter Higate and James Donnel, overseers.
Witnesses: James Donnel, John Steel.

JONES, MARY. Widow. Tredyffrin.
August 9, 1745. August 26, 1747. B. 227.
To son Joseph Jones 1 shilling. To sons John and William £5 each. To daughter Catharine wife of Isaac Evans £5. To daughter Martha wife of John Besh £5. To daughter Sarah wife of Timothy Davis £5. To daughter Mary wife of Griffith Evan £5. To daughter Ann wife of John Morris £5. To daughter Margaret wife of Richard Williams £5.
Executor: son in law Timothy Davis of Tredyffrin.
Witnesses: Richard Iddings, Owen Philip, John Davis.

GARRETT, SAMUEL.
May 4, 1747.
Adm. to Sarah and Thos.
Garrett and Benj. Hibberd.

ARTHUR, CHARLES.
May 19, 1747.
Adm. to Elanor Arthur and Nathan Evans.

COWEN, EPHRAIM.
June 15, 1747.
Adm. to Anne Cowen.

MORGAN, WILLIAM.
June 17, 1747.
Adm. to Robert Kyll.

ARMSTRONG, ANDREW.
July 10, 1747.
Adm. to Anne Armstrong.

HEWES, WILLIAM.
July 18, 1747.
Adm. to William Hewes.

GUIN, OWEN.
August 5, 1747.
Adm. to Hannah Guin.

FISHER, THOMAS. E. Caln, yeoman.
4/3/1747. August 27, 1747. B. 228.
To son Samuel 150 acres of land being the Bouth side of the tract I live on. To son Thomas at 21 the remainder of said tract being about 100 acres with the buildings subject to provision for wife Elizabeth and payment of £10 to son Francis and £5 to daughter Mary at 20. To daughter Elizabeth wife of Jos. Wilkinson a colt, contingent legacies of £5 each to sons William and James.
Executors: wife Elizabeth and son Samuel.
Witnesses: Wm. Pim, Thos. Downing, Thomas Paine.

POCK, THOMAS. Aston, yeoman.
August 30, 1747. September 17, 1747. B. 228.
To wife Ann 1/3 of all real and personal estate. To son John the mare and colt an equal share with his sisters of my estate. Executors: brother James Pock and Hugh Linn, brother in law Leard Burns to have oversight of wife and children.
Witnesses: John Carrell, James Crage. Account filed mentions Francis Scot who married Martha one of the daughters of decedent.

EVANS, OWEN. Kennett, yeoman.
August 7, 1747. October 1, 1747. B. 229.
Provides for wife not named including use of plantation I live on for 18 years or until son Owen is 21. To eldest son Aaron the plantation formerly in possession of Wm. Smith containing 200 acres when 21. To daughter Sarah Evans the messuage, formerly of John Cox containing 65 acres when 18. To youngest son Owen the plantation where I live containing 78 acres 60 per at 21 also £50. Remainder to be sold and divided among 3 children.
Executors: wife Mary and brother Thomas Evans.
Witnesses: Jos. Harlan, Wm. Mackfarson, Joshua Harlan.

REES, EVAN. Charlestown. Carpenter.
September 20, 1747. October 1, 1747. B. 231.
Directs executor to pay to the college of New Jersey £15. To only brother John Rees, all estate real and personal also executor.
Witnesses: Arnold Francis, Owen Howell, David Parry.

SHARPLESS, JOHN. Ridley.
3/22/1737. October 1, 1757. B. 232.
To son John 15 acres 99 per of land adj that I formerly gave him, also another tract containing 4 1/2 acres and lott in Chester. To son Daniel the land I now live upon with 48 acres over the creek in Chester Township in all 258 acres also stock. To daughter Phebe Hibberd the tract of land I bought in Whiteland. To daughter Hannah Howard £50. To daughter Anne Bond £50. To 2 grandsons George and Joshua Smedley £10 each. To granddaughter Hannah Sharpless £10. To sons in law George Smedley, Benja Hibberd and Samuel Bond 40 shillings each. To son in law Henry Howard, bond of £10. To kinswoman Phebe Swarford 40 shillings.
Executors: sons John and Daniel.
Witnesses: Aaron Vernon, Wm. Swarfer, Sarah Swarfer.

JONES, JANE. Widow. Coventry.
August 20, 1747. October 1, 1747. B. 233.
To eldest son John Jones £5. To son David Jones £10 being one years rent due to me also £1-10 being money paid Abraham Wideman of his account and to Luce his wife, flannel for a petticoat. To son Evan Jones a horse and to Anne his wife articles named and to his daughter Anne, a mare. To cousin Margaret Davies 20 shillings and drugget to make her little boy a tunic. To son in law John Godfrey all my other effects also executor.
Witnesses: David Morgan, Jos. Millard, Benj. Millard.

THOMPSON, PETER. Marple, yeoman.
September 10, 1747. October 12, 1747. B. 234.
Provides for wife Margery. To eldest son Peter 1/2 of plantation whereon I live when 21 paying to his brother John £40. To son Moses the other 1/2 of same at 21. To daughter Sarah £60 at 18. To youngest son Thomas £80 at 21. 3 youngest sons to be apprenticed at 14.
Executors: wife Margery and brother Joshua Thompson.
Witnesses: John Worrall, John Pearson, Mirick Davis.

STEPHENSON, JAMES. Marple.

September 29, 1747. October 14, 1747. B. 236.
To wife Agnes £30. To sons, viz John and William my freehold to be
equally divided when come to "minority." To son James £15.
Executors: Matthew Cowden and Arthur Nesmith.
Witnesses: Thos. Patton, Matthew Hopkins.

BLACK, JOHN.
August 11, 1747.
Adm. to Elizabeth Black.

CARSON, GEORGE.
August 17, 1747.
Adm. to James Carson.

BEAUMONT, WILLIAM.
August 19, 1747.
Adm. to Elizabeth Beaumont.

HOGG, ROBERT.
August 27, 1747.
Adm. to Robert Patterson.

DOUGLASS, JEREMY.
September 15, 1747.
Adm. to Elizabeth Douglass.

WELCH, THOMAS.
October 1, 1747.
Adm. to Thomas Pennell.

NORTH, JUDITH.
October 5, 1747.
Adm. to Thomas North.

HILL, WILLIAM.
October 19, 1747.
Adm. to Mary Hill.

GOOLD, WILLIAM. Mariner.
Power to attorney to William Gray of Londongrove to receive and pay
out all money due or detained from me by the Privateer "Brigantine
Revenge" commanded by Capt. Troup of New York or any other persons
whatever.
Will August 24, 1747. October 15, 1747.
To William Gray £1000 and all other estate also executor.
Witnesses: Wm. Reed, Nicholas Pile, John Sharp.

TAYLOR, MORDECAI. U. Providence.
6/7/1747. October 19, 1747. B. 237.
Provides for wife Esther including the messuage where I dwell
containing 150 acres during life, she paying to my daughters Mary and
Sarah £50 each when 18. After wifes decease plantation to said 2
daughters.
Executors: brothers Nathan and Peter Taylor.
Witnesses: Henry Camm, George Turner, George Miller.

HELSBY, JOSEPH. Uwchlan.
8/19/1747. November 12, 1747. B. 238.
To my 3 daughter Hannah, Sarah and Mary £10 each when of age. To 3
sons Joseph, Aaron and John £15 each at 21. To Uwchlan Meeting 20
shilling. To wife Mary all lands and other goods.
Executors: wife Mary and Awbrey Roberts. Letters to widow.
Witnesses: Jos. Phipps Jr, John Dennis.

LEWIS, MAGDALEN. Widow. Charlestown.
January 12, 1744/5. November 13, 1747. B. 239.
To the 3 children of son Griffith Lewis, viz Rebecca William and
Samuel 2-6 shillings each. To Isaac son of daughter Elizabeth
David deceased 5 shillings. To Anne and Magdalen daughters of
Elizabeth David 1 shilling each. To Magdalen daughter of David

137

Humphrey and my daughter Catharine 2-6 shilling and case of drawers. To Jonathan and Samuel the 2 sons of ditto, the money from the big brass kettle, equally divided to Sarah daughter of ditto and Esther daughter of ditto. Articles named when 18, also to John and Joshua the 2 sons of ditto £1-10 each.
Executor: son in law David Humphry.
Witnesses: Owen Howell, Wm. Ball, John Rees.

FINCHER, JOHN. Londongrove.
4/5/1746. November 24, 1747. B. 240.
To son Jonathan 5 shilling. To son Francis £20. To daughter Rebecca Bennett £30. To daughter Sarah Swain £30. To Thomas Cox living over the Susquehanna £5 for the use of his daughter Rebecca wife of James Fraiser. To Mary eldest daughter of son Jonathan £10 when of age. Remainder to sons Francis and John. Executors: friends Joshua Pusey and Nath. Pennock and Joshua Johnson, overseers.
Witnesses: Moses Pyle, Joseph Pennock Jr.

HOWELL, THOMAS. Charlestown.
December 9, 1747. December 12, 1747. B. 241.
Non Cupative will. To daughter Sarah £20. Provides for wife Mary, remainder real and personal to son Owen also executor. Witnesses: David Davies, Griffith James.
Will proven by the written consent of widow Mary and daughter Sarah Howell.

TAYLOR, ABIAH.
October 26, 1747.
Adm. to Samuel Taylor.

MARTIN, JOHN.
November 21, 1747.
Adm. to Phebe Martin.

ASHBRIDGE, JOHN.
November 3, 1747.
Adm. to Hannah Ashbridge.

BOYD, HUGH.
November 12, 1747.
Adm. to Robert Mackey.

BOON, ANDREW.
November 18, 1747.
Adm. to Mounce Rambo and Wm. Donaldson.

SHARP, WILLIAM.
November 20, 1747.
Adm. to Margaret Sharp.

RONELLS, JAMES.
November 26, 1747.
Adm. to Robert Hamill.

CRESWELL, JOSEPH.
November 27, 1747.
Adm. to William Creswell.

HALL, JOHN. W. Fallowfield.
March 14, 1746/7. January 14, 1747/8. B. 242.
To wife Margaret 1/3 of all estate. To sons Walter and William the plantation I now possess at valuation and all estate equally divided among sons, Walter, William, John and daughters Rose and Margaret Hall also mentions grandson Joseph Campbell. Executors: sons Joseph and Walter and brother Saml. Dickson/Dickison.
Witnesses: Wm. Willson, Cormick Maguire, Thos. Maguire.

BUFFINGTON, RICHARD. E. Bradford, Chester Co.

January 7, 1747/8. February 10, 1747/8. B. 242.
Provides for wife Alice. To daughters Hannah Dain, Mary Turner, Elizabeth Freeman and Lydia Martin, a Bible worth 30 shillings each. To son William all wearing apparel. To daughters Abigail Seed & Alice McArthur, a Bible each. To son Thomas' (deceased) heirs 5 shillings. To son Richard's (deceased) heirs 5 shillings. To daughter Ann Hickman's (deceased) heirs 5 shillings. To daughter Ruth Harlan's (deceased) heirs 5 shillings. To son John's (deceased) heirs 5 shillings. To son Joseph remainder of real & personal estate and if he dies without heirs then to daughters Abigail & Alice. To Owen Thomas minister of the Anabaptist Society held at John Bentleys in Newlin £5 also to Society £20 in annual payments of £5. To Richard Kimbel £2-10.
Executor: son Joseph.
Witnesses: Evan Jones, Wm. Bennet, Saml. Grubb.

JONES, NICHOLAS. Fallowfield.
February 16, 1747/8. February 23, 1747/8. B. 243.
To wife Mary 1/3 of moveable estate. To sons Robert and David the plantation now in my possession, they to maintain their brother Samuel Jones, during life that he may not be a charge to the Township. To son John the part of the plantation he now possesses. To my daughter Mary Hinds, Sarah McGuinnes, PatteneB Johnston and Margaret Hanson 1 shilling each.
Executors: friends Joseph Adams and Andrew Gibson and friends Joseph Willson and William Boggs, overseers.
Witnesses: James Allison, Andrew Kirkpatrick.

ROCKETT, HENRY. E. Nantmell.
February 14, 1747/8. February 24, 1747/8. B. 244.
Gives all his goods to be at the disposal of Matthias Lamey "the principal creditor I have in this province." The remainder to be at disposal of daughter Margaret Sullivan.
Witnesses: Thos. Cadigan, Will Quarry, John Mulcaster.

CLOUD, JEREMIAH. E. Marlborough, yeoman.
February 19, 1747/8. February 26, 1747/8. B. 245.
Provides for wife Anne. To son William the plantation where he now dwells being by estimation 200 acres where my son Joel formerly dwelt. To son Jeremiah the plantation whereon I dwell containing 230 acres. To son Mordecai that tract of land my father gave to my brother Daniel near Chichester. To grandson Joel that settlement on which his father dwelt by estimate 100 acres. To daughter in law Hester Cloud the profits of said land for the bringing up of the children, viz David, Daniel and Joel till they are 14. To son in law Thomas Underwood 1 shilling. To granddaughter Lydia Underwood £10 at 18. Mentions apprentice Abraham Johnston.
Executor: son Jeremiah and Daniel Baily and Joseph Davis, assistants. Testator died before he could sign the will. Witnessed by John Cloud, Geo. Baily.

TOWNSEND, JOHN. Westtown, yeoman.
January 25, 1747/8. February 29, 1747/8. B. 246.
To son John all wearing apparel besides the 100 acres of land already given him. To grandson Thomas Townsend 5 shillings besides the 100 acres already given him. To daughter Rachel wife of John Cooper bed and bedding. To daughter Phebe wife of John Taylor warming pan. Remainder of estate equally divided between son John and daughter Phebe Taylor, Rebecca wife of Daniel Mercer, Hannah wife of Isaac Vernon Jr, Anne wife of Dennis Whelen, Rachel Cooper and Mary wife of Isaac Thomas.
Executor: son John.
Witnesses: Stephen Taylor, Thos. Yearsley, Hannah Curray.

HARLAN, SARAH. Kennett.
February 5, 1747/8. March 3, 1747/8. B. 247.
To my 3 sons, viz George, Samuel and Aaron 5 shillings each. To my 3 daughters, viz Charity Baldwin, Mary Evans and Elizabeth Hollingsworth £20 each. To cousin Martha Way £4 when 18. Remainder to grandchildren.
Executrix: daughter Mary Evans.
Witnesses: John Clark, Francis Clark.

MARTIN, PHEBE. Widow of John.
December 1, 1747.
Adm. to Thomas Mercer.

MARTIN, JOHN.
December 2, 1747.
Adm. d.b.n. to Jonathan Martin.

ARCHER, ADAM.
January 8, 1747/8.
Adm. to Elizabeth Archer and Andrew Morton.

GOHEEN, EDWARD.
February 9, 1747/8.
Adm. to Anne Goheen.

FERGUSON, WILLIAM.
February 29, 1747/8.
Adm. to Mary Ferguson.

JAMES, MORRIS.
March 4, 1747/8.
Adm. to John James.

McCULLOGH, NATHANIEL.
March 7, 1747/8.
Adm. to John Galbreath.

JONES, WATKIN.
March 16, 1747/8.
Adm. to Mary Mills.

HOWARD, PETER. Coventry. Codwainer.
February 18, 1747/8. March 15, 1747/8. B. 247.
To wife Rebecca all my goods in this province. To son John if he lives to 21 my plantation whereon I dwell but if another child be born it shall have an equal share.
Executrix: wife Rebecca. David Parry of Tredyffrin and Jonathan Davies of Charlestown, guardians.
Witnesses: James John, Jacob Engers, John Llewellin.

DAVID, PHILIP. E. Nantmell.
June 3, 1742. Codicil: March 1, 1747/8. March 23, 1747. B. 248. To sister Gwan Llian David £2. To sister Janet David £2. To wife Katherine all personal estate she paying legacies also my land during life and after her deceased to my servant lad Evan son of Griffith Griffies "to him and his heirs but no assigns."

Executors: wife Katherine and neighbors John Griffies and John Rees.
Cod gives to Evan Griffies all bequeathed to his wife she being now
deceased except £5 to Thomas son of Wm. Vance at 21 and articles named
to Clement Radford and names as executors: Nathaniel Jones and John
Rees. Letters to Jones. Rees renouncing. Witnesses: Jeremiah Kyle,
John Lewis, John Cain.

JOHN, WILLIAM. Uwchlan, yeoman.
February 23, 1747/8. March 23, 1747/8. B. 249.
To son Evan John 5 shillings. To son James £5. To son Joshua £2. To
son Enoch £5. To son Elias £5. To daughter Anne Gowger £5. To daughter
Elizabeth John or Gowger £2-10. To grandson son of Evan John the smith
tools when 21.
Executors: Philip David and Awbrey Roberts.
Witnesses: Nathl. Jones and Humphrey Lloyd.
Letters to Roberts, David being deceased.

DAVID, JOHN. Of the Valley Township, Ches Co.
March 7, 1748. March 25, 1748. B. 250.
Provides for wife Mary. To daughter Christian £5 and I discharge
Jenkin David my son in law the sum of £25 he owes me. To daughter
Rachel £5. To daughter Margaret £5. To son Evan my plantation where I
live during life and after his decease the western end, to my grandson
Mezek David if 21. To grandson John David the remainder of land his
mother Mary to have use of it during life if she survives her husband.
Executor: son Evan. Friends John Havard, David Jones and Isaac David,
overseers.
Witnesses: John Jones, Thomas Jones, Malachi Jones.

GARRETT, THOMAS. Darby. Weaver.
8/13/1747. March 25, 1748. B. 252.
To sister Mary Eldridge £100. To brother Joseph £60. To sister Hannah
Lewis £50. to Sarah widow of deceased brother Samuel £10 and to the
children of said deceased brother, viz Josiah, Jesse, Samuel and Aaron
£80 to be dis at 21. To Esther Hibberd daughter of sister Jane
deceased £15 at 21. To Mary Sykes daughter of my deceased wife
articles named. To Ann Andrews sister of my wife and Catherine
Wetherill sister of ditto articles of household goods. To Johanna
Sykes ditto. To Hannah Mendenhall of Darby £30. To Mary Griffith of
Darby £20. To James Hinde, blacksmith £10. To John Hinde my late
apprentice £10. Wearing apparel to brothers Joseph and Nathan.
Remainder to Nathan.
Executors: brother Nathan and John David of Darby.
Witnesses: John Garrett, Wm. Horne, Isaac Pearson.

CARPENTER, WILLIAM. New Garden. Taylor.
February 21, 1747/8. March 28, 1748. B. 253.
Directs executors to make deed to William, Nathaniel and Isaac
Richards the 3 children of Nathaniel Richards deceased for 50
acres of land as has been already agreed upon. Provides for wife
Margaret. To son John my plantation in New Garden containing 174
acres he paying to son Thomas £50 when 21. In case all children
should die before legal age, plantation to brother John Carpenter

and heirs of Alderton in Gloucestershire, England and in default of
heirs to sister Ann Carpenter of same place she paying to each of my
sisters Sarah and Mary of London. To son Thomas £94 at 21. To daughter
Sarah and Albina £20 each at 18 or married.
Executors: wife Margaret and her son Wm. Richards.
Witnesses: Willm. Reed, Thomas Wily, Wm. Miller.
[Margaret died in W. Bradford December 4, 1796, aged 90, 113 children,
grandchildren, etc.]

SHARP, JOHN. New Garden, yeoman.
To son John 1/3 of my plantation whereon I live when 21 containing 300
acres. To daughter Elizabeth £20 at 21. To son George 1/3 of
plantation when 21. To son Benjamin the remainder of plantation sons
Geo. and Benj. paying to son Thomas £60 when 21. Provides for wife Ann
including profit of real estate until sons come of age she paying to
daughter Mary £20 when of age.
Executors: wife Ann and son John.
Witnesses: John Pyle, Thomas Bryan, Jas. Miller.

MELIN, SUSANNA.
March 23, 1747/8.
Adm. to William Melin.

YOUNG, WILLIAM. Londongrove, yeoman.
March 10, 1747/8. March 28, 1748. B. 255.
All estate to wife Mary for her maintenance and educating and bringing
up of children none of whom are named.
Executrix: wife Mary. Friend John Allen, overseer.
Witnesses: James Dannell, John Johnston, William Brown.

ASHBRIDGE, GEORGE. Chester Township.
March 1, 1747/8. March 29, 1748. B. 256.
To son Joseph the messuage, where I now dwell with the lotts of land
lately purchased. To daughter Elizabeth wife of John Sharpless £40 and
to their daughter Mary chest of drawers. To daughter Hannah wife of
Joshua Hooper £40. To granddaughter Mary daughter of Amos Yarnall and
Mary his wife late deceased £40 at
18. Remainder to son Joseph.
Executors: sons Joseph and George.
Letters to Joseph the other refusing to act.
Witnesses: John Taylor, Jo Parker, H.H. Graham.

GRIFFITH, DANIEL. Pikestown.
March 14, 1748. April 5, 1748. B. 257.
Wife Ann and son Hosea to be joint sharers in my effects and if wife
be with child, executors to pay it £10 when 21.
Executors: wife Ann and son Hosea.
Witnesses: John Meredith, Robt. Hamilton.
Brothers Timotheus and John Griffith guardians.

REECE, JOHN.
March 14, 1747/8.
Adm. to Morris Reece.

PLAIN, JOHN.
March 25, 1748.
Adm. to Mary Plain.

CULIN, JOHN.
March 26, 1748.
Adm. to Daniel Culin.

MCKEEVER, DANIEL. Newlin.
March 28, 1748.
Adm. to Thomas Willson.

WILEY, ALLEN.
March 28, 1748.
Adm. to Betty Wiley.

SCOTT, ADAM.
March 29, 1748.
Adm. to John Ranken.

MORRIS, JENNETT.
March 30, 1748.
Adm. to Theophilus Morris.

THOMAS, JOHN.
April 4, 1748.
Adm. to John Pugh and Dinah Jones.

OWEN, WILLIAM.
April 5, 1748.
Adm. to David Owen.

GRONOW, LEWIS. Cumru, Lan Co. Fuller.
March 15, 1747/8. April 5, 1748. B. 257.
To grandson Isaac David son of daughter Sarah David £10. To grand son Lewis Gronow son of my only son John £10. To granddaughter Joanna daughter of Daniel Prichard £10 at 18. To great grandson Levi Prichard £2-10. To grandaughter Anne, daughter of son George, deceased, £2-10. To 3 daughters Sarah David, Penelope Rees and Catherine Prichard 1 shilling each. All remainder to son John also executor.
Witnesses: John Melchor, Wm. Gronow, John Meredith.

JONES, REES. Uwchlan, yeoman.
March 28, 1748. April 5, 1748. B. 258.
All estate to 3 daughters Jane, Margaret and Sarah.
Executors: son in law John Williams and John Meredith.
Witnesses: Enoch Williams, John Edwards.

GRIFFITH, Thomas. Vincent, yeoman.
March 1, 1748. April 5, 1748. B. 259.
To wife Rachel £20. To children Gwenllian and Judith Griffith £30 when 18. To Gwen a Welsh Bible and to Judith an English one. Joseph Williams and Daniel Griffith to be guardians and wife Rachel executrix.
Witnesses: John Gronow, Ann Parker, Reuben William.
[The administration account show that the widow married Thomas Prowell; also a payment of £6 to James Prowell, marriage at Swedes Church, Philadelphia.]

DAVID, WILLIAM. Vincent. Taylor.
March 3, 1748. April 5, 1748. B. 259.
Provides for wife Sarah. To eldest daughter Rebecca Prichard 10 shillings and to grandson Levi Prichard El. To youngest daughter Hannah 1/4 of estate at 18. To son Isaac my right to a lease of land and remainder of estate also executor.
Witnesses: Llewellin David, Jos. David, Danl. Griffith.

JAMES, JOHN. Willistown, yeoman.
March 24, 1748. April 11, 1748. B. 260.

To friend John Rowland £10. To friend Paul Bond £5. To Lewis son of
John Gronow £5. To Morris Evan £2 and to his son Daniel Evan £1 and to
his daughter Anne £5. To Mary daughter of Anne Evan £. To Elizabeth
daughter of John Rowland walnut chest. To Ezekiel son of John Bowen
£2. To cousin John Jones of Lancaster Co. my right to the plantation
where I dwell in Willistown.
Executors: John Jones and Wm. Rowland.
Witnesses: John Bowen, Methusalem Davis.

BOWEN, JOHN. Willistown. Weaver.
March 26, 1748. April 11, 1748. B. 261.
Directs real estate to be sold. To grandmother not named £10. To aunt
Ruth Evans £5. To aunt Anne Evans £5. To aunt Elizabeth Thomas £10. To
cousin Evan Bowen £4 at 21. To cousin Levi Bowen £3 at 21. To cousin
Ezekiel Bowen £3 at 21. To apprentice David Yarnall one of the 2 looms
in my shop.
Executors: uncle Saml. Richard, Jacob Thomas and Rowland Richard.
Witnesses: Francis Yarnall, Nathan Thomas, Robert Cox.
[1st wife Mary Hannum; 2nd wife Elinor Gibson.]

SMITH, THOMAS. Birmingham.
April 7, 1748. April 12, 1748. B. 262.
Provides for wife Elinor. To son James that part of my land I bought
of Joseph Webb at 21. To son Isaac the other part of my land with 1.4
part of the mills at 21. To son William my plantation in Concord on
which he lives and that part of my land bought of Thomas West. To
daughter Sarah Scott £5. To daughter Margery Bullock 10 shillings. To
daughter Mary Smith £30 at 18. To daughter Hannah Smith £30 at 18. To
sons John and Thomas 5 shillings each.
Executors: sons John and William.
Witnesses: William McClure, Enoch Hollingsworth.

HOPTON, RACHEL. Widow. Bethel.
March 31, 1748. April 14, 1748. B. 263.
To granddaughter Rachel Nichland walnut clothes press. To son in law
Joseph Nickland 5 shillings. To granddaughters Mary and Anne Hopton
articles named. Remainder to son John Hopton also executor.
Witnesses: Joseph Booth, Saml. Savill, Hugh Blackwell. [John Hopton of
Bethel left two children John and Mary who married Joseph Nicklin Jr
and John Marshall. Deed book V. 341.]

MARIS, JOHN. Springfield. Cordwainer.
September 30, 1747. April 18, 1748. B. 263.
To wife Susanna all estate during life afterwards sold and divided in
7 equal parts to daughter Sarah, Mary and Susanna, Cathrine Pusey
daughter Alice 3 daughters and daughter Hannah's children and son
John.
Executors: wife and son George Maris.
Witnesses: John Levis, James Maris.

INDEX

-A-
ABBOT, John, 4
  Rebeckah, 4
ABERNATHEY, John, 4
ABOURN, Agnes, 72
  James, 72
ABRAHAM, Joseph, 113
ABRAM, Joseph, 129
  Noah, 129
  Sarah, 129
ABRAMS, Enoch, 129
  James, 129
  Noah, 129
  Sarah, 129
ACTION, Ann, 109
ADAMS, Agnes, 120
  Elizabeth, 1
  Hugh, 81
  James, 81, 86, 103
  Joseph, 139
  Robert, 120
  Samuel, 1
  William, 103
AILS, Mary, 19
ALCOCK, Jeffrey, 11
ALDESTON, ---, 142
ALDHAM, Mary, 61
ALEXANDER, Andrew, 111
  John, 119
  Moses, 112
  William, 125
ALISON, Fra., 130
ALLEN, Agnes, 130
  David, 104
  Hannah, 73
  Isaac, 65
  James, 65, 125, 130
  John, 14, 59, 65, 94, 142
  Mary, 65
  Morril, 65
  Nathan, 65
  William, 65, 95
ALLIN, Alice, 16
  John, 16
ALLISON, Alexander, 111
  Andrew, 86
  Annas, 86

Christiana, 86
David, 111
Elizabeth, 111
Francis, 99
Isabella, 86
James, 45, 86, 92, 139
Janet, 45
Jean, 45
Jenneh, 45
John, 45, 86
Margaret, 45, 86
Martha, 111
Mary, 86, 111
Patrick, 45
Rebecca, 111
Richard, 46
Robert, 45, 86
Thomas, 86
William, 45, 86
AMANS, Thomas, 10
ANDERSON, Elizabeth, 101
  James, 45, 101
  Jane, 109
  John, 105, 121
  Kenneth, 71
  Margaret, 104
  Patrick, 101
  Samuel, 103
  William, 66
ANDREWS, Ann, 141
  Elizabeth, 13
  Thomas, 58
  William, 70
ARCHER, Adam, 26, 95, 140
  Andrew, 26
  Christian, 95
  Eleanor, 95
  Elizabeth, 95, 140
  Gartrad, 95
  Gertrude, 95
  Gunner, 95
  Jacob, 20, 95
  John, 20, 95
ARMENT, Elizabeth, 57
ARMSTRONG, Andrew, 135
  Anne, 135

David, 53
Joseph, 105
Mathew, 97
William, 90
ARNENT, William, 57
ARNOLD, Anthony, 10, 18, 67, 128, 130
  Elizabeth, 10, 18
  Grace, 18
  Hannah, 31, 130
  John, 10, 130
  Joseph, 18
  Josiah, 10, 121
  Mary, 121, 131
  Richard, 10, 18, 94, 130
  Sarah, 10, 18
  Thomas, 10, 18, 131
  William, 10, 18, 36, 67
ARTHUR, Charles, 85, 135
  Elanor, 135
ASH, Samuel, 53
ASHBRIDGE, Elizabeth, 142
  George, 3, 8, 25, 42, 74, 106, 112, 128, 142
  Goe, 64, 81
  Hannah, 138, 142
  John, 138
  Joseph, 142
  Margaret, 105
ASHBROOK, Nathaniel, 66
ASHMEAD, Sarah, 64
ASHTON, Sarah, 16
ASKEW, Lazarus, 133
  Mabell, 133
  William, 79
ASTON, George, 28
ATHERTON, Henry, 110, 111
  Rebecca, 91
ATKINSON, John, 109
AYERS, Abraham, 50

-B-
BACKHOUS, Res.

INDEX

Richard, 120
BACKHOUSE, Anna, 100
BAILY, Abigail, 43, 63
  Ann, 59
  Daniel, 59, 63, 139
  David, 84
  George, 60
  Goe, 139
  Isaac, 43, 59, 63
  Joel, 2, 3, 51, 59, 63
  John, 59, 105
  Josiah, 59, 102
  Mary, 50, 59
  Sarah, 84
  Thomas, 59
BAKER, Aaron, 74, 75
  Adam, 100
  Ann, 74, 76
  Caleb, 43
  Elizabeth, 58
  Hannah, 9, 67
  Jane, 75
  Jesse, 75, 77
  John, 6, 67, 75, 77
  Joseph, 5, 6, 9, 44, 67, 74, 75, 77
  Margaret, 76, 100
  Martha, 77
  Mary, 6, 9, 67, 74, 75
  Nehemiah, 75, 77
  Rachel, 67, 75
  Rebecca, 67
  Richard, 58, 74, 75
  Robert, 6, 43
  Sarah, 6, 9, 75, 77
  Susanna, 6, 75
BALDWIN, Anthony, 22, 32, 52, 54, 57, 96
  Charity, 140
  Elizabeth, 6, 105
  Francis, 57
  John, 5, 47, 56, 57
  Joseph, 6, 54
  Joshua, 57
  Margary, 52
  Margery, 107
  Mary, 22, 54

Thomas, 22, 54, 57
  William, 22, 54
BALL, Elizabeth, 77
  Hannah, 77
  John, 77, 87
  Roger, 77
  William, 138
BALLAR, Ann, 64
  Lydia, 64
  Thomas, 64
BANE, Alex, 73
  Alexander, 29
BANET, Thomas, 55
BARBER, James, 3, 67
  Susanna, 74
BARNARD, Jeremiah, 105
  Richard, 59
  Sarah, 64, 80
  Thomas, 20, 64
BARNES, Elizabeth, 58
  Thomas, 15
  William, 58
BARNETT, William, 88
BARNHILL, James, 128
BARNS, Aaron, 62
BARRATT, Arthur, 24
BARRETT, Arthur, 113
  Hannah, 113
BARRY, Richard, 53, 57, 67, 89, 113
BARTHOLOMEW, Joseph, 134
BARTON, Abraham, 20
  Benjamin, 20
  Elizabeth, 20
  Isaac, 20
  Jacob, 20
  Joshua, 20
  Mary, 20
  Sarah, 20
BARTRAM, Anne, 93
  Elizabeth, 40, 65, 123
  John, 93
  William, 40, 65
BASSETT, Silvanus, 85
BATE, Humphrey, 54
BATTERTON, Henry, 36
  James, 36

Martha, 36
  Mary, 36
  Patience, 36, 86
  Robert, 36
BAXTER, William, 94
BAYLE, Mary, 112
  William, 112
BAYLISS, Jane, 2
BEAKER, Joseph, 16
BEAKES, Stephen, 25
BEAKS, Stephen, 67
BEALE, Mary Ann, 3
  Stephend, 3
  William, 117
BEALS, Ann, 31
  Jacob, 23, 31
  John, 23, 31
  Mary, 31
  Phebe, 31
  Sarah, 31
  Thomas, 31
  William, 31
BEAN, William, 119
BEARD, John, 76
BEAUMONT, Elizabeth, 137
  William, 137
BECKETT, John, 31, 68
BECKINGRAM, John, 10, 22, 27, 54, 69
BEEKE, John, 103
BEESON, Edward, 1, 14
  Elizabeth, 1
  Richard, 1
  William, 1
BELL, Abigail, 89
  John, 88
  Mary, 73
  Samuel, 73
  Thomas, 113
  William, 88
BELLARBY, Isaac, 8
BELLERBY, Mary, 46
  Susanna, 46
BENNET, Hannah, 132
  John, 60
  Rebecca, 50
  William, 139
BENNETT, Ann, 15
  Edward, 2, 4

INDEX

Elizabeth, 4
Esther, 4, 14, 109
Hannah, 129
Jacob, 4, 14, 103, 109
John, 4, 14, 15, 30, 121, 129, 132
Joseph, 4
Rebecca, 138
Sarah, 2, 4, 10, 121
William, 4, 100, 128
BENSON, Ann, 128
James, 128
John, 128
Katherine, 128
Robert, 128
William, 128
BENTLEY, John, 139
Jona, 12
Jonathan, 7
BERREY, Elizabeth, 66
Hannah, 66
John, 66
Margaret, 66
Samuel, 66
Sarah, 66
Thomas, 66, 129
BESH, John, 135
Martha, 135
BETHALL, Rose, 40
BETHEL, Ann, 4, 8
Jane, 4
John, 28
Joseph, 28
Rose, 25
Samuel, 4, 8, 87
Sarah, 62
William, 28
BETHELL, Ann, 7, 47
Eliza, 28
Elizabeth, 40
Frances, 28
Joseph, 40
Rose, 28
Samuel, 7, 42, 47
BETTLE, Samuel, 66, 121, 123
BETTY, David, 53

John, 118
William, 53, 86
BEVAN, Aubrey, 89
Barbara, 7, 8
Charles, 114
Mordecai, 85
BEVERLY, William, 39
William, 59
BEZAR, John, 36
BEZER, Edward, 18
Esther, 1, 56
John, 1, 20, 56, 57
Mary, 49
Richard, 88, 92
Sarah, 49
William, 49
BIRD, Susanna, 119
Thomas, 14
BIRON, William, 48
BISHOP, Alice, 103
Charles, 103
Ealse, 100
Esther, 100, 108
Hannah, 103
John, 100, 103
Joseph, 103
Lydia, 103
Mary, 103, 114
Priscilla, 103
Rose, 103
Samuel, 100, 103
Sarah, 103
Susanna, 103
BIZALLION, Martha, 106
Peter, 106
BLACK, David, 3
Elizabeth, 137
John, 137
Rachel, 3
Thomas, 48
BLACKWELL, Hugh, 42, 144
John, 144
Mary, 144
BLAKELY, John, 134
BLAND, Isaac, 34
Susanna, 34
BLEAKLY, John, 103
BLOAIR, Sarah, 58

BLUNSTON, Ann, 8
Hannah, 62, 75
John, 4, 8, 28, 44, 62, 75
Margaret, 28
Michael, 4, 36, 62, 75
Phebe, 75
Samuel, 62, 75
Sarah, 7, 75
William, 75
BLUNSTONE, Hannah, 24
John, 24
Margaret, 24
Samuel, 24
Sarah, 24
BOGGO, John, 61
BOGGS, Alexander, 110
James, 94, 110
Jane, 130
John, 94, 110, 130
Joseph, 110, 130
Margaret, 110, 130
William, 81, 110, 139
BOHAMEN, James, 111
BOLTON, John, 72
Sarah, 72
BOND, Anne, 136
Elizabeth, 70
Joseph, 41, 49, 70
Paul, 144
Samuel, 136
BONSALL, Abadiahl, 28
Abraham, 87, 127
Ann, 10
Benjamin, 42, 87
Enoch, 10, 11, 13, 74
Esther, 127
Hannah, 73, 117
Jacob, 10, 11, 74, 77, 87
Jesse, 87
Joseph, 64, 73, 125
Lydia, 87
Martha, 10
Mary, 87
Moses, 87
Obadiah, 24, 64

INDEX

Sarah, 33, 64
Thomas, 87, 127
BONSELL, Jacob, 76
BOON, Andrew, 28, 48, 138
Ann, 28
Barbara, 28
Bridget, 28
Hance, 28
Katherine, 28
Neels, 48
Swan, 12, 48
Swen, 28
BOOTH, Ann, 36
Charles, 6
Elizabeth, 6, 36, 116
John, 36
Jonathan, 58
Joseph, 36, 144
Marsi, 19
Mary, 36
Mercy, 36
Robert, 36
Thomas, 116
BORRADAIL, Arthur, 33
BORRAS, John, 61
BOSS, Elizabeth, 131
BOSTOCK, George, 33, 82
BOULTON, Francis, 101
BOUND, John, 109
BOUNE, John, 25
Mary, 25
BOWATER, Frances, 19
BOWEN, Anne, 45
Evan, 44, 144
Ezekiel, 144
Gainor, 45
John, 44, 144
Levi, 144
BOWES, Alexander, 83
BOYCE, John, 109
Joseph, 109
Margaret, 109
Mary, 109
Phebe, 109
BOYD, Adam, 28
Hugh, 138
James, 93, 124

John, 124
William, 27, 58, 77, 126, 132
BOYDON, James, 55
BOYLE, Agnes, 78
Alexander, 78
Daniel, 113
Hugh, 78, 90
John, 78
Robert, 78
William, 78
BRACKENBURY, John, 12
BRADFORD, David, 107
Joseph, 51
BRADISH, John, 96
BRADLEY, William, 100
BRADSHAW, Elizabeth, 35, 46, 75
Hannah, 35
Margaret, 95
Mary, 35
Samuel, 46
Sarah, 35, 46, 75
Thomas, 4, 35, 75, 95
BRAND, Adam, 26
Hans, 26
BRANDON, Elizabeth, 108
BRANTON, Hannah, 13
BRASIES, Thomas, 20
BRASSEY, Thomas, 40
BRENAMAN, Christian, 32
BREWBACK, John, 29
BRIGHT, Elizabeth, 5
BRINTON, Edward, 61, 69, 94, 117, 121, 122
Hannah, 17, 69, 94
Jane, 116
Jean, 19
John, 94, 119
Joseph, 4, 14, 69, 122, 123
Mary, 69
Thomas, 105, 116, 121
William, 4, 18, 19, 60, 61, 116

BRITAIN, Deborah, 16
Peter, 16
BRODOND, Samuel, 95
BROGDEN, Samuel, 95
BROGDON, Edward, 106
Elizabeth, 106
BROMFIELD, John, 45
Mary, 45
Thomas, 45
BROMM, Elizabeth, 107
BROOKS, David, 97
BROOM, Alexander, 21
Daniel, 56
Edith, 21
Elizabeth, 8, 52
Hester, 116
James, 21, 116
John, 83, 116
Mary, 83, 107
Thomas, 52
BROOMALL, Ellen, 48
Jean, 48
John, 48
John B., 16
Lydia, 48
Mary, 48
BROOMFIELD, John, 22, 39
Mary, 22, 39
Robert, 94
BROWN, Agnes, 52
Alexander, 22
Andrew, 128
Anne, 132
Charles, 128
Daniel, 5, 6
Dinah, 62
Eleazer, 132
Elizabeth, 98, 132
Ellen, 132
Ellenor, 22
Esther, 27
George, 10, 14, 15
Hannah, 5
Honor, 5
James, 5
Jane, 5
Jennet, 128
Jeremiah, 5, 107
John, 5, 6, 93, 98,

126, 128. 132
  Joseph, 5, 6, 98,
    128, 132
  Joshua, 98, 107
  Margaret, 6, 52
  Margary, 5
  Mary, 5, 14, 15, 52
  Mercer, 5, 57
  Messar, 38
  Messer, 5, 31, 57,
    62, 102
  Michael, 128
  Nathan, 132
  Rachel, 132
  Rebecca, 126
  Richard, 5
  Robert, 70, 90, 97,
    113
  Samuel, 5, 68, 128,
    129
  Sarah, 113
  Susanna, 126
  Thomas, 5, 65, 68,
    129, 132
  William, 5, 6, 16,
    38, 49, 52, 68,
    98, 129, 142
BROWNHILL, Mary, 107
BROWNLER, James, 45
BRUCE, Deborah, 106
  James, 26, 106
BRUSS, John, 5
BRYAN, Thomas, 142
BUCHANAN, David, 130
  James, 104
BUCHHOLTS, Jacob, 65
BUCKINGHAM, Alice,
    112
  John, 112
  Margaret, 33
  William, 33
BUCKLEY, Adam, 119
  John, 119
BUFFINGTON, Alice,
    105, 139
  Betty, 91
  Eals, 120
  Ealse, 120
  Frances, 98
  Henry, 98

  Isaac, 98
  Jeremiah, 98
  John, 79, 98, 127,
    139
  Joseph, 98, 128,
    139
  Mary, 79
  Nathan, 98
  Peter, 98
  Phebe, 98
  Richard, 66, 79,
    91, 98, 139
  Samuel, 98, 127
  Sarah, 31, 79, 130
  Susanna, 91
  Thomas, 79, 91,
    130, 139
  William, 91, 139
BUGHANON, Gilbert,
    113
BULLER, Alexander,
    109
  Elizabeth, 13, 17
  John, 13, 18, 116
  Richard, 13, 17,
    116
  Thomas, 13, 17
  William, 13
BULLERBY, Isaac, 46
  John, 46
BULLOCK, Aaron, 70
  Margery, 144
  Thomas, 78
BUNTING, Eleanor, 90
  Eleanor, 81
  John, 62, 90
  Margaret, 90
  Mary, 53, 62, 90
  Robert, 81, 90
  Samuel, 24, 35, 46,
    49, 64, 75, 76,
    77, 87
  Sarah, 53, 75
  William, 62, 90
BURCK, Bartholomew,
    91
BURNS, Leard, 135
BURTON, Mary, 9
BUSHELL, Joseph, 9
  Sarah, 9, 11, 13

BUSHELLS, Joseph, 13
BUTCHER, Edmund, 22,
    31
  Isabella, 22, 131
  Jach, 12
  Susanna, 22, 31
  Thomas, 22, 31
  William, 22
  Zachariah, 22, 31,
    63
BUTTERFIELD, Mary, 5
BUZARS, John, 132

-C-
CADIGAN, Thomas, 139
CAESAR, 89
CAIN, Ann, 15
  John, 15, 62, 141
  Thomas, 62
CALDWELL, Anne, 15
  Betty, 15, 51, 69
  Elizabeth, 132
  Hannah, 15
  Henry, 132
  James, 106
  Jane, 132
  Margaret, 132
  Mary, 15
  Robert, 120, 123,
    132
  Ruth, 11, 15
  Vincent, 3, 11, 15
CALLOEHEN, Owen, 70
CALVERT, Daniel, 41,
    80
  Elizabeth, 41
CAMM, Henry, 79, 86,
    93, 109, 118, 137
  John, 86
  Mary, 86
CAMPBELL, Colin, 53,
    58
  Joseph, 138
  Samuel, 81
CAMPEN, Mary, 7
CAMPINET, George, 20
CARLETON, Thomas, 96,
    112, 119, 131
CARLTON, Allice, 114
  Arthur, 114

John, 114
Thomas, 114
CARNAHAN, Jane, 86
  John, 86
CARNRAN, John, 77
CARNWATH, Thomas, 92, 93
CARPENTER, Albina, 142
  Ann, 142
  Isaac, 17
  James, 18
  John, 141
  Margaret, 141, 142
  Mary, 142
  Sarah, 142
  Thomas, 141, 142
  William, 141
CARR, John, 113
CARRELL, John, 132, 135
CARSON, Eleanor, 131
  George, 59, 105, 125, 131, 137
  James, 137
  John, 131
  Mary, 131
  Samuel, 58
CARTER, ---, 125
  Abraham, 80
  Ann, 34
  Edward, 22, 80
  Elizabeth, 34
  George, 34
  Jacob, 75, 134
  Jeremiah, 80
  John, 34, 56, 70, 125
  Joseph, 13, 75
  Mary, 34, 80
  Nicholas, 81
  Nineveh, 80
  Rachel, 34
  Robert, 4, 33, 126
CARTHEDGE, Elizabeth, 22
  John, 22
CARTMELL, Dinah, 30
CASEY, James, 58
  Sarah, 58

CASHWELL, Isabella, 118
  Mary, 118
CASON, Moses, 61
CASSELL, Andrew, 126
  Sarah, 122
CAUSEY, James, 58
  Sarah, 58
CAWLEY, Samuel, 76
CAYE, Ann, 129
CEARY, Hannah, 13
  John, 13
  Margaret, 13
  Samson, 13
  Samuel, 13
  William, 13
CHADS, Ann, 2
  Betty, 2
  Elizabeth, 127
  Francis, 2
  Grace, 2
  John, 2, 46, 72, 114, 127
  Sarah, 2
CHALFANT, John, 10, 53
  Solomon, 53
CHALFORT, John, 27
  Robert, 27
  Solomon, 27
CHAMBERLIN, Ciecly, 57
  Jacob, 57, 60
  James, 57
  John, 57, 60, 64, 121, 60
  Joseph, 60, 130, 131, 60
  Lettice, 64
  Mary, 11, 60
  Robert, 11, 57, 60
  Susanna, 57, 60
CHAMBERS, Elinor, 51
  Elizabeth, 51
  Joseph, 107
CHANDALAR, William, 13
CHANDLEE, Benjamin, 2
  Cottey, 2
  Sarah, 2

William, 2
CHANDLER, Anne, 130
  Elizabeth, 105
  George, 2
  Jacob, 47, 119
  John, 130
  Mary, 130
  Moses, 130
  Ruth, 2
  Swithin, 2
  Thomas, 2, 59, 130
  William, 2, 130
CHANLER, Ann, 19
CHAPMAN, John, 20, 85
CHARLTON, Alice, 114
  Allice, 114
  Edward, 122
  Elinor, 114
  Henry, 95, 114, 122
  Isabella, 122
  Jane, 114, 122
  John, 122
  Letice, 114
  Lettice, 122
  Mary, 114
  Poynton, 114
  Thomas, 95, 114, 122
CHARTER, Margaret, 121
CHENEY, John, 23, 37
  Thomas, 23
CHEVERS, James, 43
CHEYNEY, Ann, 43, 108, 124
  Elizabeth, 43
  John, 43, 69, 116, 121, 124
  Joseph, 124
  Mary, 43, 124
  Richard, 124
  Thomas, 43, 69, 124
CHILD, John, 49
CHIVERS, James, 11
  Margaret, 11
CHRISTIAN, Mary, 22
CHURCHMAN, Dinah, 27
  Edward, 27
  George, 27
  Hannah, 27

INDEX

John, 2, 24, 27, 68
Miriam, 27
Sarah, 27
Susanna, 27
Thomas, 27
William, 27
CLARK, Francis, 140
Gabriel, 133
John, 70, 85, 140
Jonathan, 34
Walter, 133
CLAYTON, Abel, 41, 55, 82
Ambrose, 41
Ann, 20
Easter, 82
Edward, 41
Elizabeth, 41, 77, 84
Grace, 84, 114
Joseph, 82
Margaret, 82
Mary, 64
Richard, 1, 41, 64, 77
Susanna, 82
Thomas, 41, 84
William, 13, 26, 40, 41
CLEMENTS, Jeremiah, 53
Nicholas, 40
CLENEAY, William, 114
CLERK, Ann, 10
CLERKE, William, 21
CLIFF, Benjamin, 28, 53, 76
CLIFFE, Benjamin, 7, 53
CLIFT, Benjamin, 47
CLINTON, Archibald, 129
Elizabeth, 130
Hannah, 130
James, 130
John, 130
Mary, 130
Sarah, 130
William, 130
CLOOSE, John, 16

CLOUD, Abigail, 123
Abner, 123
Ann, 1, 18, 119
Anne, 139
Betty, 123
Daniel, 26, 139
David, 139
Edward, 119
Elizabeth, 123
Esther, 133
Grace, 18
Hester, 139
Jason, 18, 47, 103
Jeremiah, 26, 33, 90, 123, 139
Jeremias, 12
Joel, 133, 139
John, 33, 119, 139
Joseph, 18, 24, 35, 42, 79, 80, 83, 90, 123
Mary, 90
Mordcay, 12
Mordecai, 123, 139
Richard, 18
Ruth, 42
Sarah, 123
Susanna, 18
Susannah, 123
William, 18, 47, 139
CLUSE, John, 9
William, 18
COBOURN, Mary, 44
COBOWEN, Joseph, 124
COCHRAN, James, 113, 133
Joseph, 40
COCK, James, 34
Otto Ernest, 25
COCKFIELD, Elizabeth, 27
Hannah, 27
Joshua, 27
COCKRAN, James, 27
CODRY, Elizabeth, 32
Thomas, 32
CODWELL, Ann, 78
John, 78
Lillies, 78

Margaret, 78
Rebecca, 78
Thomas, 78
COEBOURN, John, 78
Joseph, 78
Thomas, 78
COEBURN, Caleb, 24
Dinah, 24
Elizabeth, 27
Joseph, 11, 24, 76
Joshua, 24
Lydia, 24
Mary, 76
Samuel, 96
Sarah, 24, 96
Susanna, 24
Thomas, 11, 24, 27
William, 96
COHLAN, Cornelius, 36
John, 36
COHOON, John, 96
Rebecca, 96
COLBERTSON, Ann, 86
Oliver, 86
COLE, Elizabeth, 120
James, 39, 40, 120
John, 120
Mark, 120
Marth, 76
Martha, 120
Stephen, 77, 120
William, 120
COLLET, Jer., 69
Jeremiah, 16
COLLIER, James, 128, 132
John, 117, 128
Joseph, 113
Mary, 12 8
COLLINS, Andrew, 84
Anne, 97
Daniel, 66
Elizabeth, 66, 97
Henry, 73
John, 45, 67, 73
Joseph, 73
Mary, 73
Peter, 66
Robert, 66
Sarah, 73

COMPTON, John, 10
　Jonathan, 10
CONDRUN, Mary, 74
CONNELL, George, 83
CONNELLY, Edmund, 104
CONNEN, William, 100
CONNER, Charles, 132
　James, 109
　Mary, 109
CONNOLLY,
　Constantine, 104
CONSTABLE, Thomas,
　126
COOK, Ann, 83, 84
　Cornelius, 83
　Daniel, 83
　Elizabeth, 84
　James, 46
　John, 42, 83, 134
　Joseph, 91
　Katherine, 84
　Margaret, 134
　Neal, 83
　Sarah, 91
　Thomas, 35
　William, 84
　Zachariah, 25
COOKSON, Daniel, 17
　Elizabeth, 57
COOPE, Rebecca, 125
COOPER, Ann, 60

　Calvin, 84
　James, 29, 43, 60
　John, 46, 60, 140
　Mary, 60
　Phebe, 84
　Rachel, 140
　Thomas, 60
　William, 84
COPE, Charity, 86
　Rebecca, 42
COPPEOICK, Barth, 29
COPPOCK, Aaaron, 27
　Aaron, 31, 55, 119
　Bartholomew, 6, 12,
　　16, 56, 68, 123,
　　16
　Deborah, 16
　Elinor, 34

Ellen, 16
Esther, 12
Hannah, 12, 16, 34
Jane, 12
John, 24, 31, 98
Jonathan, 12
Lydia, 31
Margaret, 12
Margret, 12
Martha, 12, 119
Mary, 16, 34
Merian, 31
Miriam, 31
Moses, 12
Rachel, 12
Rebecca, 12, 68
Sarah, 12, 24, 68
CORBIT, Daniel, 121
CORNELIUS, Andrew, 91
　Catherine, 91
　Charity, 91
　Charles, 91
　Easton, 91
　John, 91
　Stephen, 91
　Windey Frett, 91
CORREY, George, 114
COTTEY, Abel, 2
　John, 2
　Sarah, 2
COUGHRON, Stephen,
　110
COUPLAND, Caleb, 7
COWDEN, Matthew, 137
COWEN, Anne, 135
　Ephriam, 135
　Hugh, 44, 70
COWMAN, Benjamin, 49
　Isaac, 49
　Jeremiah, 49
　Samuel, 49
COWPLAND, Abigail, 64
　Caleb, 41, 64
　Caled, 118
　David, 64
　Joshua, 64
　Sarah, 105
　William, 64
COX, Benjamin, 67, 64
　Elizabeth, 50

John, 30, 136
Joseph, 67
Moses, 84
Rebecca, 34, 138
Richard, 126
Robert, 144
Thomas, 138
Walter, 34
COYLE, Ann, 62
　Daniel, 62
CRAFFORD, John, 56
　Rebecca, 56
CRAGE, James, 135
CRAGHTON, John, 52
CRAMPTON, James, 134
　Susanna, 134
CRAWFORD, John, 52
　Mary, 52
CREIGHTON, John, 124
　William, 124
CRESWELL, Abraham,
　115
　James, 115, 116
　Joseph, 138
　Mary, 115
　Robert, 115
　Samuel, 115
　Susanna, 115
　William, 115, 138
CRIGHTON, John, 55
　Margaret, 55
　Thomas, 55
　William, 55
CROSBY, John, 4, 13,
　14, 22, 45, 48, 75
　Richard, 13
　Susanna, 48
　Thomas, 86
CROSS, Agnes, 112
　James, 38
CROSSLEY, charles, 86
CROYDENS, Jacob, 29
CROZER, Andrew, 48
CRUDDERS, Charles,
　128
　Margaret, 128
CULIN, Ann, 75
　Daniel, 26, 75,
　　133, 143
　Ellen, 75

George, 26, 75, 130
John, 26, 75, 143
Jonas, 26, 75
Margaret, 26, 75
Morton, 26
CUMMINGS, Alice, 103
Thomas, 56, 57,
103, 120, 122, 134
CUNINGHAM, Barnet, 45
CUNNEGAN, Thomas, 94
CUNNINGHAM, James, 91
CURRAY, Hannah, 140
CURRY, George, 120
CUTHBERT, John, 81

-D-
DAIN, Hannah, 139
DANDISON, George, 34
DANGOR, Prudence, 47
DANNELL, James, 142
DARBY, Barth, 67
DARGON, William, 78
DARLINGTON, Abraham,
90, 107, 121, 125
Eliza, 129
Elizabeth, 44, 132
Joseph, 44
DARLINTON, William,
100
DAVENPORT, Joseph,
74, 78
DAVID, Ann, 48, 76,
87, 128
Bridget, 108
Catharine, 48
Catherine, 48
Christian, 141
David, 48
Dinah, 87, 128
Elizabeth, 48, 128,
137
Ellis, 17
Evan, 48, 81, 93,
104, 141
Gwan Llian, 140
Hannah, 143
Isaac, 76, 137,
141, 143
James, 48, 87, 88,
128

Janet, 140
Jenkin, 141
John, 23, 48, 108,
128, 141
Joseph, 143
Katherine, 4, 140,
141
Lettice, 87, 128
Lewis, 37
Llewellin, 76, 143
Magdalen, 76
Margaret, 87, 128,
141
Mary, 23, 87, 128,
141
Methusilah, 72
Mezek, 141
Morgan, 23, 87
Philip, 140, 141
Rachel, 141
Reece, 30
Roger, 72
Sampson, 87, 128
Sarah, 48, 143
Solomon, 55
Thomas, 23, 30, 48,
49
William, 143
DAVIES, Amos, 127
David, 128, 138
Elizabeth, 22, 30,
81
James, 30
Jonathan, 140
M., 115
Margaret, 136
Thomas, 22
DAVIS, Abraham, 14
Ann, 4, 102, 110
Anne, 87, 133
Benjamin, 134
Bethel, 87
Bridget, 37
Cathrine, 98
Charitie, 14
Daniel, 14, 15, 57,
111
David, 73, 85, 105
Eleanor, 71
Elizabeth, 44, 105,
110
Hannah, 14, 102
Hazehiah, 39
Hugh, 17, 44, 110
Isaac, 14, 134
Jane, 87, 105
Jenkin, 95
John, 4, 14, 17,
46, 53, 62, 65,
68, 75, 77, 80,
93, 99, 102, 110,
113, 135
Jonathan, 105
Joseph, 39, 40,
102, 123, 139
Lewis, 4, 29, 102,
113
M., 127
Margaret, 103, 105,
134
Mary, 14, 31, 57,
87, 100, 102, 112
Maudlin, 29
Methusalem, 144
Mirick, 102, 108,
136
Myrick, 41
Philip, 105
Rachel, 47
Rebecca, 14, 68,
102
Samuel, 87
Sarah, 102, 135
Susanna, 14
Thomas, 44, 45, 105
Timothy, 135
Valentine, 96
William, 4, 37
DAVISON, John, 70
DAWSON, ---, 29
Elizabeth, 29, 104
James, 104
DAY, John, 31, 46, 68
DEACON, Martha, 53
DEAN, Hannah, 101
Jeremiah, 79, 91,
101
Lydia, 91, 132
DEEBLE, Elizabeth, 59
George, 59, 84, 114

INDEX

Jane, 59
DELL, Thomas, 17, 21
DELWARTH, Sarah, 14
  William, 14
DELWORTH, Anthony, 88
DENESTON, Elizabeth, 118
  James, 118
  Margaret, 118
  Martha, 118
DENING, William, 134
DENISTON, Martha, 118
DENNER, James, 104
DENNIS, John, 137
DENNY, Walter, 125
DERITT, John, 97
  Mary, 97
DETTERS, William, 87
DEVENPORT, Johan, 5
DEVONALD, Daniel, 72
  Hannah, 72, 126
  John, 55, 72
  Judith, 72
  Mary, 72, 126
  Rachel, 72
  Sarah, 72
DEVOR, John, 28, 134
DICK, John, 103
DICKEN, James, 30, 45
DICKENSON, Joseph, 115
  Margaret, 115
DICKEY, Martha, 60
  Samuel, 116
DICKINSON, Elizabeth, 106
  Joseph, 106
DICKISON, Samuel, 138
DICKS, Nathan, 34
  Peter, 39, 56, 57, 59, 134
DICKSON, Samuel, 138
DIERS, Roger, 29
DILBECK, Abraham, 85
DILWORTH, Goe, 78
DIX, Deborah, 17
DIXON, Joseph, 78
  Sarah, 77, 78
DOBSON, Henry, 131
  John, 131

DODSON, John, 4
DONACHE, William, 92
DONALD, James, 36
DONALDSON, William, 138
DONAVAN, Elizabeth, 78
DONEGAN, David, 100
DONELSON, Florence, 65
  Mary, 65, 66
DONNEL, James, 70, 100, 135
DONNELL, Joseph, 119
DORSON, ---, 5
DOUGHERTY, Owen, 23
DOUGLAS, Elizabeth, 131
  Jeremiah, 131
DOUGLASS, Elizabeth, 137
  Jeremy, 137
  John, 77
  Sarah, 77
  William, 118
DOUHERTY, Edward, 23
DOWNER, Michael, 42
DOWNING, Thomas, 111, 113, 135
DRUIT, John, 92
DRUITT, Elizabeth, 97
  John, 97
DUBLE, Jerome, 8
DUCKER, John, 113
DUGAL, 55
DUGLAS, Elizabeth, 131
  Joseph, 131
  Mary, 131
DUN, Martha, 134
DUNBABIN, John, 4
  Margaret, 4
  Thomas, 4
DUNN, Edward, 72
  Sarah, 78
DUNWOODY, John, 115
  Susanna, 115
DUPLESE, John Bernard, 33
DUTTON, David, 55

Edward, 57
Elizabeth, 19, 76
Elizabeth Abeth, 19
Gwin, 57
Hannah, 19, 76
Harman, 41
Jacob, 19, 76
John, 4, 55, 57, 76, 103
Jonathan, 55, 127
Joseph, 19, 76
Kinsman, 19, 76
Lydia, 55
Mary, 19, 55, 57, 76
Richard, 55, 127
Robert, 76
Sarah, 55
Thomas, 55
William, 57
DWYER, Esther, 28
  Thomas, 28

-E-
EACHES, Elizabeth, 43
EACHUS, Alice, 45
  Ann, 45
  Daniel, 45
  Elizabeth, 45
  Enoch, 45
  John, 45
  Robert, 45
  William, 45
EAKIN, Jane, 130
EARL, John, 24, 33, 123
EASE, Edward, 49
EASTO, John, 53
EAVENSON, Grace, 10, 18, 80, 116, 121, 131
  Jacob, 116, 121
  Joseph, 71, 116, 121, 131
  Katherine, 91
  Mary, 90
  Nathaniel, 90
  Phebe, 116
  Ralph, 18, 57, 80, 91, 116, 121

INDEX

Richard, 43, 79, 90, 91
EBERNATHY, James, 101
EBY, Dorus, 42
  John, 42
ECKHOFF, David, 51
EDGE, Abigail, 17, 62
  Hannah, 17
  Jacob, 17
  Jane, 17
  John, 17, 23, 70
  Mary, 70
  Sarah, 17
EDMOND, Thomas, 61
EDMONSTON, Mary, 83
  Robert, 83
EDMUNDS, Thomas, 99
EDWARDS, Edward, 70, 92
  Elizabeth, 92, 104
  Hannah, 104
  Jane, 12, 104
  Jemima, 83
  John, 25, 104, 143
  Joseph, 11, 111
  Lettice, 104
  Margaret, 92
  Mary, 11, 104
  Owen, 92
  Richard, 10, 83, 88, 92, 104, 132
  Sessil, 92
  Sibilla, 25
  Susanna, 104
  Thomas Owen, 92
  William, 12
EFFORD, Thomas, 22
ELDRIDGE, Mary, 67, 116, 141
  Obadiah, 116
  Thomas, 67
ELGAR, Elizabeth, 68
  Joseph, 67, 68
  Margaret, 68
  Mary, 67, 68
  Susanna, 68
  Thomas, 68
ELLAM, John, 88
ELLEMAN, John, 35
ELLIMAN, John, 54

ELLIOT, Hannah, 117
ELLIOTT, Abraham, 132
  Benjamin, 132
  Enoch, 95
  Joseph, 132
  Samuel, 132
ELLIS, Benjamin, 37, 47, 108, 112
  Bridget, 108
  Eleanor, 104
  Evan, 37, 69, 108, 112
  Humphrey, 104
  Jane, 104
  Jeremiah, 104
  Joseph, 37, 108
  Lydia, 37, 108, 112
  Margaret, 104
  Mary, 104
  Perthiana, 104
  Rachel, 104
  Rebecca, 37, 108
  Sarah, 69, 104, 112, 113
  Subilnus, 104
  Subilynus, 104
  Thomas, 37
  William, 37, 47
ELLY, Joseph, 1, 3
ELWELL, Richard, 1
ELY, Joseph, 27
EMANUEL, David, 81, 101
EMBRUGH, John, 26
EMERSON, Lambert, 49
EMMICH, Abraham, 39
EMMIT, Abraham, 38, 58, 123
EMMITT, Abraham, 50
  David, 50
  Jane, 5 0
  Josiah, 50
  Josias, 50
  Sarah, 50
  William, 50
ENGERS, Jacob, 140
ENGLE, Ann, 35, 79
  Frederick, 79
  John, 79
  Mary, 79

Paul, 79
Susanna, 79
ENGLISH, Hannah, 28
  John, 28
  Joseph, 28
  Rachel, 28
  Thomas, 28
  William, 28
ENOCH, David, 47
ENTRIKEN, George, 77, 93
ERANSON, Joseph, 66
ERWIN, Edward, 44
  James, 90
  Robert, 44
  Sarah, 44
  William, 11, 88, 90
ESTAUGH, John, 40
EVAN, Anne, 144
  Daniel, 7, 144
  Griffith, 135
  Isabel, 84
  James, 84
  Jane, 84
  John, 3, 72, 84, 100
  Mary, 44, 135, 144
  Morris, 144
  Robert, 84
  Thomas, 54
EVANS, Aaron, 136
  Amos, 83
  Anne, 144
  Cadwallader, 112, 118, 124
  Catherine, 135
  David, 72, 76, 84, 88
  Deborah, 117
  Eleanor, 86
  Elizabeth, 37
  Ellen, 82, 83
  Evan, 54, 83, 94
  George, 29, 83, 94
  Griffith, 102
  Hannah, 102, 105
  Hezekiah, 102
  Hugh, 111
  Isaac, 135
  Isabel, 84

INDEX

Jane, 83, 94, 105
Joel, 87
John, 15, 29, 44,
  61, 66, 81, 82,
  83, 94, 100
Lettis, 86
Lowry, 105
Lydia, 83, 94
Margaret, 54, 84,
  94
Mary, 44, 72, 83,
  84, 86, 94, 136,
  140
Nathan, 135
Obadiah, 102
Owen, 91, 126, 136
Peter, 83, 94
Rebecca, 102
Roger, 86
Ruth, 144
Samuel, 128
Sarah, 136
Stephen, 101
Thomas, 73, 44,
  117, 136
EVAT, Francis, 11
EVENSON, Joseph, 31,
  130
  Margaret, 31
  Ralph, 31
  Richard, 31
  Thomas, 31
EVERSON, Mary, 50
  Ralph, 17
EVITT, Mary, 73
EWING, Elizabeth, 96
  James, 96
  Jane, 96
  John, 53, 74
  Joshua, 74
  Margaret, 96
  Rebecca, 96
  Sara, 74
  Sarah, 74
  Thomas, 74, 96
  William, 74, 96
EYRE, Ann, 32
  Robert, 32
  William, 32

-F-
FABIAN, Elizabeth, 35
  Sarah, 35
  William, 35
FAGG, John, 32
FAGGS, John, 32
FAIRLAMB, Katherine,
  4, 24
  Nicholas, 3, 5, 7,
  14, 24
FAMSON, James, 89
FAROKS, John, 62
FARR, Alice, 118
  Edward, 118
  Richard, 118
  William, 118
FAWCETT, Joseph, 88
FAWKES, John, 107
FEAGAN, Rebecca, 34
FEARN, Josiah, 52,
  53, 70, 76
  Rebecca, 53, 70, 75
  Sarah, 75
FEENCERS, Mary, 14
FELL, John, 66
FEN, Jane, 54
FEREE, Ruth, 91
FERGUSON, Charles, 88
  Mary, 140
  William, 88, 140
FERN, Josiah, 35
  Sarah, 24
FERRY, Fughny, 60
FERVIS, Francis, 19
  Rachel, 19
FESTER, Mark, 46
FEW, Isaac, 70
  James, 58, 62, 70,
  80, 103
  Richard, 70
FIERRE, John, 6
  Mary, 6
FINCHER, Francis, 50,
  138
  John, 50, 65, 138
  Jonathan, 50, 138
  Mary, 138
  Susanna, 65
FINIKIN, Richard, 47
FINLER, Samuel, 6

FINLEY, Charles, 81,
  86
  John, 86
  Mary, 103
  Robert, 83, 103
  Samuel, 83
  Sarah, 103
  William, 103
FINNEY, Catherine, 98
  Lazarus, 98
  Robert, 27
  William, 120
FISHER, Elizabeth,
  135
  Francis, 135
  James, 135
  Mary, 135
  Samuel, 135
  Thomas, 135
  William, 135
FLEMING, David, 110
  James, 95
  Jane, 110
  John, 110
  Mary, 29, 35, 95
  Robert, 110
  Sarah, 78
  William, 29, 36, 95
FLING, David, 93
  William, 109
FLOWER, Edward, 48
  Enoch, 10
  John, 10, 83
  Margaret, 83
  Mary, 8 3
  Richard, 47, 83,
  126
  Sarah, 10
  Thomas, 83
  William, 10, 83
FOLWELL, Denesse, 66
  Edward, 66
  Gouldsmith
  Edward, 54
FOREMAN, John, 120
  Susanna, 120
FORGUSON, David, 108
  James, 108
FORRESTER, Ralph, 38
  Tamer, 38

INDEX

FOSTER, Francis, 101
  Mary, 101
FOULK, Esther, 123
  Stephen, 123
FOX, George, 7
FRAISER, James, 138
  Rebecca, 138
FRANCIS, Arnold, 136
  Margaret, 72
  Richard, 61
  William, 72
FRAZER, Sarah, 31
FRED, Ann, 24, 102
  Benjamin, 15, 25,
    39, 50, 59, 63,
    101
  Cathrine, 102
  John, 15, 24, 102
  Joseph, 102
  Katherine, 59
  Mary, 24, 102
  Nicholas, 15, 24,
    102
  Rachel, 15
  Sarah, 102
FREDD, Benjamin, 25,
    63, 74, 88
  Deborah, 24
  Katherine, 24
FREDERICK, Isaac, 22
  John, 9, 22
FREE, Abraham, 84
  Anne, 84
  John, 84
  Martha, 84
  Mary, 84
  William, 84
FREEMAN, Elizabeth,
    139
  John, 98
FRETWELL, Ellen, 40
FREVILLER, Catherine,
    49
FREY, Hance, 42
FRIEND, John, 45
FRINSTER, John, 104
FULTON, John, 78
FUREY, Catherine, 107
  Elizabeth, 107
  Hugh, 107
  Margaret, 107
  Mary, 107
  Thomas, 107
  William, 107
FURMAN, John, 78

-G-

GALBREATH, John, 140
GAMBLE, William, 123
GANDOVELT, Alexa, 74
GANDOVETT, Francis,
    13
GARDNER, James, 106
  John, 106
  Stephen, 109
GARRAT, Elizabeth,
    110
  Hannah, 110
  Isaac, 110
  John, 110
  Joshua, 110
  Martha, 110
  Mary, 110
  William, 110
GARRATT, Jane, 116
  John, 116
  Joseph, 116
  Nathan, 76, 116
  Samuel, 76, 116
  Thomas, 116
GARRET, John, 84
  Mary, 4
  William, 4
GARRETT, Aaron, 141
  Ann, 97
  Elizabeth, 35, 36
  George, 8, 97
  Hannah, 8, 36
  Isaac, 35, 36, 87
  Jane, 46
  Jesse, 141
  John, 33, 36, 97,
    141
  Joseph, 33, 141
  Joshua, 35, 36
  Josiah, 141
  Martha, 35, 36
  Mary, 7, 8, 35, 36,
    87
  Nathan, 85, 141
  Rebecca, 8
  Samuel, 8, 46, 53,
    62, 75, 85, 135,
    141
  Sarah, 135, 141
  Susanna, 8
  Thomas, 8, 97, 135,
    141
  William, 7, 8, 35,
    36, 97
GARTEN, John, 17, 67
  John F., 17
  Rebecca, 67
GARTRIL, John, 99,
    129, 132
GARTWRIGHT, Thomas, 9
GATCHELL, Elisha, 25,
    44, 61, 89
GATES, Josiah, 47
GATLIVE, Charles,
    111, 113
  Elizabeth, 111
  James, 111
  Margaret, 111
  Mary, 111
  Rees, 111
GAY, Robert, 89
GEARY, James, 58
GEATENBY, Ann, 114
GEERY, James, 103
GEESBRED, Henry, 56
GELASPY, William, 50,
    58
GELLSON, Mr., 55
GELSTON, Samuel, 52
GEORGE, 69
  Ellis, 108
  Jane, 35
  Lydia, 108
  Mary, 77
  Rebecca, 108
  Richard, 108
  Thomas, 4, 77
GESS, James, 131
  Joseph, 131
  Phebe, 131
GIBB, John, 83
  Samuel, 83
GIBBONS, Ann, 24, 61,
    69

INDEX

James, 3, 11, 15, 19, 24, 61, 67, 122, 124
Jane, 122
John, 19, 58, 122
Joseph, 61
Mary, 58
Rebecca, 19
Robert, 19
Sarah, 19, 58
Thomas, 122
William, 122
GIBSON, Andrew, 139
Ann, 62
Elinor, 144
John, 20
GIBY, David, 81
Elizabeth, 81
John, 81
William, 81
GIFFING, Thomas, 82, 83
GILBERT, Thomas, 121
GILBERTHARP, Ann, 8
GILKEY, Mary, 105
William, 105
GILPIN, Alice, 11
Esther, 91
George, 91
Hannah, 91
Isaac, 126
Joseph, 11, 14, 91, 131
Mary, 126
Moses, 91
Rachel, 11
Samuel, 91
Thomas, 57, 71, 94, 112, 116
GLEAVE, John, 16
GLEAVES, John, 96
GLEN, John, 113
GLENN, John, 91
GLESFORD, Esther, 99
Henry, 99
GODFREY, John, 136
GODSHETT, George, 10
GOHEEN, Anne, 128, 140
Edward, 140

John, 128
GOLDING, John, 42, 69
GOLDSMITH, Elinor, 65
John Edward, 66
GOODBOLT, Sibella, 40
GOODWIN, John, 54
Sarah, 100
Thomas, 118
GOOLD, William, 137
GOOR, John, 60
GORDON, John, 114, 122
GORE, John, 67
Margery, 67
GORSUCH, Ebenezer, 118
Hannah, 118
John, 118
Lydia, 118
Mary, 118
Rebecca, 118
Thomas, 118
William, 118, 134
GOSS, Charles, 61, 78
Evan, 78
GOTTY, Mary, 2
Sarah, 2
GOULDING, John, 3
GOWGER, Anne, 141
Elizabeth, 141
GRACE, Robert, 98
GRAGE, Martha, 106
William, 106
GRAHAM, Agnes, 120
Anne, 120
Cathrine, 120
Daniel, 124
Elizabeth, 108
Frances, 120
H. H., 142
James, 58, 120
Jane, 108
John, 108, 120
William, 108, 120
GRASHOE, Peter, 38
GRAVE, Samuel, 49
Sarah, 49
GRAY, Allen, 81
Elizabeth, 67
George, 58, 67, 86

James, 58
Loranna, 81
Mary, 58
Nigel, 58
William, 131, 137
GREAG, John, 81
GREAGHTON, John, 52
GREEN, John, 51
Rachel, 28, 51
Robert, 56
Thomas, 28
GREER, Robert, 58
GREGORY, Ann, 38
Esther, 38
John, 38
Margaret, 38
Mary, 38
Rebecca, 38
Thamer, 38
William, 38, 81
GRESWELL, David, 115
GRICE, Martha, 54
GRIEST, John, 22
GRIFFEY, Abel, 85
Gwen, 85
GRIFFIES, Evan, 140, 141
Griffith, 141
GRIFFITH, Ann, 50, 142
Benoni, 101
Catherine, 101
Christopher, 50
Daniel, 143
David, 76
Garterce, 89
Gwenllian, 143
Henry, 133
Hosea, 142
John, 50, 87, 134, 142
Jonathan, 11
Judith, 143
Mary, 141
Morris, 101, 128
Nathan, 101
Rachel, 143
Richard, 93
Solomon, 99
Thomas, 133, 143

INDEX

Timotheus, 142
William, 19, 118, 124
GRIFFITHS, Joseph, 20, 44
GRIMES, Catherine, 111
GRIMSON, William, 98
GRIST, Hannah, 64
Jacob, 64
GROGAN, Hugh, 101
GRONOW, Anne, 143
George, 143
John, 143, 144
Lewis, 143, 144
William, 143
GROVE, Ann, 32
John, 32
GRUBB, Henry, 98
Samuel, 98, 127, 139
GUESS, James, 121
Phebe, 121
GUEST, Henry, 86, 88
John, 86, 88
Sarah, 100
Thomas, 100
GUIN, Hannah, 135
Owen, 135
GUNSTON, Ann, 51
Henry, 51
GUNTER, Blanch, 129
GUTEY, Alexander, 112
Ilender, 112
GUYAN, Gavin, 123
GWEN, Robert, 58

-H-

HACKNEY, Charity, 117
Joseph, 117
HAGGATHY, Nicholas, 47
HAIL, Thomas, 85
HAINES, Jacob, 107
Jeremiah, 107
Joseph, 32, 107
Joshua, 107
Mary, 97, 107
Prudence, 107
Sarah, 107
Stephen, 107
HAINS, Isaac, 81
HAIR, Abraham, 29
HALE, Frances, 120
William, 120
HALL, Charles, 84
Dinah, 84
Elizabeth, 84
George, 84
Hannah, 84
Jacob, 95
James, 84
John, 9, 10, 82, 111, 138
Joseph, 138
Margaret, 84, 138
Mary, 9, 82, 84, 95, 103, 126
Phebe, 84
Rose, 138
Samuel, 3, 82, 84
Sarah, 9, 84
Susanna, 84
Thomas, 9, 10, 82, 98, 126
Walter, 138
William, 138
HALLIDAY, Mabel, 100
Robert, 100, 101
William, 50, 100
HALLOWAY, Mary, 64
HALLOWBURTON, John, 26
HALLOWELL, John, 40, 87
HAMETTON, Sarah, 65
HAMILL, Robert, 138
HAMILTON, John, 128
Patrick, 94
Robert, 142
William, 64
HAMMANS, William, 59
HAMMONS, William, 21, 65
HAMPTON, Simon, 108
Thomas, 31
HANBY, Daniel, 66
Elizabeth, 66
John, 26, 66
Mary, 66
Richard, 66
William, 66
HANES, Dorothy, 4
John, 4
HANGEL, Gerrard, 37
HANGELL, Katherine, 37
HANIGEN, Patrick, 116
HANNAMS, Hannah, 62
John, 63
William, 7
HANNAUM, Mary, 144
HANNUM, Ann, 11, 52, 107
Elizabeth, 52, 107
George, 11
James, 11, 107
John, 11, 52, 79, 107
Margary, 52
Margery, 11, 52, 107
Mary, 52, 107
Robert, 11, 52, 88, 107
Sarah, 11, 52, 107
HANRY, Barbary, 46
Henry, 46
Ulrich, 46
HANSON, Margaret, 139
HARLAN, Aaron, 1, 63, 140
Anne, 126
Benjamin, 55, 115
Betty, 79
Caleb, 117
Charity, 63
Deborah, 117
Dinah, 47, 48, 59
Elizabeth, 55, 63
Ezekiel, 1, 49, 55, 79, 102, 103, 106, 115, 131
George, 1, 47, 48, 59, 63, 102, 140
Hannah, 58, 79, 102, 131
Isaac, 126
Jacob, 63
James, 47, 58, 59,

INDEX

61, 79, 117
  Joel, 102
  Joseph, 55, 115,
    117, 119, 136
  Joshua, 15, 52, 63,
    78, 117, 136
  Lydia, 126
  Mary, 49, 55, 59,
    63, 102, 115, 117,
    126
  Michael, 1, 14, 47,
    102
  Rebecca, 117
  Ruth, 55, 115, 139
  Samuel, 63, 117,
    140
  Samuel
    Hollingsworth, 1
  Sarah, 117, 140
  Solomon, 48, 58, 59
  Stephen, 48, 58
  Susanna, 79, 126
  Thomas, 48, 69,
    103, 126
  William, 49, 55,
    106, 115
HARLEM, Thomas, 77
HARPER, Elizabeth,
  128
  Moses, 128
  Samuel, 88
HARR, John, 26
HARRED, Katharine, 5
HARREY, Sarah, 16
HARRIS, Ann, 65
  Edward, 7
  Elizabeth, 3
  James, 106
  John, 19, 24, 31,
    48
  Mary, 37
  Rachel, 3
  Rebecca, 3
  Robert, 106
  Rodger, 3
  Sarah, 3, 24
  William, 7, 48
HARRISON, Caleb, 27,
  96, 134
  Hannah, 27

HARROLD, Elizabeth,
  31
  Jonathan, 31
  Mary, 31
  Rachel, 31
  Richard, 31
HARRY, 134
  David, 21
  Lydia, 21
  William, 43
HARRYS, Ann, 43
  Daniel, 43
  Elizabeth, 43
  Evan, 43
  Hannah, 43
  Mary, 43
HARVEY, Anne, 125
  Benjamin, 73, 121,
    125
  Eleanor, 125
  Henry, 125
  Job, 76, 117
  John, 125
  Joseph, 81, 95, 125
  Mary, 121, 125
  Sarah, 125
  Susanna, 81
HARVY, Job, 28
HARY, William, 37
HASLUM, Richard, 86
HASTINGS, David, 113
  Henry, 17
  Jennet, 113
HATHORN, Agnes, 97
  Martha, 97
  Mary, 97
  Samuel, 97
HATTON, Hannah, 41
  Peter, 41, 68, 97
HAVARD, John, 141
HAVERD, Margaret, 82
HAWKLY, Henry, 105
HAWLEY, Joseph, 45,
  76
HAY, John, 8
HAYCOCK, Jonathan,
  20, 23
HAYDON, Andrew, 46,
  68
  Catherine, 68

  Sarah, 68
  W., 22
HAYES, Anne, 125
  Elizabeth, 125
  George, 111
  Hannah, 70
  Henry, 12, 56, 111,
    125
  Isabella, 125
  James, 125
  Jesse, 111
  Joanna, 125
  John, 125
  Jonathan, 72, 111
  Joseph, 70, 111,
    125
  Lydia, 125
  Margaret, 111, 125
  Mary, 86, 111, 125
  Rachel, 125
  Richard, 13, 19,
    111
  Ruth, 125
  Stephen, 125
  Thomas, 86
  William, 111, 125
HAYS, Henry, 51
  Richard, 12, 33, 59
HAYWARD, Adam, 120
  James, 98
  Jennett, 120
  Mary, 98
  Thomas, 67
HEACOCK, Ann, 34
  Jona, 34
  Jonathan, 16
HEAD, Benjamin, 21
  Mary, 21, 26
  Sarah, 21, 26
HEAL, Sarah, 30
HEALD, Dinah, 63
  Hannah, 96
  James, 96
  Joanna, 61
  John, 58, 95, 96
  Joseph, 58, 78, 96
  Lydia, 96
  Martha, 95, 96
  Mary, 78
  Samuel, 4, 78

INDEX

Susanna, 96
Thomas, 61, 95, 96
William, 78
HEARD, Stephen, 36
HEATH, John, 33
HEDGES, Andrew, 114
  Catharine, 71
  Charles, 71, 114
  Dorcas, 71
  Ezekiel, 114
  John, 114
  Jonas, 71
  Joseph, 71, 114
  Joshua, 71
  Josiah, 71
  Peter, 114
  Ruth, 71
  Samuel, 71
  Solomon, 71
HELSBY, Aaron, 137
  Hannah, 137
  Joan, 18
  John, 137
  Joseph, 18, 137
  Mary, 137
  Sarah, 137
HENDERSON, Anne, 120
  Daniel, 124
  David, 58, 124
  Edward, 58
  Isabel, 124
  Jane, 58
  John, 52, 55, 58, 91, 120, 124
  Joseph, 124
  Margaret, 52
  Mathew, 124
  Michael, 124
  William, 55, 124
HENDRA, Richard, 30
HENDRICK, John, 40
  Magdalen, 35
HENDRICKS, Andrew, 20
  Israel, 20
  John, 20
  Magdalena, 20
  Mary, 20
  Tobias, 10, 40, 89
HENDRICKSON,
  Albertus, 5

Albertus Steve, 5
Andrew, 22
Elinor, 22
Gabriel, 22
Helchey, 5
Henry, 22
Jacob, 22
James, 5
Johannes, 5
John, 22, 35
Katharine, 22
Katherine, 22
Maudlin, 130
Peter, 22
Rebecca, 22
Tobias, 5
HENRICKSON, John, 130
HENRY, Ann, 70
  Janes, 70
  John, 70
  Robert, 70
  Samuel, 81
  Susanna, 32
HERR, Hance, 46
HESTERMARRY,
  Margaret, 116
HETHERINTON, John, 118
HEWES, Mary, 133
  William, 133, 135
HEWS, Joseph, 130
  Margaret, 130
HEWSTON, James, 62
  Thomas, 62
HIBBARD, Josiah, 36
HIBBERD, Aaron, 109
  Anne, 120
  Benjamin, 120, 135, 136
  Elizabeth, 75, 83
  Esther, 141
  Jacob, 102, 120
  Jane, 141
  John, 120
  Joseph, 83
  Josiah, 77, 102, 120
  Phebe, 136
HIBBERT, Elizabeth, 53

Joseph, 51
HICKIN, William, 6
HICKMAN, Ann, 43, 97, 139
  Benjamin, 37, 43, 108
  Bery, 25
  Francis, 108
  John, 108, 124
  Robert, 40
HICKS, Christopher, 125
HIDDINGS, Richard, 40
  William, 40
HIDEY, Christian, 47
HIGATE, Peter, 135
HIGGINS, Annanias, 31
  Dennis, 110
HIGHET, Peter, 86
HIGHGATE, Peter, 70
HILL, James, 15
  Mary, 76, 137
  Thomas, 15, 26
  William, 9, 11, 79, 137
HILLARD, John, 71
  Thomas, 71
HIND, Elizabeth, 67
  James, 67
  John, 76
HINDE, Elizabeth, 76
  James, 77, 141
  John, 141
HINDMAN, John, 104
HINDS, Mary, 139
HINES, James, 62
HITCHING, John, 100
HOBSON, Francis, 78
HOCKLEY, Esther, 87
  Henry, 109
HOCKLY, Henry, 95
HODGE, Andrew, 70
  Samuel, 101
HODGEN, Robert, 130
HOGG, Robert, 105, 137
HOLLINGSWORTH,
  Elizabeth, 140
  Enoch, 60, 144
  George, 63

John, 24
Katherine, 24
Samuel, 63, 78, 113, 116, 125, 127, 131
Thomas, 63, 57
HOLLMAN, Charles, 21
HOLSTEN, Benjamin, 133
John, 133
HOLT, ---, 51
Moses, 51
HOOD, Ann, 8, 10
Hannah, 10
John, 1, 8, 11, 40, 53
Jonathan, 11, 44
Martha, 10, 49
Mary, 10
Sarah, 10
Thomas, 4, 10
HOODE, John, 131
HOOPER, Hannah, 142
Joshua, 142
HOOPES, Abraham, 128
Ann, 44
Joshua, 113, 124
HOOPS, Daniel, 3
HOPE, John, 59
HOPES, John, 102
Thomas, 114
HOPKIN, Mathew, 69
HOPKINS, Matthew, 137
HOPTON, Anne, 144
John, 36, 51, 133, 144
Mary, 144
Rachel, 51, 144
HORN, William, 68
HORNE, Elizabeth, 114
William, 4, 114, 141
HOSKINS, John, 8, 89
Joseph, 74, 89
Mary, 89
Ruth, 8, 89
Sarah, 89
Stephen, 89
HOULDSTON, Ann, 62
Benjamin, 62

Elizabeth, 62
Hannah, 62
John, 41, 62
Rebecca, 62
Sarah, 62, 63
HOULSTON, John, 62
HOULTON, John, 134
Martha, 74
Nathaniel, 74
HOUSE, George, 34
William, 31
HOUSTON, Christopher, 99
Esther, 99
James, 14, 89, 99
Joseph, 27, 50
Martha, 99
Robert, 99
Samuel, 99
HOWARD, Hannah, 136
Henry, 136
James, 91
John, 140
Peter, 140
Rebecca, 140
Robert, 42
Samuel, 91
Thomas, 42
HOWELL, Abraham, 77
Ann, 52, 71
David, 26, 35, 71, 81
Elizabeth, 71
Evan, 70, 75
Griffith, 26
Howell, 71, 72
Hugh, 52
Jacob, 7, 8, 17, 27, 38, 46, 78, 89
Jenkin, 82
John, 3 5
Mary, 71, 138
Mordecai, 117
Owen, 136, 138
Penelope, 26
Rachel, 41
Reece, 70, 71, 115
Reeces, 84
Rees, 11
Reynold, 83

Reynolds, 94
Sarah, 27, 70, 75, 138
Thomas, 41, 92, 138
William, 5, 15, 83
HOWRY, Barbary, 26
Wolrick, 26
HUBART, Thomas, 127
HUBBARD, John, 65
Mary, 65
HUBBERT, Alice, 101
HUDSON, El'lzabeth, 27
HUESTON, Elizaabeth, 62
HUFF, Jennet, 65
Susanna, 65
HUGH, Edward, 73
Evan, 73
Hugh, 73
Mary, 16, 73
Morgan, 73
Owen, 73
Susanna, 73
William Thomas, 73
HUGHES, Elizabeth, 126
John, 21
Samuel, 38
Thomas, 126
William, 98
HUGHS, Benjamin, 37, 66
Dorothy, 37
Edward, 37
Elizabeth, 37
Margaret, 66
Mary, 6 5
Morgan, 37
Richard, 35, 66
William, 49
HULBERT, John, 117
HUMPHREY, Anne, 137
Catharine, 138
Catherine, 81
David, 76
Esther, 138
John, 138
Jonathan, 76, 138
Joshua, 138

INDEX

Magdalen, 76, 137
Samuel, 138
Sarah, 138
HUMPHREYS, John, 3
HUMPHRY, David, 138
HUNT, Elizabeth, 117
  James, 117
  John, 117
  Joseph, 116
  Mary, 108, 117
HUNTER, Alex, 35, 67
  Esther, 53
  George, 76
  James, 76
  John, 76
  Jonathan, 53, 67
  Margaret, 76
  Margery, 67
  Mongey, 134
  Peter, 53, 76
  Peter H., 20
  Rachel, 67
  William, 76
HUNTLY, Francis, 26
HURLY, Stephen, 131
HURTEEN, William, 8 9
HUSTON, Eleanor, 119
  Thomas, 119
HUTCHISON, Alex, 46
HUTTON, Benjamin, 74
  Ephraim, 74
  John, 74
  Joseph, 2, 74
  Mary, 24, 39, 51, 74
  Nehemiah, 74
  Samuel, 74
  Sarah, 39, 51
  Thomas, 74, 101
  William, 74
HYNMAN, Robert, 111

-I-

IDDINGS, Ann, 30
  Elizabeth, 30
  John, 30
  Richard, 30, 37, 60, 65, 135
  Sarah, 30
  William, 30
IGNEW, Andrew, 51
INGRAM, George, 88
  Samuel, 111
IRELAND, Nicholas, 87
IRISCALL, Elizabeth, 38
IRWIN, David, 115
  James, 90
  Jane, 44
  John, 44
  Martha, 115
  Mary, 115
  Samuel, 115
  Theophilus, 44
  Thomas, 115
  William, 115

-J-

JACK, Andrew, 134
  Anne, 93
  Elinor, 34
  Elizabeth, 93
  Jane, 93
  John, 93
  Mary, 93
  Patrick, 34, 93
  Samuel, 93
  Thomas, 93
JACKSON, Ann, 43
  Barbara, 86, 100
  Ben, 38
  Benjamin, 38, 86, 100, 105, 133
  Ealis, 44
  Elizabeth, 65
  Ephraim, 9, 23, 41, 44, 46, 63, 65, 75
  Hannah, 44, 46
  Isaac, 25, 38, 74
  Jacob, 86, 100
  John, 53, 65
  Jonathan, 125
  Joseph, 44, 65, 74, 86, 100
  Lydia, 127
  Margaret, 86
  Mary, 25, 28, 38, 39, 49, 65, 115, 126
  Nathan, 65
  Nathaniel, 65
  Rachel, 9, 44, 65
  Robert, 53, 86, 100
  Roger, 5
  Samuel, 25, 38, 39, 43, 65, 85, 126
  Stephen, 24
  Thomas, 28, 25, 38, 42, 127
JAMES, Aaron, 61
  Abel, 92
  Anne, 16, 127
  Daniel, 71
  Elizabeth, 16, 71, 92, 133
  George, 16, 87, 101
  Griffith, 138
  Hannah, 16, 108
  Jane, 16
  John, 92, 104, 111, 140, 143
  Joseph, 33, 71, 82
  Margaret, 82
  Mary, 16, 82
  Mordecai, 16
  Morgan, 71, 82
  Morris, 127, 140
  Rachel, 91
  Samuel, 82, 91, 120
  Sarah, 16
  Sessil, 92
  Susanna, 71
  Thomas, 61, 79
  William, 54
JAMSON, Elizabeth, 112
JANE, Hannah, 62
JARMAN, Jeremiah, 19
JEFFERIES, Elizabeth, 128
JEFFERIS, Abigail, 125
  Ann, 87
  Anne, 87
  Benjamin, 86
  Eleanor, 80
  Eliza, 83
  Elizabeth, 125
  Emmor, 124
  George, 86, 103,

INDEX

108
  James, 72, 80, 86, 124
  Jane, 87
  John, 87
  Mary, 87
  Richard, 87
  Robert, 86
  Thomas, 80, 87
  William, 78, 83, 86, 132
JEFFREY, Robert, 14
JEFFRY, 68
JENKEN, John, 120
JENKIN, Anne, 101
  David, 112
  Elizabeth, 104
  Evan, 112
  Gwin, 112
  John, 104, 112
  Mary, 112
JENKINS, David, 19, 61, 74
  Enoch, 103
  Isaac, 61
  Mary, 103
  Nathaniel, 104
  Sarah, 61
  Thomas, 61
JERMAN, Elizabeth, 101
  Jerermy, 3
  John, 87, 97, 102
  Mary, 102
  Thomas, 101
JERVIS, Joseph, 17, 57
JESSOP, Robert, 77
JO, 35
JOB, Abigail, 58
  Abraham, 22, 25
  Andrew, 1, 2, 5, 22
  Caleb, 23
  Elizabeth, 23
  Enoch, 22, 58
  Hannah, 23
  Jacob, 22
  Joshua, 23
  Nathan, 22
  Patience, 23

  Thomas, 22, 25
JOHN, David, 19, 61
  Elias, 141
  Elizabeth, 141
  Enoch, 141
  Evan, 141
  Griffith, 29, 120
  Gwen, 54
  James, 140, 141
  Joshua, 141
  Morris, 87
  Owen, 35
  Rees, 87
  Samuel, 25, 44, 100, 111
  Thomas, 29, 44, 54, 101
  William, 141
JOHNS, Elizabeth, 30
JOHNSON, Abigail, 63
  Abraham, 68
  Ann, 63
  Barbara, 25
  Benjamin, 43, 63
  Caleb, 43
  Cales, 33
  David, 109
  Elizabeth, 25, 74
  Henry, 80
  Hugh, 109
  James, 15, 25, 39, 43, 63, 82, 102, 129
  John, 25, 103
  Joshua, 43, 63, 106, 138
  Kattren, 80
  Margaret, 43, 110
  Mary, 82
  Robert, 43, 63
  Sarah, 92, 106
  Thomas, 92
  William, 82
JOHNSTON, Abraham, 139
  James, 40
  John, 142
  Pattenes, 139
  William, 110
JONES, Aaron, 82

Abram, 107
Ann, 39, 56, 85, 135
Anne, 136
Arthur, 62
Benjamin, 117
Cadwallader, 86, 110
Catherine, 135
Charity, 31
David, 13, 81, 85, 110, 136, 139, 141
Dinah, 143
Edward, 105, 110, 117, 129
Eleanor, 86
Elinor, 82
Eliza, 49
Elizabeth, 28, 85
Ellen, 107
Esther, 107
Evan, 136, 139
Hannah, 117
Jacob, 93, 107
Jane, 73, 136, 143
John, 39, 55, 73, 83, 86, 94, 105, 107, 111, 117, 119, 135, 136, 139, 141, 144
Jonathan, 110
Joseph, 135
Judith, 31
Lydia, 117
Malachi, 141
Margaret, 81, 135, 143
Martha, 135
Mary, 31, 39, 56, 81, 107, 135, 139
Morgan, 60, 86
Nathaniel, 141
Nathiel, 141
Nicholas, 139
Patience, 31
Peter, 39, 56
Price, 73
Rebecca, 113
Rees, 3, 65, 143
Ress, 105

INDEX

Richard, 17, 29, 36, 45, 54, 65, 69, 72, 73, 83, 100, 101, 105, 122
Riche, 3
Robert, 15, 18, 34, 95, 101, 139
Ruth, 47, 59, 110
Samuel, 139
Sarah, 31, 117, 135, 143
Thomas, 22, 35, 37, 39, 81, 92, 141
Watkin, 140
William, 105, 106, 117, 135
JORDAN, John, 32, 119
Margaret, 119
Marth, 39
Martha, 50, 51
Mary, 50
Thomas, 119
JOY, John, 14

-K-

KARGIN, William, 125
KEASBY, Mathew, 42
KEATH, Robert, 16
KEES, John, 111
KELLER, Owen, 104
KELLY, James, 36
Joseph, 38
KENDALL, Benjamin, 57
Ellin, 103
Jane, 103
John, 103
Thomas, 103
KENDRICK, Barbary, 26
Henry, 26
Jacob, 42
Martin, 26
KER, Daniel, 118
Josiah, 99
KERLIN, Margery, 105, 120
Mary, 35, 90
Mathias, 35
Susanna, 35
KERR, Josiah, 98
KETTON, John, 58

KEY, Elizabeth, 4, 41, 96
Moses, 4, 14, 41, 57, 122
KEYSER, Nicholas, 120
KILGORE, John, 58
KILPATRICK, Anne, 125
James, 125
Robert, 125
Samuel, 125
William, 125
KIMBEL, Richard, 139
KING, James, 1, 6, 31
KINIKAN, Joseph, 52
KINIKIN, James, 52
KINNISON, Charles, 79
Edward, 79
Hannah, 79
James, 79
Mary, 79
William, 79
KINSMAN, John, 1, 19
KIRK, Alfhonsus, 2
Alphonsus, 1
Deborah, 102
Elizabeth, 3, 102, 121
Katharine, 121
Rebecca, 102
Roger, 66, 102
Samuel, 102
Timothy, 102, 104
William, 21, 82, 102, 121
KIRKPATRICK, Andrew, 139
KIRKUM, Robert, 109
KITCHEN, John, 15
KNOWLS, Francis, 54
KOWELL, Rees, 71
KYLE, Jeremiah, 141
KYLL, Robert, 135

-L-

LACKEY, Alexander, 133
LACY, William, 61
LAMBE, Mammas, 115
LAMEY, Matthias, 139
LAMPLUGH, Jacob, 92,

109
John, 92
Mary, 92
Nathaniel, 6, 109
Samuel, 92, 121
William, 92
LANG, William, 44, 113
LANGWORTHY, Henry, 37
Jenesis, 36
Margaret, 37
Mary, 37
Sarah, 37
William, 37
LARKE, Donti, 53
Thomas, 53
LARKIN, Esther, 122
John, 122
LAROW, George, 106
LASLEY, Sarah, 125
LATIMORE, Arthur, 107
James, 107
LATTIMER, Arthur, 130
LAWRENCE, Daniel, 12, 93
David, 12
Edward, 23, 29
Evan, 93
Henry, 12, 13
John, 95
Joshua, 54
Margaret, 129
Mary, 29, 95
Rachel, 12, 93
Sarah, 93
Thomas, 12, 13, 93
William, 13, 93
LE TORT, Ann, 18
James, 18
LEA, Anthony, 15, 44
George, 54
Hannah, 33, 73
Isaac, 33, 46, 51, 54, 73, 80
John, 16, 21, 33, 42, 73
LECOCK, John, 49
LEEPER, Isabella, 123
LEES, George, 116
LEET, Edward, 92

166 INDEX

Mary, 92
LEONARD, Daniel, 115
  George, 4, 27
  Ruth, 115
LEPER, Alexander, 99
  Andrew, 99
  Blanch, 99
  Gayen, 99
  Gien, 99
  Isabel, 99
  James, 99
LERRETT, Edward, 88
  Susanna, 88
LESTER, Daniel M., 28
LEVIS, Abraham, 82
  Elizabeth, 14, 68,
    75, 133
  John, 68, 144
  Joseph, 68, 110
  Lydia, 133
  Mary, 133
  Samuel, 1, 14, 15,
    23, 33, 35, 36,
    40, 41, 46, 47,
    68, 75, 76, 119,
    130, 133
  Sarah, 14, 133
  William, 1, 14, 15,
    33, 68, 75, 96,
    97, 119, 133
LEWELLIN, David, 23
  John David, 37
  Margaret, 23
LEWELYN, Elizabet,
  100
LEWIN, Edward, 12
  Mary, 12, 13
LEWIS, Abraham, 37,
  85
  Abram, 37
  Ambrose, 54
  Amos, 56, 104
  Ann, 21, 54, 72
  Anne, 21
  Catharine, 35
  David, 13, 26
  Elizabeth, 9, 35
  Ellen, 72, 115
  Ellin, 123
  Ellis, 9, 47, 50,
    56, 59, 61, 78, 80
  Enoch, 104
  Enos, 54
  Evan, 7, 16, 21,
    22, 35, 71, 72
  Gideon, 54
  Griffith, 7, 35,
    49, 76, 81, 137
  Hannah, 21, 23,
    116, 141
  Harry, 23
  Henry, 6, 13, 19,
    23, 29, 37, 65,
    114
  Jabez, 84
  Jane, 26, 65, 82
  Japhet, 54
  Japheth, 54
  Jephtha, 54
  Jeptha, 54
  John, 97, 109, 141
  Jonathan, 72, 115
  Joseph, 5, 14, 54
  Josiah, 108, 127
  Lewis, 21, 71, 72,
    82, 84, 115
  Lowry, 54
  Magdalen, 137
  Margaret, 81
  Mary, 21, 35, 37,
    41, 50, 71, 72,
    76, 81, 85, 115
  Maud, 35
  Mordecai, 72, 84,
    115, 123
  Nathan, 54
  Phebe, 46
  Phineas, 21
  Rebecca, 76, 81
  Robert, 71, 84, 96,
    119
  Samuel, 19, 76, 81,
    82, 85, 107, 137
  Sarah, 23
  Stephen, 64
  Thomas, 65, 75
  William, 6, 11, 17,
    23, 54, 71, 72,
    76, 81, 82, 95,
    115, 116, 124
LIGHTER, Samuel, 31
LIGHTFOOT, Jacob, 28,
  49, 62, 89
  Margaret, 28, 62
  Michael, 28, 39,
    51, 62, 78
  Samuel, 28, 62
  Thomas, 28, 78
  William, 28, 78
LILLY, Samuel, 127
LINDLEY, Elinor, 32
  Elizabeth, 32
  Hannah, 32
  James, 32
  Jonathan, 32
  Margarey, 32
  Rachel, 32
  Robert, 32
  Thomas, 32
  William, 32, 57
LINDLY, James, 67
  Thomas, 74
LINLEY, Deborah, 100
LINN, Charles, 82,
  129
  David, 115
  Hugh, 99, 129, 132,
    135
  Jennet, 99
  Jennett, 129
  John, 129
  Margaret, 99, 129
  Martha, 99, 129
LINSEY, Margaret, 96
  William, 96
LINTON, Robert, 56
LINVAL, Thomas, 20
LINVILL, Dinah, 74
LINVILLE, Thomas, 13
LITTLER, John, 36, 53
  Joshua, 36
  Mincher, 36
  Rachel, 36
  Samuel, 36
  Sarah, 36
LIVINGSTON, Robert,
  56
LLEWELLIN, John, 140
LLEWELLY, Parry, 88
LLOYD, David, 5, 54

Elizabeth, 75
Erasmus, 75
Grace, 54
Humphrey, 141
John, 75
Lydia, 75
Thomas, 30, 75, 88
LLOYED, Thomas, 127
LOBB, Benjamin, 53, 74
LOCKHART, John, 54
LOCKRY, James, 52
LOGAN, Ann, 119
  Anne, 119
  James, 119
  Jane, 119
  Katherine, 119
LONG, Allen, 133
  Matthew, 134
  Rebecca, 132, 133
LOUGHLIN, Terrence, 106
LOUGHRIG, Robert, 99
LOVE, John, 81
  Robert, 45
  Samuel, 113
LOWDEN, Jane, 125
LOWDIN, John, 6
  Margaret, 6
LOWDON, Jane, 90
  William, 34
LOWE, Joshua, 40
  Margaret, 38
LOWNES, Ann, 96
  Benanuel, 96
  Esther, 96
  George, 96
  James, 96, 97
  Mary, 96
  Susanna, 12
LOWRY, William, 87, 98
LUSK, David, 131, 132
  Hugh, 131
  James, 131
  John, 116, 131, 132
  Martha, 131
  Mary, 131
  Samuel, 131
  Sarah, 131, 132

William, 131
LYNCH, Michael, 111

-M-
MCAFEE, William, 123
MCARTHUR, Alice, 139
MCCAIN, Susanna, 52
  Thomas, 52
  William, 52
MCCALL, Thomas, 90
  William, 90
MCCLANARAN, Robert, 81
MCCLEHAN, John, 58
MCCLELLAN, Daniel, 97
  Elizabeth, 96, 104
  James, 113
  John, 96
  Martha, 113
  Robert, 96, 104
  Samuel, 113
  William, 96
MCCLELLAND,
  Elizabeth, 96
MCCLEMAN, Robert, 92
MCCLENAHAN, John, 52
MCCLINTOCK, Mary, 129
MCCLUER, Thomas, 132
MCCLURE, William, 144
MCCONAHEE, Janet, 128
  Robert, 128
MCCONNEL, Alexander, 52
MCCONNELL, Elizabeth, 52
MCCORD, George, 99
MCCORMOCK, Henry, 134
MCCOY, Ann, 101
MCCUIN, John, 104
  Sarah, 104
MCCULLOCH, William, 130
MCCULLOGH, Nathaniel, 140
  Thomas, 96
MCCULLOUGH, William, 126
MCDANIEL, Janet, 44
  John, 44
MCDONALD, Alexander,

114
  Isaac, 114
  John, 114
  Mary, 114
MCDOWELL, Joseph, 99, 115
  Robert, 114
MCELDUFF, Jane, 99
MCFARSON, Daniel, 2, 96
MCGARR, Michael, 106
MCGEE, Bryan, 101
MCGHEE, Mary, 134
  Susanna, 134
MCGLOUGHLIN, Jane, 86
MCGUINNES, Sarah, 139
MCGUISTON, David, 61
MCHENDY, Barnet, 59
MACK, Ann, 80
  William, 80
MACKALL, Mary, 57
MCKANE, Thomas, 55
  William, 55
MCKEAN, Thomas, 52
  Thomas, 112
  William, 52
MCKEE, Alex, 84
MCKEEB, Catherine, 84
MCKEEVER, Daniel, 143
MACKEY, Frances, 70
  James, 70
  Robert, 115
MACKEYD, Robert, 138
MACKFARSON, William, 136
MCKILLIP, John, 39
MCKIM, Thomas, 90
MCKINLEY, Matthew, 47
  Samuel, 44, 47
MCKNIGHT, William, 106
MCKOLLAGH, Edmond, 52
MCKRAKIN, John, 39
MCLAUGHLIN, Jane, 100
  Robert, 130
MACLERY, John, 67
MCLISTER, Daniel, 15
MCMICHAEL, Jorg, 129
MCMULLIN, James, 31
MCNABB, John, 103

MCNEES, Samuel, 99
MCNEILE, Archibald, 113
  Elizabeth, 113
MCNEILL, Elizabeth, 126
MCNIGHT, Jorg, 129
MCNUTT, Robert, 78
MCTEAR, Henry, 109
  Margaret, 109
MCTEER, Henry, 67
  James, 67
MADCAFF, William, 29
MADDOCK, James, 80
  Nathan, 2
MAFFITT, Samuel, 97
  William, 97
MAGEE, Ann, 77
  Richard, 77
MAGIL, Daniel, 45
MAGILL, Daniel, 26
MAGINLY, James, 33
MAGU, Archibald, 67
MAGUIRE, Cormick, 138
  Thomas, 111, 138
MAKOMSON, Andrew, 104
MALIN, David, 122
  Isaac, 37, 48
  Jacob, 37
  Randal, 37
  Sarah, 73
  Susanna, 37
  Thomas, 73
  William, 122
MANSON, William, 126
MARGARET, 69
MARIA, 89
MARIO, Elizabeth, 21
MARIS, Alice, 144
  Ann, 96
  Elizabeth, 123
  George, 71, 96, 144
  Hannah, 144
  James, 144
  Jane, 82
  John, 11, 16, 44, 60, 144
  Jonathan, 123
  Joseph, 123
  Mary, 144
  Richard, 22, 96, 123
  Sarah, 144
  Simon, 72
  Susanna, 144
MARK, James, 46, 64, 87
MARLBOROUGH, Mary, 49
  Thomas, 49
MARLIN, John, 97
MARRAN, John, 112
MARRIS, John, 62
MARRS, George, 124
MARSDEN, Richard, 10
MARSH, Deborah, 118
  Eleanor, 118
  Elizabeth, 118
  Gravener, 98
  Gravner, 118
  Henry, 98, 118, 132
  James, 118
  John, 118
  Lydia, 118
  Mary, 118
  Rachel, 118
  Sarah, 118
  Susanna, 118
  William, 20, 98, 118
MARSHALL, Abraham, 29, 49, 101
  Ann, 49, 50
  Benjamin, 49, 96
  Elizabeth, 117
  Hannah, 93, 96, 97
  Joanna, 49
  John, 8, 36, 49, 50, 97, 117, 119, 144
  Margaret, 49
  Martha, 97
  Mary, 38, 97, 144
  Samuel, 94
  Sarah, 7, 8, 49
  Thomas, 41, 49, 93, 94, 96
  William, 38, 50
MARTEN, Elizabeth, 14
  Feoffe, 14
  Hannah, 13
  John, 14
  Mary, 13
  Thomas, 14, 17
MARTER, Elizabeth, 13
  Sarah, 13
MARTIN, Ann, 11, 13
  Elizabeth, 129
  George, 66
  John, 18, 109, 138, 140
  Jonathan, 140
  Joseph, 38
  Lydia, 138
  Mary, 1, 13, 26
  Mathias, 28
  Phebe, 138, 140
  Ruth, 38, 49
  Stephen, 13
  Thomas, 96
  Walter, 2, 13
MASON, Richard, 3
MASSAR, Elizabeth, 24
  Mary, 24
MASSER, Joseph, 24
  Thomas, 24
MASSEY, Hannah, 12
  James, 71
  Mordecai, 6, 12, 29, 39, 58, 68
  Thomas, 71, 124
MATHER, James, 89, 120
  John, 47, 89, 120
  Joseph, 89
  Margaret, 105
  Ruth, 89
MATHERS, Peter, 94
MATHEW, George, 46
MATHEWS, Chidley, 71
  Edward, 52
  Francis, 47
  Margaret, 15
  Margret, 15
  Mary, 1
MATHIAS, John, 70
MATTISON, Benjamin, 31
MATTSON, Hannah, 118
MAXEL, Jane, 3
  John, 3

INDEX

MAXWELL, Elish, 32
MELCHOR, John, 143
MELIN, Isaac, 30
  Susanna, 142
  William, 142
MENARN, Jane, 58
MENDENHALL, Aaron,
  18, 88
  Alice, 47, 59
  Ann, 93
  Anne, 93, 133
  Benjamin, 18, 46,
    61, 93, 112
  Caleb, 59, 93, 133
  Eales, 19
  Hannah, 93, 112,
    141
  John, 9, 11, 24, 26
  Joseph, 59, 61, 91,
    93, 96, 97, 107,
    119, 129, 132
  Joshua, 112, 131
  Lydia, 112
  Martha, 112
  Mary, 112
  Moses, 19, 47, 59,
    93
  Phebe, 47, 59
  Robert, 93, 97
  Ruth, 91
  Samuel, 112
MERCER, Ann, 7, 62
  Daniel, 7, 140
  Elizabeth, 7
  Hannah, 46
  Joseph, 7, 62
  Mary, 7, 129
  Rebecca, 140
  Thomas, 7, 140
MEREDITH, David, 49,
  129
  Eleanor, 97
  John, 142, 143
  Simon, 25
MERICK, Rachel, 21
MESSAR, Robert, 37
MIER, Woolrich, 40
MILEN, Martin, 40
MILINOR, Mary, 113
MILLARD, Benjamin,
  136
  Henry, 8
  Joseph, 136
MILLEMAN, Gasper, 85
  Peter, 85
MILLER, Andrew, 50
  Ann, 39
  Barbary, 42
  Benjamin, 106, 115
  David, 50
  Deborah, 106, 59
  Dorothy, 59
  Elinor, 2, 39
  Elizabeth, 2, 39,
    106
  Gayen, 2, 106, 115
  Gayon, 3
  George, 59, 106,
    107, 115, 137
  Henry, 17, 37, 42,
    46, 59
  Hugh, 101
  Isaac, 39
  James, 106, 2, 39,
    49t 50, 51, 59,
    74, 88, 92, 106,
    107, 133, 142
  Jane, 106
  Jesse, 106, 59
  John, 106, 2, 39,
    59, 115
  Joseph, 106, 2, 39,
    106
  Katherine, 28
  Margaret, 100, 107,
    115
  Martha, 2
  Mary, 106, 2, 50
  Mathew, 101
  Patrick, 106, 115,
    119
  Rachel, 24, 25, 59,
    107
  Rebecca, 106
  Robert, 106
  Samuel, 106, 63,
    106
  Sarah, 106, 2, 25,
    59, 106
  Susanna, 2, 39, 50,
    51
  William, 2, 39, 48,
    50, 51, 74, 78,
    106, 107, 115, 142
MILLHOUS, Thomas, 78
MILLISON, Ann, 118
  Hannah, 118
  James, 118
  John, 118
  Jonathan, 118
  Mary, 118
MILLS, Jane, 128
  John, 128
  Mary, 140
  Thomas, 23
MILLSOM, Edward, 58
MILLSON, Edward, 58
  John, 58
  Kathrine, 58
  Mary, 58
  Thomas, 58
MILSAM, Edward, 31
MINHALL, Isaac, 39
MINIARD, John, 96
MINNER, Mary, 15
MINSHALL, Aaron, 56,
  93
  Edward, 56
  Griffith, 56
  Griffithe, 69
  Hannah, 77
  Isaac, 56, 75
  Jacob, 56, 69
  John, 35, 69, 77
  Joshua, 77
  Martha, 77
  Moses, 69, 110
  Rebecca, 55, 56, 75
  Samuel, 56
  Sarah, 59, 69
  Thomas, 27, 56, 59,
    69
MITCHELL, Thomas, 97
MOLE, James, 27, 112
MONEY, James, 70
MONTGOMERY, Alice, 50
  Ann, 50
  Hugh, 101
  Joan, 50
  John, 50

INDEX

Margaret, 50
Michael, 50
Robert, 50
William, 50
MOOR, Andrew, 60
   Elizabeth, 39, 100
   Francis, 39
   James, 27, 39
   Jane, 39
   Jean, 39
   Jenneh, 39
   John, 84, 103
   Margaret, 39
   Mary, 80
   Thomas, 73, 80
MOORE, Andrew, 70
   Benjamin, 35
   David, 32
   Eliza, 60
   Elizabeth, 67, 97
   Ephraim, 40
   Gabriel, 67
   John, 35, 66, 97, 111, 129
   Joseph, 84
   Mary, 32, 51, 67
   Patrick, 27
   Rachel, 100
   Samuel, 67
   Stacy, 35
   Thomas, 35, 126
   William, 120
MOOT, James, 107
MORDAH, Robert, 112
MORGAN, Ann, 11
   Anne, 91
   Benjamin, 11
   Blanch, 11
   David, 42, 54, 65, 136
   Edward, 87
   Elizabeth, 11, 127
   Evan, 8, 54
   George, 83, 127
   Hugh, 41, 42
   Jacob, 120
   John, 41, 54, 112, 120
   Joseph, 42
   Lettis, 86

Margaret, 54
Mary, 41, 42, 130
Mordecai, 11
Moses, 42
Robert, 42
Sarah, 42, 120
Susanna, 127
Thomas, 54, 86, 104
William, 135
MORIS, Ann, 21
   Elizabeth, 21
   Mary, 21
   Richard, 21
MORISON, Alexander, 123
MORRIS, Ann, 135
   Anthony, 61, 63
   David, 18, 19, 45, 47
   Elinor, 55
   Elizabeth, 18
   Evan, 55
   Gennett, 128
   Hannah, 102
   Isaac, 18
   Jennett, 143
   John, 23, 102, 135
   Jonathan, 18, 45, 47, 102
   Katherine, 102
   Lettice, 87
   Mary, 19, 47, 102
   Mordecai, 18, 102, 107
   Phebe, 102
   Samuel, 87, 102
   Terrence, 97
   Theophilus, 143
   Thomas, 55, 63
MORRISON, John, 38
   Rebecca, 88, 102
   William, 88
MORTIMER, James, 23
MORTON, Andrew, 22, 140
   Bridgett, 80
   David, 85
   Eleanor, 85
   John, 26, 95
   Margret, 22

Mary, 26, 35
Mathias, 80
MORTONSON, Andrew, 12
   David, 12
   John, 12
   Katherine, 12
   Margaret, 12
   Mathias, 12
   Morton, 12
MOULDER, Benjamin, 22, 55
   Deborah, 55
   Elizabeth, 55
   Joseph, 55, 82
   Mary, 55
   Peter, 55
   Prudence, 55
   Robert, 55
   Thomas, 55
   William, 55
MULCASTER, John, 139
MULLIN, Martha, 50
MUNDAY, Henry, 92
MUNROE, Jonathan, 57
MURPHY, Mary, 36
MURRAH, Barbara, 52
MURRAY, Barbara, 55
MUSGRAVE, Aaron, 129
   Abraham, 6
   Elizabeth, 29
   Gainer, 6
   John, 29, 60
   Moses, 29
MUSGROVE, Jean, 29
   John, 29
MYER, Woolrich, 40
MYLEN, John, 42

-N-

NATSELLERS, Catharine, 25
   Christian, 25
   Dorothy, 25
   Elizabeth, 25
   Margaret, 25
   Mary, 25
   Mathias, 25
   Otto, 25
NAYLE, Deborah, 30
   Henry, 3, 14, 30

NEDDHAM, John, 56
NEED, Ann, 14
  Joseph, 102
NEEDHAM, John, 55,
  130, 134
NEELDS, John, 55
NEELY, John, 113, 134
  Robert, 113
  William, 134
NEIL, John, 30, 103
  William, 103
NEILD, Elizabeth, 26
  John, 26
NEILL, William, 58,
  106
NESBIT, James, 60
NESMITH, Arthur, 137
NETHERMERK,
  Christian, 25
  Gunrod, 25
NETSELLIS, Mathias,
  12
NEWLIN, Edith, 91
  Elizabeth, 9, 56,
  80, 98
  Jane, 56, 80
  Jean, 56
  Jemima, 9
  John, 9, 50, 56,
  80, 91, 94, 98
  Joseph, 56, 80, 98
  Kezia, 9
  Martha, 56, 80
  Mary, 9, 50, 52,
  56, 80, 98
  Nathan, 14, 19, 50,
  56, 80, 98
  Nathaniel, 6, 7, 9,
  34, 50, 52, 56,
  80, 98, 118
  Nicholas, 4, 9, 52,
  56, 68, 80, 98
  Rachel, 56
  Sarah, 50
NICHLAND, Joseph, 144
  Rachel, 144
NICHOLAS, Amos, 45
  Ann, 45
  Edward, 45
  John, 45

NICHOLS, Mary, 38
  William, 38
NICHOLSON, Mary, 97
  William, 97
NICKALSON, Richard,
  124
NICKINSON, John, 121
  Sarah, 121
NICKLES, Hannah, 28
NICKLIN, Joseph, 144
  Mary, 144
NICKOLS, John, 126
NIXON, Thomas, 64
NOBLET, Francis, 71
NOBLETT, Anne, 92
  Margaret, 92
  William, 92
NOOKS, Ann, 66
  Elizabeth, 66
  Jane, 66
  Joseph, 66
  Mary, 66
  Moses, 66
  Ruth, 66
  Sarah, 66
  Susanna, 66
  Thomas, 66
  William, 66
NORBURY, Elizabeth,
  108
  Philip, 108
NORREY, John, 105
NORTH, Judith, 137
  Thomas, 137
NORTHUM, Margret, 8
  William, 8
NOSSET, Jane, 100
NOWLAN, Hannah, 128
  James, 128
  John, 128
  William, 128
NOX, Catherine, 104
  William, 104
NUBROUGH, John, 72
NUTT, Ann, 87
  Rebecca, 87, 88
  Samuel, 4, 34, 67,
  88

-O-
OATWAY, George, 23
OBORN, Ann, 79
  Elizabeth, 57
  Hannah, 57, 79
  Henry, 57, 79
  Susanna, 57, 79
  William, 57
OBOURN, Henry, 63
OBRYAN, Henry, 106
ODGEN, Esther, 96
  Samuel, 96
OGDEN, Martha, 38
OGDON, David, 38
  Jonathan, 38
  Joseph, 38
  Katherine, 38
OLDHAM, Mary, 116
  Robert, 42
  William, 84
OLIVER, John, 94
  William, 44
O'NEAL, Abigail, 134
ORAN, John, 73, 83
  Mary, 73
ORSON, Ann, 99
  George, 99
  Rachel, 99
  Tamson, 99
  William, 35, 99
OSBORN, Frances, 98
  Richard, 31
  Samuel, 98
OSBORNE, Samuel, 130
OSBOURN, Henry, 60
O'SHANACH, Owen, 133
OSSON, Damson, 66
OTLEY, Thomas, 71
OWEN, Alexander, 29
  David, 143
  Elinor, 29
  Elizabeth, 110
  John, 28
  Owen, 12, 54
  Rachel, 29
  Rebecca, 29
  Richard, 28
  William, 76, 100,
  143
OWENS, Ann, 42

Elizabeth, 101
Owen, 42
Thomas, 101

-P-
PACKER, John, 117
PAGETT, Elizabeth, 9
  William, 9
PAINE, Thomas, 135
PAINSTON, James, 64
PAINTER, Susanna, 34
PALMER, Eleanor, 10
  John, 10, 41, 52,
    79, 105, 116, 120,
    121, 131
  Margaret, 88
  Martha, 41
  Mary, 105, 107, 120
PARK, Ann, 92
  Arthur, 45, 92
  David, 92
  Jean, 92
  John, 92
  Joseph, 92
  Mary, 92
  Samuel, 92
PARKE, Arthur, 28, 45
  Robert, 81
  Thomas, 81, 108
PARKER, Abraham, 78
  Ann, 143
  Jo., 11, 142
  John, 2, 7, 47, 76
  Joseph, 19, 27, 38,
    47, 55, 57, 62,
    64, 76, 89, 95,
    110, 122, 134
  Martha, 4, 7, 8,
    47, 76, 77, 87
  Mary, 47, 76
  Richard, 4, 7, 8,
    12, 13, 25, 28,
    36, 47, 53, 64, 76
  William, 7, 47, 76
PARKS, Benjamin, 65
  John, 65
  Richard, 65
  Samuel, 65
  Susanna, 65
  Thomas, 65

PARRY, Ann, 30
  David, 30, 95, 134,
    136, 140
  Elizabeth, 30, 134
  Emma, 95
  Esther, 134
  Hannah, 95, 134
  Hester, 30
  James, 30
  John, 30, 64, 72,
    88, 95, 134
  Lettice, 30, 134
  Lewellin, 45
  Margaret, 30, 95,
    134
  Martha, 95
  Mary, 30, 95, 134
  Rowland, 95, 134
  Sarah, 95
  Susanna, 95
  Tobitha, 134
PARSONS, Joseph, 121
PARTRIDGE, Edward, 27
PARVIN, Thomas, 61
PASCHALL, Hannah, 64
  John, 47, 110, 117
  Margaret, 47
  Thomas, 47
  William, 30, 48,
    49, 64
PASSMORE, Augustine,
    131
  Elizabeth, 3
  Enoch, 119
  George, 119, 131
  Hannah, 119
  Humphrey, 119
  John, 3, 131
  Joseph, 119
  Lydia, 119
  Mary, 96, 119, 131
  Phebe, 119
  Samuel, 131
  Susanna, 119
  William, 118, 131
PATRICK, Blanch, 99
PATTEN, James, 108
  John, 108
  Robert, 108
  William, 86, 108

PATTERSON, Anne, 97
  James, 23, 97
  John, 60
  Margaret, 97
  Mary, 97
  Rebecca, 97
  Robert, 137
  Samuel, 97
  William, 12, 126
PATTESON, Samuel, 108
PATTISON, Agnes, 112
  James, 112
  Margaret, 112
  Mary, 112
  Mole, 112
  Robert, 112
PATTON, Robert, 61
  Thomas, 137
PAULL, John, 89
  Margaret, 89
PAXTON, Alexander, 77
PEARCE, George, 9
  Henry, 52
PEARSON, Abel, 68
  Benjamin, 24, 25,
    28, 35, 40, 46,
    48, 53, 116, 121
  Enoch, 39, 40, 68
  Francis, 33
  Isaac, 110, 125,
    141
  John, 23, 51, 68,
    125, 136
  Lawrence, 68
  Margery, 68
  Mary, 68
  Robert, 68, 121
  Samuel, 40
  Sarah, 68
  Thomas, 68, 87, 125
  Thomas, 87, 121
  William, 40
PEDRICK, Elizabeth,
    24
  Philip, 124
PEERSALL, John, 100
PEIRCE, Ann, 69
  Caleb, 29, 60, 94,
    108, 122
  Elizabeth, 30, 69

Gainer, 7, 69
George, 7, 15, 69
Henry, 30, 97, 107,
  108, 110
Joseph, 91
Joshua, 7
Rachel, 91, 107
Sarah, 69, 128
Susanna, 69
PEIRSAL, Jeremiah,
  102
Jeremy, 102
Mary, 102
PEIRSEY, Thomas, 90
PEIRSON, Thomas, 2,
  24
PENAL, Mary, 24
PENICK, Christopher,
  57
Edward, 56, 57
Hannah, 56, 57
John, 6, 56, 57
Joshua, 56, 57
Roman, 56
Ruth, 56
Sarah, 56, 57
PENIL, William, 5
PENISTON, Roger, 15
PENNELL, Alice, 46
Ann, 44, 46
Elizabeth, 44
Evan, 115
Hannah, 46, 72, 115
James, 46
Jane, 46
Joseph, 36, 44, 46
Joshua, 82, 115
Mary, 44, 46
Robert, 46
Thomas, 46, 109,
  118, 122, 137
William, 46, 55
PENNICK, John, 53
PENNIL, Robert, 14
William, 7
PENNOCK, Christopher,
  56
Jane, 105
Joseph, 68, 138
Mary, 68

Nathaniel, 121, 138
William, 133
PENTLAND, Alexander,
  78
George, 78
John, 78
PERESS, Eliza, 74
PERKINS, Ann, 25
Caleb, 25
Humphrey, 42
Jane, 42
Mary, 56, 57
PERRY, Isabella, 114
PERTT, Simon, 40
PETERS, William, 92
PETERSON, William,
  115
PHIBO, Joseph, 15
PHILIP, Daniel, 6
Owen, 135
PHILIPS, Henry, 127
Mary, 19
Susanna, 127
PHILLIPS, Griffith, 7
Jemnnet, 7
John, 7, 82
Mary, 32, 82
Nathaniel, 76
Thomas, 32
William, 19, 82
PHIPPS, Joseph, 8,
  137
Samuel, 63
Sarah, 105
PHIPS, Mary, 8
PICKLES, Nathan, 35
PIERCE, Ann, 69
Caleb, 69
Gainer, 69, 128
George, 11, 69
Hannah, 69
Henry, 31, 68, 121
Joshua, 69
Mary, 69
PIERSON, Rose, 7
Thomas, 7, 18
PIGOT, Jeremiah, 5
John, 5
Margary, 5
Patience, 5

PIKE, Elizabeth, 110
John, 54, 83
PILE, Betsy, 100
Joseph, 100
Mary, 100
Nicholas, 137
Ralph, 100
William, 100
PILKINGTON, Ann, 73
Edward, 15, 23, 73
Hannah, 73
Mary, 73
Sarah, 73
Thomas, 73
PIM, William, 106,
  135
PIPE, Samuel, 78
PIPER, Mary, 123
PLAIN, John, 142
Mary, 142
PLAMER, William, 19
PLUMOR, Eleanor, 79
Robert, 41, 79
PLUMSTEAD, Clement,
  118
POAK, John, 114
POCK, Ann, 135
James, 135
John, 135
Thomas, 135
PORTER, Andrew, 88
David, 91, 113
James, 88, 91
John, 101
Mary, 80
William, 36, 119,
  120
POSTLETHWAIT, John,
  40
POSTON, Ann, 133
Anthony, 133
John, 133, 134
Martha, 134
Robert, 133
POTTER, Ann, 124
John, 124
POTTS, Jere., 97
Jeremiah, 102
John, 101, 105
Ruth, 87

POULSTON, Mary, 4
  Thomas, 4
POWELL, Ann, 21
  Anna, 1, 2, 3
  Benjamin, 3
  David, 21, 72
  Elizabeth, 21, 69, 103
  Evan, 61, 77, 78
  John, 3, 17, 19, 21, 40, 54, 69, 70, 103
  Joseph, 1, 3, 26, 69, 70, 99, 103
  Lydia, 21
  Margaret, 3, 69
  Mary, 3, 21, 69, 103
  Samuel, 21, 118
  Sarah, 1, 69
  Susanna, 1, 69
  Thomas, 1, 21 3, 5, 69, 103
  William, 70
POWER, James, 79
  Pierce, 18, 29
PRATT, Alice, 108
  Ann, 108
  Joseph, 12, 108, 118
  Mary, 108
PRESSOLL, Valentin, 98
PRESTON, John, 65
PREW, Betty, 33
  Caleb, 33
  Hannah, 33
  Mary, 33
  Sarah, 33
  Susanna, 33
PRICE, Ann, 80, 81, 93
  David, 25
  Elizabeth, 37, 81, 108
  James, 73
  Jane, 73
  John, 80
  Margaret, 73
  Martha, 81

Rees, 37, 93
Rice, 81
  Sarah, 81
  Tamer, 73
  Thomas, 60, 66, 80
  William, 80
PRICHARD, Catherine, 143
  Daniel, 143
  Joanna, 143
  Levi, 143
  Rebecca, 143
PRIOR, Silas, 22
PRISE, Susanna, 73
PRITCHARD, Elizabeth, 18
  Philip, 40
  Richard, 18
  Samuel, 40
PRITCHET, John, 128
PRITCHETT, Ann, 64
  Edward, 41, 80
  Elizabeth, 41
  Richard, 41
  Samuel, 41
PROWELL, James, 143
  Rachel, 143
  Thomas, 143
PRYOR, Elizabeth, 133
  James, 61
  Joanna, 61
  Joseph, 61
  Silas, 61
  Susanna, 61
PUGH, David, 25
  Edward, 30
  Hugh, 25, 110, 117
  James, 19, 25
  Joan, 25
  John, 25, 101, 143
  Jonathan, 111
  Mary, 110
  Sible, 25
  Thomas, 25
PULE, Robert, 19
PULFORD, Thomas, 62
PULLAN, Francis, 69
PULLEN, Francis, 7, 10, 11
  Kate, 1

PUMMELL, Henry, 106
PURTELL, James, 31
PUSEY, Caleb, 34
  Cathrine, 144
  Eliza, 19
  Elizabeth, 54, 105
  Hannah, 105
  John, 105
  Joshua, 105, 131, 138
  Mary, 105, 131
  William, 19, 54, 105
  William L. Caleb, 34
PUTCON, Peter, 25
PYLE, Alice, 11
  Ann, 9, 71, 72
  Betty, 127
  Daniel, 51, 60, 77
  Edith, 9
  Eleanor, 127
  Elizabeth, 1, 11
  Hannah, 1
  Isaac, 71, 72
  Jacob, 11
  James, 68
  Job, 71, 72
  John, 51, 60, 71, 72, 127, 142
  Joseph, 9, 51, 56, 58, 127
  Mary, 51, 60, 71, 72, 77, 100, 127
  Moses, 125, 138
  Nicholas, 4, 9, 68, 131
  Olive, 43, 71, 72
  Phebe, 71, 72
  Philip, 68
  Ralph, 15, 68, 127
  Robert, 1, 9, 11, 19, 36, 49, 51, 125
  Samuel, 9, 19, 29, 51, 63, 68, 69, 117, 127, 131
  Sarah, 1, 9, 51, 58, 68, 108, 127
  Susanna, 51, 59,

60, 133
William, 4, 9, 11,
21, 29, 43, 51,
71, 72, 127
PYLES, Joseph, 17
Ralph, 17
Robert, 17
PYLY, Nicholas, 13
William, 10

-Q-
QUARRY, Will, 139
QUINN, William, 91
QULAND, John, 63

-R-
RACHEL, 52
RADFORD, Clement, 141
RAMBO, Catherine, 48
Mary, 75
Mounce, 138
RAMMELS, James, 115
RAMSEY, Samuel, 124
William, 112
RANKEN, Alexander, 112
John, 143
Mary, 112
RANKIN, John, 94
Samuel, 94
RASAMOND, Nathan, 109
RATTEW, Mary, 70
Thomas, 70
William, 4, 9, 54, 63
RAWLINS, Thomas, 32
RAWSON, Andrew, 58
Charles, 97
Elizabeth, 97
Gantree, 58
John, 88
Lydia, 88
Margaret, 88
Martha, 88
Mary, 88
Sarah, 58
READ, John, 113, 124
Margaret, 113
William, 50
READING, Mathew, 104

REARDON, Margaret, 88
Martin, 88
REDDICK, Robert, 81
REECE, Caleb, 124
David, 123, 124
Jane, 124
John, 12, 37, 124, 142
Joseph, 124
Morris, 142
Thomas, 37, 124
REED, David, 134
Eleanor, 119
Elizabeth, 44
James, 44
John, 44, 119
William, 137, 142
REES, Catharine, 101
Evan, 136
James, 120
John, 73, 89, 101, 136, 138, 141
Lettice, 72
Lewis, 73
Penelope, 143
Reece, 73
Samuel, 72
REESE, Grace, 85
REGISTER, David, 16
REILLY, William, 109
REINEY, Hugh, 38
REMINGTON, John, 5
RENTFROES, John, 42
RETTEW, William, 118
REYNERS, Hannah, 73
Isaac, 73
J., 47
Joseph, 35, 73
Mary, 73
Rachel, 73
Stephen, 73
REYNOLDS, Agnes, 36
David, 36
Deborah, 26
Francis, 25, 42
Hannah, 26
Henry, 16, 25, 26, 42, 62, 66, 99, 107, 132, 89
James, 133

John, 26, 47
Margaret, 26, 52, 133
Martha, 36, 47
Mary, 36
Prudence, 26, 42
Robert, 36, 52
William, 16, 26, 36, 104
RHOADS, Adam, 76
Benjamin, 109
Catherine, 75, 109
Elizabeth, 75, 114
Hannah, 75
John, 76
Joseph, 75
Katherine, 75, 76
Mary, 75
Samuel, 75
Sarah, 75
RHODES, Katharine, 24
RICE, Catherine, 35
Edward, 35
Evan, 83
Henry, 35
John, 6, 35
Mary, 83
RICHARD, John, 45
Nathaniel, 3
Rowland, 144
Samuel, 144
Thomas, 87
RICHARDS, Dinah, 110
Edward, 74
Hugh, 110
Isaac, 141
Joseph, 74, 84
Margaret, 53
Mary, 74
Nathaniel, 3, 6, 51, 53, 141
Richard, 110, 129
William, 6, 141, 142
RICHARDSON, Anne, 95
Catherine, 30
Elinor, 30
Elizabeth, 30
Isaac, 30
John, 30, 95

INDEX

Lettice, 95
Martha, 30
Mary, 30, 95, 122
Robert, 23, 88
Thomas, 95
RICHISON, Richard, 79
RICKESON, Richard, 75
RICKISON, Ann, 49
  Richard, 49
RIGG, John, 111, 112
RILEY, John, 88, 92, 132, 10, 84, 122
  Margaret, 88
  Mary, 132
RING, Bathsheba, 114
  Benjamin, 114
  Elizabeth, 126
  Nathaniel, 91
RITTER, Frederick, 37
  George, 37
  John, 37
  Margaret, 37
  Paul, 37
  Sarah, 37
ROADES, Adam, 37, 121
  Elizabeth, 88
  Jacob, 121
  John, 88
  Joseph, 121
  Katharine, 121
  Mary, 121
  Samuel, 121
ROADS, Abigail, 58
  Adam, 62
  Benjamin, 42
  Elizabeth, 42
  John, 58
  Joseph, 58
  Rebecca, 122
ROBB, George, 126
  Margaret, 126
  Mary, 126
  Robert, 126
  Sarah, 126
  William, 126
ROBERTS, Aubrey, 86, 85
  Awbrey, 105, 128, 137, 141
  Hannah, 43

Hugh, 87
John, 121
Jonathan, 105
King, 93
Robert, 43
Ruth, 128
Thomas, 81
ROBERTSON, John, 56
ROBINETT, Allen, 13
  Samuel, 69
ROBINSON, Aaron, 119
  Catherine, 40
  George, 9, 10
  John, 10, 94, 119
  Joseph, 55
  Margaret, 10
  Martha, 31, 119
  Mary, 127, 119
  Miriam, 119
  Ralph, 127
  Richard, 127
  Ruth, 119
  Sarah, 9, 10
  Sicilly, 10
  Thomas, 40
ROBISON, Andrew, 19
  Elizabeth, 23
  George, 38
  John, 23, 62
  Mathew, 62
  William, 89
ROCKERFIELD, John, 67
  Martin, 67
  Mary, 67
ROCKETT, Henry, 139
RODES, Christian, 82
  Hannah, 82
  Jacob, 82
  Joseph, 82
ROE, Elizabeth, 40
  Joseph, 39, 40
  Priscilla, 40
  Sarah, 40
  William, 50
ROGERS, Deborah, 102
  Elizabeth, 113
  Mary, 68
  Nicholas, 4, 68
  Philip, 113, 102
  Thomas, 48, 65, 68, 102

ROMAN, Dorothy, 49
  Hannah, 13
  Jacob, 13, 43, 49
  Jonah, 49
  Joshua, 49
  Martha, 49
  Mary, 49
  Philip, 43, 49
  Rachel, 49
  Robert, 13, 49
  Ruth, 57
  Thomas, 49
  William, 49
RONELLS, James, 138
ROSE, John, 30
ROSS, Alexander, 36
  Eleanor, 119
  Jane, 119
  John, 52, 114, 119
  Margaret, 119
  Thomas, 119
ROSSEN, Andrew, 58
  Sarah, 58
ROUTH, Francis, 13, 26
ROWAN, Abraham, 27
  Ann, 27
  Cornelius, 27
  David, 27
  James, 134
  William, 113
ROWELS, Elizabeth, 127
  John, 127
ROWLAND, Anne, 127
  Catherine, 127
  Elizabeth, 144
  James, 83, 127
  John, 87, 127, 144
  Letitia, 127
  William, 127, 144
RUDDELL, Ann, 84
  John, 42, 84, 36, 61
  Mary, 8 4
RUDDERFORD, Samuel, 88
RUE, William, 34
RUHYON, Richard, 79

RUMFORD, Jonathan, 117
RUNDELS, Richard, 90
RUSSEL, Jacob, 114
  Joseph, 114
  Sarah, 114
RUSSELL, Alexander, 128, 132
  Dinah, 122
  Edward, 124
  Elizabeth, 132
  Isabel, 132
RUTHLEDGE, William, 84
RYALL, Peter, 32
RYAN, Richard, 88, 108
RYANDEL, ---, 52

-S-
SALKELD, Agnes, 12, 75, 89, 109, 110
  David, 89, 109
  Jane, 89
  John, 3, 5, 7, 19, 21, 24, 62, 75, 89, 109
  Joseph, 89
  Mary, 89, 109
  Thomas, 89
  William, 89, 109
SAMPLE, William, 86
SAMUEL, Michael, 49
SANDELANDS, Jonas, 30, 32, 42
  Mary, 30, 42
SANFORD, Robert, 20
SANGER, James, 78
SAVAGE, Anna, 105
  Anne, 104
  Joseph, 87, 95
  Martha, 105
  Mary, 105
  Ruth, 105
  Samuel, 43, 87, 95, 104, 109
  Thomas, 87, 105
SAVILL, Samuel, 117, 127, 144
SCALL, William, 49

SCARLET, Anne, 126
  Else, 126
  Hannah, 76
  Humphrey, 20, 84, 126, 132
  John, 126, 132
  Mary, 132
  Nathaniel, 76, 126
  Phebe, 126, 19
  Shadrach, 126
SCARLETT, Nathaniel, 94
  Shadrack, 94
SCARRIOT, Joseph, 34
SCAWTHORN, Mary, 54
  Nathan, 54
SCHOLAR, Jane, 16
  John, 16
SCHOLLAR, Jane, 23
  John, 23
SCOT, Francis, 136
  Martha, 136
SCOTT, Adam, 143
  Archibald, 52
  John, 6, 32, 64, 67
  Mary, 6
  Samuel, 10, 46, 77
  Sarah, 107, 144
  Thomas, 84
SEAL, Caleb, 107, 129, 132
  Hannah, 91, 107, 129
  Joseph, 91, 107, 129, 132
  Joshua, 107, 129, 132
  Rachel, 107, 129, 132
  William, 90, 107, 125, 129, 132
SEARES, Catherine, 120
SEED, Abigail, 139
  Edward E., 128
SELBY, Joseph, 6, 9, 12, 21, 34, 39, 47
  Mary, 29
SELLARS, Samuel, 64
SELLER, Samuel, 36,

49, 76, 119
SELLERS, Ann, 64
  Anna, 64
  Samuel, 4, 21, 64, 77, 87
  Sarah, 4, 7, 8, 87
SELLUS, Samuel, 53
SEYMOUR, Israel, 102
SHANK, Christian, 32
  Henry, 32
SHANTON, Rachel, 62
SHARMAN, Ann, 88
  Eleanor, 88
  Elizabeth, 88
  Judith, 88
  Robert, 63, 88
  Sarah, 88
SHARP, Abigail, 9, 131
  Ann, 142
  Benjamin, 142
  Elizabeth, 51, 131, 142
  George, 142
  John, 78, 106, 137, 142
  Joseph, 9, 108, 131
  Margaret, 138
  Mary, 9, 131, 142
  Samuel, 131
  Thomas, 142
  William, 92, 138, 88
SHARPE, William, 13
SHARPLESS, Caleb, 19
  Daniel, 136
  David, 130
  Elizabeth, 142
  Esther, 130
  Hannah, 136
  James, 130
  John, 8, 17, 19, 41, 46, 72, 136, 142
  Lydia, 130
  Mary, 130, 142
  Rachel, 130
  Samuel, 60
  Sarah, 130
SHAW, Anthony, 77, 89

INDEX

John, 65
Mary, 89
SHELDON, Joseph, 123
SHELLEY, Elizabeth, 122
  James, 122
  Lydia, 122
  Nathan, 122
  Roger, 122
SHELLY, Roger, 79
SHELTON, Elinor, 37
  John, 93
SHEPARD, Matildith, 109
SHEWARD, Elizabeth, 58
  James, 58
  Jane, 59
SHEWIN, Hannah, 50
SHIELDS, James, 94
SHIELL, Arthur, 89
  Mary, 89
SHIPLEY, Eliza, 68
  Mary, 40
  Thomas, 123
  William, 40, 97
SHIPPARD, Robert, 112
SHIVERS, Samuel, 53
SHOEMAKER, Jenkin David, 87
SHORTLIDGE, Hannah, 93
  James, 93
SHUAN, Sarah, 113
SIDWELL, Abraham, 99
  Anne, 99
  Elizabeth, 48
  Henry, 99
  Hugh, 48, 99
  Isaac, 99
  Jacob, 99
  John, 48, 99
  Joseph, 99
  Mary, 99
  Richard, 48, 99
SILL, Ann, 74
  James, 75, 108
SIMCOCK, Benjamin, 8
  Jacob, 8, 16, 40, 44, 62
  John, 2, 44
  Joseph, 8
  Sarah, 8
SIMONSON, Henry, 131
  Stephen, 131
  Susanna, 131
  William, 131
SIMPSON, George, 10, 122
  Ruth, 122
  Zebulon, 122
SIMSON, William, 90
SINCLAIR, Mary, 31, 91
  Robert, 91
SINKLER, Aaron, 98
  Elizabeth, 98
  Mary, 98
  Robert, 98
  William, 98
SKEARS, Catherine, 105
SKEEN, Joseph, 34
SKELTON, John, 68
  Susanna, 108
SLACK, John, 88
SLEIGH, Joseph, 129
SLOAN, Isabel, 81
  John, 81
  Patrick, 81
SLONE, George, 118
  Hannah, 118
SMART, Mary, 117
SMEDDLEY, Sarah, 21
SMEDLEY, George, 21, 23, 59, 136
  Joshua, 136
  Sarah, 6
  Thomas, 6, 23, 25, 37, 69, 79
SMEDLY, Thomas, 16
SMITH, Abraham, 116
  Andrew, 31
  Ann, 21, 34, 116
  Edward, 40, 41, 53
  Elinor, 144
  Elizabeth, 7, 21, 40, 41
  Hance Adam, 91
  Hannah, 144
  Isaac, 144
  James, 38, 50, 58, 70, 78, 116, 144
  Jane, 7, 8, 54
  John, 4, 7, 8, 24, 34, 40, 47, 53, 59, 62, 87, 109, 115, 116, 144
  Joice, 40
  Lydia, 34
  Martha, 4, 40, 53
  Mary, 4, 21, 40, 41, 46, 52, 53, 60, 107, 116, 144
  Richard, 21
  Robb, 39
  Robert, 38, 50, 70, 119
  Samuel, 80
  Sarah, 4, 40
  Simon, 40
  Thomas, 11, 21, 52, 54, 60, 116, 144
  William, 1, 4, 7, 8, 36, 40, 44, 46, 53, 65, 80, 120, 136, 144
SNADDEN, William, 104
SOUTH, Elizabeth, 84
SPARK, Mary, 3
SPEAKMAN, Ann, 64
  Micajah, 134
  Thomas, 43, 64
  Thomas, 59
SPEARY, James, 105
SPENCER, Dinah, 48
  Elizabeth, 48
  John, 38, 48
  Thomas, 48
SPIKMAN, Thomas, 43
SPRAY, Christopher, 14, 85
  Elizabeth, 85
  James, 85
  Jane, 85
  Mary, 85
  Phebe, 85
  Rebecca, 85
  Sarah, 85

Thomas, 85
SPRINGER,
    Christopher, 114
SPRINT, Jacob, 65
SPRUCE, John, 86
    Lydia, 86
SQUIBB, Mary, 78
    Robert, 96
SQUIRE, Adam, 66
STACKHOUSE, Sarah, 64
STANTON, John, 90
STAPLER, James, 26
    Stephen, 26
STAPLETON, Rachel,
    56, 57
STARR, Deborah, 24
    Isaac, 62
    James, 2, 39
    Jer., 48
    Jeremiah, 48
    Margaret, 49
    Mary, 28
STEDMAN, John, 18
    Joseph, 18
STEDWELL, Dinah, 35
    Ebenezer, 35
    Thomas, 35
STEEL, Andrew, 38, 70
    Elizabeth, 76, 135
    Francis, 135
    James, 112, 135
    Jennet, 135
    John, 70, 94, 100,
        125, 135
    Joseph, 58, 86
    Martha, 112, 125
    Mary, 125
    Moses, 112
    Ninian, 125
    Robert, 70, 125
    Samuel, 125
    Susana, 125
    William, 125, 135
STEEN, John, 97
    Margaret, 97
STEPHENS, Edward, 4
STEPHENSON, Agnes,
    137
    James, 137
    John, 137

William, 137
STEVENS, Mary, 27
    Robert, 10, 14, 131
STEVENSON, Gaien, 15
    Grace, 15, 46
    Robert, 103
STEWART, Alexander, 3
    Ann, 3, 59
    Hugh, 56
    Jane, 3
    John, 3
    Mary, 3
    Robert, 3
    Walter, 124
STIDMAN, Joseph, 62
STOCK, Mary, 90
STOCKIN, Ann, 49
    Francis, 49
    Thomas, 49
STOCKTON, Frances,
    114
    Thomas, 114
STONEMAN, Nicholas,
    32
STORY, Richard, 4, 22
STREATOR, James, 13
    Robert, 13
STRINGER, Daniel, 83
    George, 83
    John, 83
    Martha, 83
    William, 83
STRODE, John, 59,
    105, 111, 133
    Thomas, 63
STRONG, Sarah, 38
STUART, George, 94,
    126
    Robert, 102
SULLIVAN, Darby, 133
    Margaret, 139
SUMERILL, David, 123
    Jean, 123
SUMMERS, Thomas, 109
SWAFER, Ann, 17
    Jacob, 17
    Joseph, 17
    Mary, 17
    Phebe, 17
    Rebecca, 17

Sarah, 17
Thomas, 17
William, 17
SWAFFER, Ann, 41
    Elizabeth, 1
    Hannah, 41
    Jacob, 41
    James, 1
    Joseph, 41, 96
    Mary, 41
    Phebe, 41
    Sarah, 41
    Thomas, 41
    William, 1, 41
SWAIN, Elizabeth, 73,
    111
    Sarah, 50, 138
    William, 34, 50,
        73, 111
SWAINE, Edward, 21
    Francis, 21
    Jean, 21
    Sarah, 21
    William, 21
SWARFER, Sarah, 136
    William, 136
SWARFORD, Phebe, 136
SWOAP, John, 42
    Yoast, 42
SYKES, Johanna, 141
    Mary, 141

-T-
TALBOT, Benjamin, 20,
    85
    Elizabeth, 20, 85
    Hannah, 85
    John, 20, 85
    Joseph, 20, 85
    Mary, 20
    Rachel, 20
    Sarah, 20, 85
TALFORD, Joseph, 124
TASEY, Ann, 60
TATE, Magnus, 39, 79
TATNALL, Anne, 134
    Edward, 134
    Elizabeth, 134
    Jonathan, 134
    Thomas, 97, 134

INDEX

TAYLOR, ---, 33
  Abiah, 34, 138
  Ann, 43, 63, 64
  Benjamin, 30, 87,
    95, 117
  Catharine, 94, 117
  Christopher, 30
  Deborah, 108
  Eleanor, 119
  Elizabeth, 93, 94,
    117
  Ellen, 30
  Esther, 29, 137
  Hannah, 29, 30, 62,
    117, 119
  Isaac, 7, 9, 10,
    11, 21, 29, 43,
    49, 93, 116, 126
  Israel, 30
  Jacob, 43, 69, 90,
    108, 127
  Jeremiah, 64, 117
  Jo., 29
  John, 7, 14, 17,
    18, 21, 25, 34,
    43, 49, 53, 60,
    63, 72, 77, 93,
    94, 100, 105, 111,
    113, 117, 118,
    119, 126, 127,
    140, 142, 133
  Jonathan, 29
  Joseph, 15, 43, 59,
    64, 87, 93, 94,
    115, 117, 119
  Margaret, 93
  Martha, 30, 43, 49,
    72
  Mary, 29, 43, 62,
    64, 91, 117, 126,
    137
  Mordecai, 29, 93,
    137
  Nathan, 93, 118,
    137
  Pete, 39
  Peter, 17, 55, 56,
    63, 93, 137
  Phebe, 63, 64, 113,
    140

Philip, 4, 29, 33,
  43, 58, 63, 64
Rachel, 15
Richard, 94, 117,
  119
Robert, 29, 46
Samuel, 17, 30, 40,
  117, 138
Sarah, 11, 21, 93,
  117, 119, 137
Simeon, 33
Stephen, 63, 140
Susanna, 29, 94,
  117
Thomas, 11, 16, 26,
  29, 30, 33, 62,
  113, 123
William, 17
TEMPLE, Hannah, 117
  William, 117
TEMPLIN, William, 111
TERRET, Edward, 33
TERRETT, Edward, 131
  Elizabeth, 131
  Mary, 131
  Peter, 131
TERRY, 129
TEST, John, 12
  Margaret, 12
  Thomas, 12
THATCHER, Jonathan,
  67
  Richard, 67, 130
  Sarah, 18
  Zerubabel, 18
THOMAS, Ann, 47
  Anne, 105
  Daniel, 23
  David, 10, 11, 12,
    28, 40, 53, 55,
    62, 71, 85, 88,
    102, 105
  Edward, 30
  Elinor, 55
  Elizabeth, 23, 71,
    85, 86, 117, 144
  Evan, 70, 85
  Ezekiel, 71
  Grace, 117, 7
  Gwen, 23, 71

Hannah, 117, 121
Isaac, 140
Jacob, 144
James, 3, 42, 64,
  73, 109
Jane, 75
John, 23, 37, 143
Joseph, 37
Joshua, 23
Katharine, 121
Lewis, 37, 80, 87
Margaret, 71, 109,
  130
Martha, 57
Mary, 71, 77, 85,
  105, 117, 140
Michael, 82
Nathan, 144
Owen, 32, 54, 55,
  69, 83, 92, 94,
  111, 139
Philip, 71, 105,
  101
Philips, 105
Reece, 33, 61, 63
Richard, 3, 7, 17,
  25, 110, 111, 117
Sarah, 10, 37, 110,
  125
Solomon, 105
Susanna, 37
Thomas, 75, 82,
  101, 105, 108,
  110, 130
Watkin, 86
William, 64, 81,
  85, 87, 125
THOMLINSON, Samuel,
  10
THOMPSON, Alexander,
  114
John, 111, 114,
  136, 99
Joseph, 133
Joshua, 122, 136
Lidia, 22
Margaret, 41
Margery, 68, 136
Mary, 114
Mathew, 99

INDEX

Mordecai, 113
Moses, 136
Peter, 68, 136
Samuel, 99
Sarah, 136
Thomas, 136
THOMSON, Aaron, 122
Daniel, 122
Jane, 122
Joshua, 122, 123
Mary, 122, 123
Moses, 122
Ralph, 31
THORNBURY, Elizabeth, 106
Robert, 124
Susanna, 124
Thomas, 106
TIPPING, Robert, 79, 82, 109
TITUS, Sarah, 63
TODD, James, 4
John, 4
TODHUNTER, Ann, 25
John, 3, 25
Margaret, 3, 25
Mary, 25
Sarah, 3
TOMKINS, John, 57
TOMLINSON, Benjamin, 46
Mary, 46
Samuel, 7
TOOBY, John, 29
Mary, 29
TOOL, Garret, 66
TOS, John, 51
TOWNSEND, Amos, 62
Ann, 62
Hannah, 60
James, 60, 126
John, 63, 71, 91, 118, 140, 63
Joseph, 10, 21, 34, 72
Mary, 62
Nathaniel, 63
Phebe, 140
Rachel, 140
Sarah, 63, 126

Thomas, 62, 63, 140
TRAGO, Hannah, 17
Jacob, 17
John, 17
Mary, 17
Rachel, 17
William, 17
TRANTAR, Hester, 100
TRANTER, Priscilla, 108
Richard, 108
Samuel, 108
TRAVILLA, Hannah, 64
TREECE, Anne, 120
Thomas, 120
TREESE, Joshua, 134
Thomas, 134
TREGO, Elizabeth, 121
James, 121
Peter, 93
TREHEARN, Catherine, 89
William, 89
TREHERN, William, 89
TREVILLER, Ann, 15, 33
Henry, 15, 33
James, 14, 15, 33
Katherine, 15
Mary, 33
Richard, 15, 80
Thomas, 33, 80
William, 49
TRIMBLE, Ann, 105, 120
Hugh, 129
Mary, 105, 121
William, 121, 131
TROAK, Ann, 80
John, 80
TROUP, Capt., 137
TUNECLIFF, Isaac, 40
TURNER, Charles, 14, 79, 115
Dorothy, 51
Eleanor, 90, 125
Eliza, 106
George, 51, 59, 137, 133
James, 51, 59

John, 8, 67
Mary, 139
Sarah, 67, 85
William, 90, 106
TYLER, Deborah, 10
Esther, 10
John, 3, 8, 10
Katherine, 10
William, 10
TYSON, Morgan, 30

-U-

UNDERHILL, Hannah, 63
UNDERWOOD, Alen, 43
James, 15
Lydia, 139
Thomas, 139

-V-

VALLELEY, Arthur, 38
VANCE, Andrew, 61, 74
Thomas, 141
William, 141
VANCULIN, George, 22
VANLEER, Bernhard, 53
VASTOW, John, 9
VAUGHAN, Thomas, 104
VENABLE, Richard, 134
VENAMAN, Isabel, 5
VERNON, Aaron, 51, 136
Abraham, 94
Ann, 18, 41
Anne, 90, 94
Eleanor, 101
Elizabeth, 108
Hannah, 27, 94, 140
Isaac, 45, 79, 94, 140
Jacob, 17, 27, 41, 94, 134
Joseph, 27, 85, 130, 134, 19
Lydia, 85, 134
Mary, 64, 94
Nathaniel, 85
Randle, 27
Sarah, 27, 94
Thomas, 17, 21, 41, 85, 100, 106, 130,

INDEX

134
VESTAL, Elizabeth, 5
 William, 5
VICHAN, Abednego, 23
 Griffith, 23
 Thomas, 23
VINING, Benjamin, 15
VOGAN, Hugh, 104

-W-
WADE, Ann, 118
 John, 34, 80
 Robert, 80
 Thomas, 118
WADKIN, Evan, 85
 Mary, 105
WAIT, Moses, 126
WALDERON, Cheyneyd, 23
WALDRUM, John, 95
 Mary, 95
WALKER, Alex, 110
 Alexander, 130
 Andrew, 90
 Anne, 99
 Enoch, 101
 Gabriel, 90
 Isaac, 90
 James, 90, 130
 Jane, 90
 John, 90, 115
 Joseph, 90
 Margaret, 101, 130
 Mary, 90, 101
 Nathaniel, 90, 113
 Robecca, 90
 Sarah, 101
WALL, Absalom, 124
 Ann, 82
 James, 52
 John, 98, 123, 124
 Joseph, 38
 Martha, 52
 Mary, 38, 123
 Phebe, 98
WALLACE, David, 50
WALLIS, Dorothy, 4
 James, 9
 John, 4
WALLN, Richard, 8

WALN, Mary, 115
WALTER, Ann, 121
 Elizabeth, 60, 61, 98
 Jane, 116
 John, 29, 60, 61
 Joseph, 116, 121
 Martha, 60
 Mary, 60, 61
 Rachel, 80, 98
 Thomas, 121
 William, 60, 98
WARD, Hannah, 88
 Sarah, 123
 Thomas, 34, 123
 Timothy, 66, 88
WARNER, Sarah, 118
WARREN, Mathew, 74
WARRILAW, John, 3
WASHBORN, Jane, 109
 John, 109
 Nicholas, 109
 Richard, 109
 Samuel, 109
 Sarah, 109
WATSON, John, 85
 Jonathan, 21
 William, 90
WAUGH, William, 52, 55
WAY, Ann, 52
 Benjamin, 29
 Caleb, 29
 Edward, 120
 Elizabeth, 29
 Francis, 29
 Jacob, 29, 52, 107
 James, 29
 Jane, 120
 John, 52, 107
 Joseph, 29, 116
 Joshua, 29
 Martha, 140
 Robert, 18, 29, 107
 Sarah, 52
WAYNE, Abraham, 89
 Anne, 89
 Anthony, 89
 Francis, 76, 89
 Gabriel, 89

 Hannah, 89
 Humphre, 89
 Isaac, 89
 John, 89
 Mary, 89
 Sarah, 89
 William, 89
WEAIT, Moses, 85
WEAVER, Eliza, 80
 Elizabeth, 54
 Joshua, 102
 Mary, 40, 80
 Richard, 80
 William, 40
WEBB, Ann, 123
 Benjamin, 14
 Daniel, 14, 55, 102, 115
 Elizabeth, 11, 14, 102
 Esther, 14
 Ezekiel, 103
 George, 103
 Hannah, 73
 James, 11, 14, 60
 John, 14
 Joseph, 14, 32, 73, 87, 123, 144
 Joshua, 103
 Mary, 11, 14, 55, 73, 102, 103, 115
 Rebecca, 117
 Richard, 11, 14, 15
 Samuel, 11
 Sarah, 14, 73
 William, 11, 14, 15, 33, 43, 55, 59, 60, 69, 77, 78, 103, 116, 117, 126
WEBBER, Jacob, 73
WEBLE, William, 3
WEBSTE, William, 124
WEBSTER, Thomas, 124
 William, 21
WEIGHT, Thomas, 36
WELCH, Thomas, 137
WELDON, Benjamin, 84
 Jacob, 20
 John, 24, 41, 84

INDEX

Joseph, 11, 84
Margaret, 84
William, 35, 55
WELLDON, Elizabeth, 106
John, 106
WELLS, Hannah, 28
Jean, 28
John, 28
WELSON, John, 92
WEST, Deborah, 16
John, 16, 68, 96
Mary, 14
Sarah, 68
Susanna, 133
Thomas, 11, 16, 71, 133, 144
William, 16
WESTON, Thomas, 3
WETHERILL, Catherine, 141
WHAREY, Margaret, 121
WHARLEY, Daniel, 1
WHARREY, David, 116
James, 116
WHELEN, Anne, 140
Dennis, 140
WHITACRE, Mary, 84
Peter, 91
Robert, 84
WHITAKER, Abel, 20
Charles, 15
Edward, 20, 79
Hannah, 20
James, 14, 20
Lydia, 56, 57
Mary, 20
Sarah, 20
WHITE, Alexander, 86, 112
Ann, 81
Arthur, 20
Catherine, 114
David, 112
Elizabeth, 31, 55, 61, 115
James, 110
Jane, 112
Jean, 81, 112
John, 22, 31, 81,
98, 112, 114
Joseph, 61, 93, 112
Mary, 22
Peter, 28
Robert, 49
Samuel, 31, 91
Sarah, 61
Stephen, 115
Susana, 112
Thomas, 81, 114
William, 22, 55, 98
WHITEKAR, Edward, 76
WHITEKER, Edward, 126
Susanna, 126
WHITELY, Edward, 102
Frances, 102
James, 102
John, 101, 102
Margaret, 102
Robert, 102
William, 102
WHITESIDE, Elizabeth, 84
Robert, 84
WHITING, Samuel, 53
WHITSITT, George, 78
Rebecca, 78
WHITTAKER, Ann, 44
Charles, 44
Elizabeth, 44
Hannah, 44
Mary, 44
Samuel, 44
Sarah, 44
Susanna, 44
WHITTING, Anne, 111
Benjamin, 111
Elizabeth, 111
Hannah, 111
John, 111
Mary, 111
Richard, 55, 72, 83, 111
Thomas, 111
WHITTINGTON, Hannah, 18
Samuel, 18
WHITTSITT, Richard, 78
WHITTYMAN, William, 46
WICKERSHAM, Abigail, 33, 39
Alice, 51
Ann, 33, 51
Elizabeth, 51
Hannah, 33
Isaac, 51, 106
James, 51
Jane, 51
John, 21, 33, 51, 106
Richard, 33, 51
Robert, 33
Sarah, 33
Thomas, 33, 51
William, 51
WIDDOWS, James, 43
WIDEMAN, Abraham, 136
Luce, 136
WILCOCKS, Susanna, 32
WILCOCKSEN, Elizabeth, 91
George, 91
WILCOCKSON, Elizabeth, 95
WILEY, Abigail, 28, 49
Allen, 143
Betty, 143
David, 114
John, 28, 49
Thomas, 104
WILKINSON, Edward, 34
Elizabeth, 135
Joseph, 135
WILLEY, Joseph, 62
WILLIAM, Ann, 93
Anne, 93
Daniel, 13
David, 29, 66, 92, 111
Elinor, 13
Frances, 40
John, 30, 75, 143
Joseph, 72
Lettice, 30, 72
Lewis, 30, 64, 72
Margaret, 92, 93
Rebecca, 137

INDEX

Reuben, 143
Robert, 127
Sarah, 13
WILLIAMS, Amos, 98
Anna, 98
Benjamin, 101
Catherine, 127
Edward, 73
Ellis, 128
Enoch, 143
Evan, 101
Griffith, 101
Hannah, 101
Hugh, 101
Isaac, 86
James, 67, 98
Jane, 101, 104
Joan, 25
John, 76
Joseph, 101, 143
Lewis, 101
Margaret, 134, 135
Mary, 101
Mordecai, 101
Rachel, 98
Richard, 135
Robert, 5
Sara, 101
Studney, 101
Thomas, 84, 127
William, 19, 25, 104
Zacharius, 67, 98
WILLIAMSON, Daniel, 13, 16, 34, 41
Hannah, 16, 34
John, 16, 23, 32, 41, 60, 128
Joseph, 41
Mary, 41
Robert, 16, 34, 41
Thomas, 41, 63
WILLIS, Ann, 60, 116, 123
Benjamin, 123
Edward, 62, 123
Esther, 60, 123
Henry, 123
John, 32, 60, 62, 116, 123
Katherine, 62
Mary, 60, 123
Richard, 128
Sarah, 123
WILLS, Michael, 49
WILLSON, Andrew, 130
Arthur, 104
David, 5
James, 104
John, 63
Joseph, 139
Robert, 57
Thomas, 143
William, 138
WILLY, John, 62
WILSON, Abigail, 126
Ann, 27
Gideon, 27
Hugh, 27
John, 68
Joseph, 27
Katherine, 27
Marth, 27
Martha, 96
Robert, 115, 125
Samuel, 27
Sarah, 27
William, 27, 28, 45, 81, 92
WILTON, William, 36, 51
WILY, John, 2
Thomas, 142
WINDLE, Francis, 39
WINDOWS, James, 110
WITHERS, Elizabeth, 16
Jane, 16
John, 22
Ralph, 16, 40
Robert, 16
Thomas, 16
WITTERSIN, Margaret, 65
WITTMORE, John, 47
WOGAN, John, 44
WOOD, Abraham, 42
Ann, 42
Aubrey, 38, 42
Ellen, 38
George, 10, 11, 42, 74, 76, 121
Hannah, 10, 42, 51
John, 42, 74
Joseph, 42, 51
Mary, 74
Mathew, 1, 42
Nathan, 20, 42
Rebecca, 42, 51
Thomas, 128
William, 42, 74, 76
WOODS, Dinah, 92
Mary, 128
William, 128
WOODWARD, Abigail, 62
Alice, 23
Ann, 71
Anna, 79
Edward, 5, 56, 79, 130
Elizabeth, 5
Enoch, 116, 121, 131
Hannah, 103, 116
Jane, 5, 103
Jesse, 103
John, 30, 71
Joseph, 5, 7
Margaret, 62, 103
Mary, 16, 30, 38
Mordecai, 74, 80
Richard, 4, 16, 30, 34, 38, 53
Sarah, 130
Thomas, 5, 80, 96, 103
William, 93
WOODWORTH, Mary, 34
Richard, 34
WOODY, John, 79
WOODYER, George, 8
WOOLASON, Samuel, 70
WOOLISTON, Catherine, 84
WORLEY, Francis, 34
Henry, 34
WORLY, Caleb, 34
Daniel, 34
Francis, 34
Henry, 34

WORRALL, Hannah, 6,
   39, 45
 Henry, 6, 39
 John, 6, 66, 136
 Joshua, 6, 39, 45
 Margaret, 45
 Mary, 6, 39, 45
 Peter, 6, 39, 45
 Thomas, 94, 115,
   117
WORRELL, Peter, 1, 39
WORRILOW, ---, 69
 Ann, 9
 John, 6, 34
 Thomas, 45
WORROW, Ruth, 74
WORSLEY, Daniel, 3
WORTH, Ebenezer, 53
 Hannah, 53
 John, 12, 53
 Kathrine, 12
 Lydia, 53
 Mary, 53
 Rebecca, 53
 Samuel, 53
 Sarah, 53
 Susanna, 53
 Thomas, 4, 26, 42,
   51, 53, 74, 77,
   85, 93, 125, 128,
   130
WORTHINGTON, Daniel,
   72
WORTHS, Thomas, 82
WRAY, Joseph, 60, 79,
   130
WRIGHT, Jacob, 72, 90
 James, 5, 27, 31,
   36
 John, 5, 30, 106
 Mary, 72
 Samuel, 67
 Sismer, 50
WRY, Robert, 14
WYETH, John, 22
WYTH, John, 26

 Amos, 20, 32, 142
 Ann, 85
 Caleb, 85
 Daniel, 20, 32
 David, 144
 Dorothy, 69, 113
 Francis, 20, 32,
   44, 74, 102, 124,
   144
 Hannah, 44
 Isaac, 85
 James, 97
 Jane, 85
 Job, 69, 97
 John, 20, 69, 112,
   113
 Joseph, 20, 82
 Joshua, 85
 Mary, 62, 69, 142
 Mordecai, 20, 32
 Moses, 20
 Nathan, 69, 85, 113
 Peter, 20
 Philip, 21, 66, 69,
   95, 113
 Rebecca, 69, 97
 Samuel, 69, 113
 Sarah, 20, 97
 Susanna, 97
 Thomas, 69, 113
YEARSLEY, Ann, 41
 Elizabeth, 41
 Hannah, 41
 John, 41, 64
 Martha, 41
 Phebe, 96
 Thomas, 140
YORTE, Peter, 46
YOUNG, Archibald, 126
 Harry, 60, 77
 John, 45, 47, 64,
   109
 Mary, 77, 142
 William, 142
YUNG, Alexander, 119

-Y-
YARD, Benjamin, 53
YARNALL, Abigail, 41

Other books by F. Edward Wright:

Abstracts of Bucks County, Pennsylvania Wills, 1685-1785

Abstracts of Cumberland County, Pennsylvania Wills, 1750-1785

Abstracts of Cumberland County, Pennsylvania Wills, 1785-1825

Abstracts of Philadelphia County Wills, 1726-1747

Abstracts of Philadelphia County Wills, 1748-1763

Abstracts of Philadelphia County Wills, 1763-1784

Abstracts of Philadelphia County Wills, 1777-1790

Abstracts of Philadelphia County Wills, 1790-1802

Abstracts of Philadelphia County Wills, 1802-1809

Abstracts of Philadelphia County Wills, 1810-1815

Abstracts of Philadelphia County Wills, 1815-1819

Abstracts of Philadelphia County Wills, 1820-1825

Abstracts of Philadelphia County, Pennsylvania Wills, 1682-1726

Abstracts of South Central Pennsylvania Newspapers, Volume 1, 1785-1790

Abstracts of South Central Pennsylvania Newspapers, Volume 3, 1796-1800

Abstracts of the Newspapers of Georgetown and the Federal City, 1789-99

Abstracts of York County, Pennsylvania Wills, 1749-1819

Bucks County, Pennsylvania Church Records of the 17th and 18th Centuries Volume 2: Quaker Records: Falls and Middletown Monthly Meetings
Anna Miller Watring and F. Edward Wright

Caroline County, Maryland Marriages, Births and Deaths, 1850-1880

Citizens of the Eastern Shore of Maryland, 1659-1750

Cumberland County, Pennsylvania Church Records of the 18th Century

Delaware Newspaper Abstracts, Volume 1: 1786-1795

Early Charles County, Maryland Settlers, 1658-1745
Marlene Strawser Bates and F. Edward Wright

Early Church Records of Alexandria City and Fairfax County, Virginia
F. Edward Wright and Wesley E. Pippenger

Early Church Records of New Castle County, Delaware, Volume 1, 1701-1800

Frederick County Militia in the War of 1812
Sallie A. Mallick and F. Edward Wright

Inhabitants of Baltimore County, 1692-1763

Land Records of Sussex County, Delaware, 1769-1782

Land Records of Sussex County, Delaware, 1782-1789
Elaine Hastings Mason and F. Edward Wright

Marriage Licenses of Washington, District of Columbia, 1811-1830

Marriages and Deaths from the Newspapers of Allegany and Washington Counties, Maryland, 1820-1830

Marriages and Deaths from The York Recorder, 1821-1830

Marriages and Deaths in the Newspapers of Frederick and Montgomery Counties, Maryland, 1820-1830

Marriages and Deaths in the Newspapers of Lancaster County, Pennsylvania, 1821-1830
Marriages and Deaths in the Newspapers of Lancaster County, Pennsylvania, 1831-1840
Marriages and Deaths of Cumberland County, [Pennsylvania], 1821-1830
Maryland Calendar of Wills Volume 9: 1744-1749
Maryland Calendar of Wills Volume 10: 1748-1753
Maryland Calendar of Wills Volume 11: 1753-1760
Maryland Calendar of Wills Volume 12: 1759-1764
Maryland Calendar of Wills Volume 13: 1764-1767
Maryland Calendar of Wills Volume 14: 1767-1772
Maryland Calendar of Wills Volume 15: 1772-1774
Maryland Calendar of Wills Volume 16: 1774-1777
Maryland Eastern Shore Newspaper Abstracts, Volume 1: 1790-1805
Maryland Eastern Shore Newspaper Abstracts, Volume 2: 1806-1812
Maryland Eastern Shore Newspaper Abstracts, Volume 3: 1813-1818
Maryland Eastern Shore Newspaper Abstracts, Volume 4: 1819-1824
Maryland Eastern Shore Newspaper Abstracts, Volume 5: Northern Counties, 1825-1829
F. Edward Wright and Irma Harper
Maryland Eastern Shore Newspaper Abstracts, Volume 6: Southern Counties, 1825-1829
Maryland Eastern Shore Newspaper Abstracts, Volume 7: Northern Counties, 1830-1834
Irma Harper and F. Edward Wright
Maryland Eastern Shore Newspaper Abstracts, Volume 8: Southern Counties, 1830-1834
Maryland Militia in the Revolutionary War
S. Eugene Clements and F. Edward Wright
Newspaper Abstracts of Allegany and Washington Counties, 1811-1815
Newspaper Abstracts of Cecil and Harford Counties, [Maryland], 1822-1830
Newspaper Abstracts of Frederick County, [Maryland], 1816-1819
Newspaper Abstracts of Frederick County, 1811-1815
Sketches of Maryland Eastern Shoremen
Tax List of Chester County, Pennsylvania 1768
Tax List of York County, Pennsylvania 1779
Washington County Church Records of the 18th Century, 1768-1800
Western Maryland Newspaper Abstracts, Volume 1: 1786-1798
Western Maryland Newspaper Abstracts, Volume 2: 1799-1805
Western Maryland Newspaper Abstracts, Volume 3: 1806-1810
Wills of Chester County, Pennsylvania, 1766-1778

www.ingramcontent.com/pod-product-compliance
Lightning Source LLC
Chambersburg PA
CBHW070658100426
42735CB00039B/2265